THE INSPIRED AUTHOR PRESENTS

Romance Storyline Tropes

ROMANCE WRITER'S ENCYCLOPEDIA

JESSICA BARBER
TARA G. ERICSON

Romance Storyline Tropes: What Readers Expect from
Marriages of Convenience, Matchmakers, Instant Families and more

Romance Writers Encyclopedia Vol. 2
By Tara Grace Ericson and Jessica Barber

Print ISBN: 978-1-949896-65-7
E-book ISBN: 978-1-949896-66-4

Cover design by Tara Grace Ericson
Edited by Heather Wood and Laurie Sibley
The Inspired Author Press, Rogersville, MO

PRAISE FOR THE ROMANCE WRITER'S ENCYCLOPEDIA SERIES

"I am in love with this book . . . It goes so in depth on so many tropes and gives examples of how authors use tropes to build their story. I will be using this book is to brainstorm ideas for new stories my readers will love."

-Pamela Kelley
WALL STREET JOURNAL AND USA TODAY BEST-SELLER

"What a great resource for romance writers! This book is well researched and has such great information about all the tropes that a romance writer should know about and use. This book will help you use tropes more effectively! Fantastic read."

-Victorine E. Lieske
NEW YORK TIMES BEST-SELLER

". . . a well-researched tool for any romance author, with each area of the book incredibly insightful and thorough. It has quickly become a staple in my business library."

-Mandi Blake
USA TODAY BEST-SELLER

"I didn't know I was looking for this exact book until I read it. Romance Character Tropes will [help authors create] characters and situations that are more complete, compelling, and satisfying for the reader."

-Ellie Hall
USA TODAY BEST-SELLER

"The authors don't just list out tropes and wish you well. Instead they provide a comprehensive and thought-provoking explanation of why conscious trope use is necessary and beneficial to your writing."

-Elizabeth Maddrey
USA TODAY BEST-SELLER

"This book is packed with advice on how (and how not) to use these tropes . . . a must-have for authors of any level, and I'll be reaching for it every time I create new heroes."

-Jess Mastorakos
SWOONY AWARD WINNER

"I was blown away by the amount of detail and information included. Much more than just a list of tropes, the authors are thorough and knowledgeable about each and every one."

-Hannah Jo Abbott
USA TODAY BEST-SELLER

"This is definitely not just another book to set on your reference shelf and forget about . . . I highly recommend this to any author, at any level . . . !"

-Christina Butrum
USA TODAY BEST-SELLER

"It's all the things you never knew you needed to know about romance tropes! . . . I was blown away by their attention to detail and how much I was able to glean. It's well organized and well thought out, and I can't wait to collect the rest of the series."

-A.M. Heath
SELAH AWARDS FINALIST

Tara:

Dedicated to B, C, and L . . . my little plot twists.

Jessica:

To Mrs. Winkle (Attreed)—I probably didn't appreciate you enough when I was in your class, but thanks for giving me the tools to bring the key concepts of this book together. I heard your voice on repeat in my head during the brainstorming and drafting process. I hope I held true to your lessons on universal truth and collective unconsciousness.

And to Huma—because I never would have transferred to Winkle's class if I hadn't been trying to get just one extra class period with you.

ABOUT THE BOOK

In this one-of-a-kind resource, you'll find more than a list of tropes or broad advice for genre fiction.

The Romance Writer's Encyclopedia Series breaks down our method for categorizing tropes into four types of framework tropes—Character Tropes, Storyline Tropes, Setting Tropes, and Relational Tropes.

This second volume of the encyclopedia includes detailed entries on favorite romance Storyline Tropes like Marriage of Convenience, Matchmaker Gone Wrong, Instant Family, and Time Travel.

But this isn't just a trope list—it's an encyclopedia!

Each encyclopedia entry includes an introduction to the trope itself, as well as information on why readers love the trope, what expectations exist in the stories, potential pitfalls that authors should avoid, common plot devices, potential themes, and key moments for the narrative.

Locking your characters together for a week isn't enough to have a Forced Proximity story that readers will love—but we'll tell you what will. And then we'll do it for Renovation and Arranged Marriage and Fish out of Water too.

Romance Storyline Tropes is a book designed to be used at every stage of planning, writing, and publishing your books. If used effectively, it will help you write a romance that readers will love, but it will also help you market that book to get it into the hands of readers who will devour it.

We've studied thousands of books and movies, polled readers, and studied the market to understand not just which storyline tropes work—but WHY they work.

Now we're sharing that information with you, so you can use it to make your book marketable, multi-dimensional, and satisfying.

ABOUT THE AUTHORS

Best-selling author and marketing coach Tara Grace Ericson has published over twenty-five novels in Christian romance and romantic suspense. She was a Carol Award finalist for Best Christian Fiction by the American Christian Fiction Writers in 2022.

Jessica Barber is the chief editor at New Life Editing Solutions where she offers editing and story coaching services for both traditionally and independently published authors. She is the author of *Beyond the Beats: How to Write a Romance Readers Can't Resist*.

Jessica and Tara co-founded The Inspired Author in 2022 with a vision of creating books, courses, and other resources to encourage and equip authors. Learn more at www.theinspiredauthor.net

TABLE OF CONTENTS

Part One

INTRODUCTION AND GUIDE

CHAPTER 1

INTRODUCTION TO TROPES

To some writers, trope is a dirty word, marking you as a sellout genre fiction writer—pleasing the masses with predictable drivel.

To others, tropes are effective building blocks to crafting a beloved story. We know that no story is created in a vacuum, and we recognize that tropes are derived from classic and beloved stories. Because of this, we know that tropes are not something to avoid at all costs. We know that in commercial fiction, they can make the difference between a book that sells a thousand copies and a book that sells ten. They can help you solidify your conflict, lean into the tension, build dynamic characters, and deliver a story that strikes a chord and resonates deep within your readers' hearts.

We know that even authors who profess disdain for tropifying their work will inevitably include tropes of some kind, whether they like it or not.

CHAPTER 1

Let's back up though. Maybe you're neither, because this "trope" word people keep throwing around is just another writerly word you're afraid to ask about.

Like pantsing.

Or NaNo.

And why does everyone have so many WIPs? Do you need a safe word?

(Admittedly, that joke is funnier in audio, but you got it, right?)

Let's untangle this literary term that gets thrown around so often.

WHAT IS A TROPE?

To put it in the most basic terms, a literary trope is any element that is used many times by many different writers. These elements include figures of speech, themes, symbols, settings, characters, or plot devices. Tropes have been used throughout the entire history of the written world across cultures, genres, and yes, even in literary fiction.

In a broad sense, tropes are the very product of the saying "There is nothing new under the sun." As writers, we know that can be a bit discouraging. How can my story be unique and interesting if everything has already been done?

The truth actually lies somewhere in the middle of the two. Your story will never be exactly like any other story. Because no other writer is exactly like you. But your story is guaranteed to share elements with hundreds of storytellers reaching back generations.

Your novel may take place in a fictional land unlike any other ever written, where people travel on giant bunnies and fight battles by blowing poison bubbles at one another. But tropes like The Chosen One or Unlikely Band of Heroes are likely to sneak into your manuscript, even if you have no idea what they are.

It's okay!

This is NOT a bad thing.

As a storyteller, you may profess to love them or hate them, but the truth is, tropes exist for a reason. They've been repeated in stories again and again because they are compelling to the audience. From the beginning of civilization, there has always been something exciting about hearing a story of a normal (often orphaned) boy finding out he has extraordinary gifts and an adventure awaiting him (see Harry Potter, Percy Jackson and the Olympians, Star Wars, King David in the Bible). A clandestine affair makes us hold our breath, waiting for the other shoe to drop—whether it is feuding families or a regal prince disobeying his father and falling for the servant girl (see West Side Story, Titanic, or Twilight).

Tropes exist in all genres of fiction, but in this series, we will specifically dive into tropes within the romance genre.

Can you think back to the first romantic movie you remember loving? If you were a 90s kid, maybe it was *She's All That* with a young Freddie Prinze Jr. Or, if you're older, perhaps it was *Pretty Woman* or *Dirty Dancing*, *The Way We Were* or *My Fair Lady*.

If we leave the big screen, we could look at books from Shakespeare to Jane Austen to Georgette Heyer. All of these works use tropes as tools for engaging their audiences, shaping characters and conflict, and deepening the story.

CHAPTER 1

Earlier, we defined a trope as a repeated element of speech, themes, symbols, settings, characters, or plot. We will focus on Storyline Tropes in this book, with the other elements being mentioned only when relevant to the Storyline Trope. Our goal is to help you understand the purpose of the tropes, identify the key elements of popular tropes, and teach you how to utilize them effectively in your writing to create a story that captures your readers' attention and delivers on the unwritten expectations each trope promises *without* being predictable, cookie cutter, or derivative.

A Note from the Authors

Before we start, there's something you should know. Here at The Inspired Author, we LOVE romance, but we don't do steam. It's not something we write, read, or enjoy based on our personal faith convictions. This isn't a book to bash or exclude authors and readers of steamy romance, but you won't find it addressed in any of the Inspired Author Network materials.

As we take apart the tropes one-by-one, you might think we've missed something crucial. In many cases, it will probably be true because we're human, but especially when it comes to things that are unique to the expectations of steamy romance. While we still think much of this book will be relevant to the higher-steam market, just know that there MAY be steam-related expectations of the trope that we don't cover.

We are speaking from our places of expertise in sweet, clean, or inspirational romance, so don't expect to find Trope Encyclopedia *entries based on tropes that are unique to steamy or dark romance (such as Why Choose/Reverse Harem, Mafia, or Bully romance). You can, however, extrapolate the material in our encyclopedias to create your own set of reader expectations, fulfilled reader desires, and pitfalls that are relevant for these other tropes. Hopefully, the content of this book will make you feel well-equipped for such a task.*

Learning how the framework of these trope categories works will help you to dissect any trope you may encounter in your reading or writing. And reading a few of your favorite books using this trope will allow you to identify what makes it work, the most exciting and memorable elements for you as a reader, and how the trope is driving the story.

All that said, let's examine some myths about tropes before we go deeper into Storyline Tropes specifically.

CHAPTER 2

THE PURPOSE OF TROPES (What Tropes Do and Do Not)

Tropes DO NOT build the foundation of your story.

Jane Austen didn't sit down with a list of plot devices, scan the list, and think, "I'll write an **Enemies to Lovers** story today." What she did was create deep, rich characters with a complex transformation arc who happen to also move from outright disdain (in the delightfully complex subtext of proper society) to "ardent admiration."

The main trope in *Pride and Prejudice* of **Enemies to Lovers** serves the story of a proud, arrogant man and a witty, stubborn woman. Characters and emotional arcs should be the foundation of a story. The relational trope of **Enemies to Lovers** is a way to help provide the context and conflict for that transformation to take place. The setting trope of regency England also provides unique challenges and situations for the characters' journey to unfold.

Tropes have developed over time because they are elements that audiences have connected with. But without well-rounded characters, emotional connection, and conflict, even stories that hit every trope just fall flat. In each book, we'll address how the type of trope works as a framework *on which to build* the foundation of your story.

The primary unit of story is the plot, or the sequence of events. The plot will be influenced by elements such as genre, premise, and—you guessed it—tropes. The plot includes the central conflict, the actions and decisions of the characters, and the resolution of the conflict. But plot alone will not give your story the solid foundation that it needs; it needs the support of characters, setting, and theme. Together these elements create the foundation of a story, providing a structure that supports the narrative and guides the reader through the events that unfold.

By creating a sense of familiarity and shaping reader expectations, tropes provide a valuable framework for the plot. They can influence plot structure or provide archetypes and themes which can be used to craft a compelling narrative. Layering tropes can maximize their effect on your story's foundation. A Storyline Trope can flesh out the conflict, and a Character Trope can develop a strong character arc and backstory.

Tropes DO make promises to the reader.

Whether readers acknowledge it or not, they carry expectations into every book they read. It might be based on a familiar author. It might be based on the cover or the title or the blurb. For some genres, the expectation might even be that the reader "expects" to be totally surprised. But for romance, we all know there is one GIANT expectation: This couple will end up together in a happily ever after (HEA) or a happy for now (HFN) by the end of the story.

Romance readers have other expectations, often laid by the trope. If you pick up a story where a woman is falling for her brother's best friend, you have the general expectation that there will be some conflict about how the brother will react or some reason the couple will want to keep things low-key. If that unwritten expectation isn't met, the reader may finish a totally enjoyable romance and feel like there was something missing. They might not even be able to articulate why they felt let down by the story—but it's likely because the setup promised something that the story didn't deliver. While you may choose to subvert the expectations of the trope, it's important to understand what readers are looking for so that you can delight them with your surprises and plot twists without ignoring their general expectations.

This is why authors can write books that deliver the same things over and over again and have readers eagerly awaiting their next book. The author promised a Cowboy Romance, and that is exactly what the reader happily received.

By intentionally choosing the tropes and delivering what was promised, you build trust with the reader. And while we might think readers don't want to know what they are getting in a story, the market dynamics tell us the exact opposite. Readers want "familiar but different" stories—which brings us to the next function of tropes.

Tropes DO provide
"familiar but different" stories.

We've already established that it's the familiarity of tropes that resonates so strongly with readers—but it is the variation, the twists, and the subversions that create a fresh and unique take on a well-loved story and a compelling narrative. We like to think of any good story as a tapestry. Every author's story will look different. They'll choose different colors and different patterns to tie it all together. They might even choose different fibers. Even if they start with the same end goal—to make a tapestry—how they get there will be completely different.

But tropes help add something familiar to the tapestry of a story that the reader is examining. It might be the setting of an idyllic **Small Town** that they are drawn to, or the setup of a **Workplace Romance** with the undercurrent of an off-limits relationship that they can't resist.

The rest of the story will still be unique, infused with the artistic touch of the author, but a reader will naturally be drawn to something within the story that is slightly familiar.

Tropes help us create a framework for our tapestry: something creative and different, but not so different that a reader is confused and hesitant to buy it. It allows the reader to look at the story and latch onto something they enjoy so they are willing to take a risk on the rest. That's what we want as authors. They have to be intrigued with the premise enough to have a chance to fall in love with the story, and in turn—the author.

Tropes CAN fulfill common reader wishes or desires.

One of the biggest things we will do in Part 3 of this book is examine different tropes and dive into why readers love stories featuring that trope. What we'll find is that so many tropes can be traced back to some deep longing or wish within the reader. And many of these are generally shared by the larger population.

Why set your story in a **Small Town**? A longing for simpler times and a place where people truly know and appreciate each other.

Why **Law Enforcement**, **Bodyguards**, **Firefighters**, and **Military**? A deeper wish for protection and provision from a strong, honorable hero.

Why **Friends to More**? An underlying desire to have a romantic relationship with the person who understands you better than anyone in the whole world.

Why **Fake Relationship**? The longing for a life with a little more drama—for shared secrets and being "on the inside" of the excitement.

There are more of course, and perhaps not all tropes tie into a secret wish of the reader, but we would argue that most do. And by acknowledging that and leveraging that secret longing—you can make your book satisfy those deeper, unacknowledged desires. And you can use them in your marketing to make your book irresistible.

Tropes DO NOT make up for lazy writing.

Please don't misunderstand us. We do not want you to slap a few tropes together, add a kiss here and there, and call it a romance. Even the most powerful tropes will not save your manuscript from lazy writing, cookie-cutter characters, lackluster conflict, poor grammar or editing, or any other number of writing and publishing pitfalls!

Well executed tropes will elevate your story, make it easier to sell, and give readers a more satisfying ending.

But you still have to write the story.

You still have to make it engaging.

You still have to make the reader feel the pain, the angst, the joy, and the excitement of falling in love and reaching the end goal.

WELL EXECUTED TROPES WILL ELEVATE YOUR STORY, MAKE IT EASIER TO SELL, AND GIVE READERS A MORE SATISFYING ENDING

A trope cannot do that for you. It can help set up the framework for a good story. But in and of itself, a trope will not carry you.

If you want to work on other aspects of your craft, we recommend reading *Beyond the Beats* by Jessica Barber. It covers everything from conflict to backstory and specific elements of prose such as effective dialogue and description.

Tropes DO NOT mean an author has to "plot" their story.

One of the most unique aspects of our relationship (that is, the relationship of your authors, Jessica and Tara) is our completely different approach to writing stories. Jessica is a proud plotter. Tara, despite multiple attempts to put on a plotter mentality, has embraced her intuitive nature to proclaim herself a pantser.

One of the things we have come to understand about plotting or pantsing or anywhere in between, is that a deeper understanding of story and conflict and characters is beneficial no matter which point in the process those pieces of information are put into play. The same goes with tropes. Perhaps, like Jessica, you want to know exactly where the story is going before you ever start writing. Which means, you identify the tropes ahead of time and can be very intentional about adding the conflict, emotion, romance, and world building into the story.

For the rest of us though, we can still use tropes super effectively!

For some, it might be more intuitive, and you might not recognize you were utilizing a specific trope until it shows up in the manuscript. Or perhaps you are a premise writer—so you know ahead of time the two people you are matching and the scenario or relationship that will bring them together. In either case, you might want to flesh out the trope and expectations during the editing phase so it is as powerful as it can be.

CHAPTER 3

THE CATEGORIES OF FRAMEWORK TROPES

We are far from the first people to compile and categorize tropes, especially romance tropes. We've seen and used many of those lists—and they absolutely *can* be helpful. Heck, we even created our own (and this is our shameless plug for The Inspired Author "Ultimate Romance Trope List"). But as we talked extensively about what we saw happening in the romance market, we realized the problem wasn't that people couldn't recognize specific tropes, or even why they are a functional element of story.

The issue we saw time and again when editing, story coaching, and offering marketing and business consultations was that authors didn't understand *how* tropes were functioning in their story. What made one **Billionaire** or **Marriage of Convenience** story a success and the other a total flop?

Even among talented writers, or authors using similar covers and the same blurb writer!

We discovered that the greatest impact on these stories was how tropes were utilized and how they were mixed and layered with one another. And quickly, the four categories of romance tropes became very clear to us. These four categories are the basis for the first four volumes of this series, and we think it's important for you to understand *why* we've chosen to break them down like this.

The four categories are as follows:

CHARACTER TROPES

On the surface, these tropes may seem like nothing more than labels or marketing hooks, but when done well, your choice of Character Tropes will significantly impact the development of your character arcs. They will inform your choice of attributes, and they will affect the way your character responds to their situation and the actions of others.

These *are* extremely powerful marketing tools, and authors can build entire careers on one single Character Trope. There is a reason we chose to make *Character Tropes* the first volume of *The Romance Writer's Encyclopedia.* They are that important. In that volume, we discussed over thirty Character Tropes—what they are, what makes them work, and why they fail.

STORYLINE TROPES

Storyline Tropes will drive the external plot and conflict of your story, and along with Relational Tropes, these are some of the most commonly discussed by readers and authors. They may also influence critical story beats, and they will inform the progression and content of your scenes.

Most of these will be adhesion tropes that force our characters together and make it oh-so-fun to read. Some examples include **Marriage of Convenience, Fake Relationship, Forced Proximity, and Renovation**. In this volume, we will dig into all the working parts of Storyline Tropes, why they work, and how to capitalize on those key moments that keep readers coming back page after page.

RELATIONAL TROPES

When tropes are discussed, Relational Tropes often top the lists—we're talking **Friends to More**, **Enemies to Lovers**, **Second Chance**, or **Childhood Sweethearts**. These tropes are all about how the characters' existing relationship will influence the romance arc as the narrative develops. They will play a role in major story beats such as the meet cute, midpoint, and black moment (also known as dark night of the soul).

The key to these tropes lies in the shifting of values on what we call a "hate-to-love scale." This means that as your characters progress through scenes, chapters, and acts, there should be a change in attitude toward one another. These values will start somewhere on the negative side of the spectrum, which spans from hate to disinterest, eventually making their way through the stages of attraction, intimacy, and commitment. Each trope in this category will move through the scale differently, but each will end at their happily ever after.

CHAPTER 3

SETTING TROPES

Setting tropes play a major role in the world-building of your book or series. They can aid you in description of place, time, customs, and archetypes. Place and time may indicate the region, the type of environment (like **Urban** or **Small Town**), and time period. Most Setting Tropes also carry specific side character archetypes like the small-town busybody, the Regency wallflower, or the Western sheriff.

In addition to this, elements like figures of speech, colloquialisms, local dress, and customs will all be heavily influenced by the Setting Trope you choose. We'd all be surprised to see your beach bunny heroine show up to the meet cute in a parka—and if your hero is a mountain man, your readers will have to give up their dreams of finding him wandering the woods in a tuxedo. Many readers choose books exclusively based on the Setting Tropes, and creating the setting as a character itself is a powerful tool to draw readers in and keep them coming back book after book.

***

That's it! Remember, there are tons of tropes that don't fall into these categories, since tropes are any element used many times by many authors. A kiss in the rain is a trope. But in the grand scheme of your book, it is far less likely to impact a full arc or major part of your story. Same for the swoony, protective *Who did this to you?* line when the heroine is hurt. These are delicious little fun scenes within a story, but they aren't *framework* tropes, and that's what we want to focus on here.

If you're looking for a list of these framework tropes broken down into these categories, but you don't want to wait for or reference four separate books, our easy-to-download "Ultimate Romance Trope List" is available as a PDF on The Inspired Author website. It also includes a quick reference guide for combining and layering tropes—but let's go into a little more depth here.

MIXING AND LAYERING TROPES

When looking to add depth, complexity, and tension to your romance story, one of the most effective methods is to layer tropes, allowing you to craft a narrative that engages readers on multiple levels. If the idea is to avoid your reader picking up the blurb and thinking "I've read this book before," then we need to break the formula and create something unique. Layering tropes allows us to do this.

Looking at things from a numbers perspective, you might say there are X number of romance books that feature **Marriage of Convenience**, Y number of stories with a **Small Town** setting, and Z with **Brother's Best Friend** . . . but how many books will feature all three of those tropes working in tandem? That number is going to be much smaller, making your story a truly unique experience for the reader.

And while authors may find their niche in a single trope or create series that utilize the same trope for several books, if each book feels like a carbon copy with nothing more than different names and slightly different sources of conflict, readers are not likely to stay engaged through an entire series. This is where the practice of layering tropes can take a common story pattern to create one compelling book after another.

To start mixing tropes, think about which ones lend themselves easily to others in different categories. You'll find a helpful chart of Commonly Paired Tropes in each encyclopedia entry. These ideas may be used to guide your selection of tropes, or you can shake things up and surprise your reader with two tropes they don't expect to see together (such as an **Urban Cowboy**).

Consider options like combining two Storyline Tropes into a dramatic **Forbidden Forced Proximity** romance or a **Mistaken Identity Amnesia** premise. You could do the same with any framework trope, whether relational, storyline, or even setting-related. You might ask yourself a few what-if questions to drum up some intriguing possibilities. What if your characters had a shared history? What if they were forced to collaborate despite their differences? What if they found themselves stranded in a challenging situation together? These questions lay the groundwork for weaving intricate layers of tension and connection. For an even more captivating tale, don't limit yourself to a single framework category—mix and match tropes from different categories to construct a rich tapestry of elements. This systematic approach not only stimulates your authorial creativity but also generates unique and appealing story premises.

ONE OF THE MOST EFFECTIVE METHODS TO ADD DEPTH, COMPLEXITY, AND TENSION TO YOUR STORY IS TO LAYER TROPES

In the last volume, we used a few theoretical examples to illustrate the process. This time, we'll use examples from popular movies to demonstrate the pervasiveness of this practice:

(Character) + (Relational) + (Storyline) + (Setting)

Athletes + Friends to More + Disguise + Academy

Two athletes meet as roommates at their private academy and gradually form a strong friendship as they train together for a critical game against a rival school—the only problem is, one of them is a female student disguised and pretending to be her twin brother.

Sound familiar? This is how the tropes were layered in the Amanda Bynes high school classic *She's the Man.*

(Character) + (Setting) + (Storyline)

Playboy + Wedding + Fake Relationship

A woman hires a charming escort to be her date and fake boyfriend at her half-sister's wedding in order to save face in front of her ex-fiancé (who is in the wedding party) and her family. When her date convinces her family that they are madly in love, they soon begin believing their own lie.

This one might not have been as familiar to you, but this is the premise and layered tropes of *The Wedding Date*, starring Debra Messing and Amy Adams.

(Character) + (Storyline) + (Storyline) + (Storyline)

Slacker + Accidental Marriage + Forced Proximity + Jilted Bride

This storyline triple whammy takes a slacker and a woman left unexpectedly by her fiancé to a drunken night in Las Vegas where they wake up married. After winning a three-million-dollar jackpot at the casino, the judge presiding over their divorce case declares that they must cohabitate for six months and see a marriage counselor before granting the divorce and dividing the casino winnings. As you might expect, they fall in love in earnest before this time is up.

This is the complex and tropey narrative from *What Happens In Vegas*, starring Cameron Diaz and Ashton Kutcher.

Identifying a trope for your story doesn't have to be hard! Choosing one or two from each category can help you ensure your story has a balance of character growth, conflict, tension, adhesion, and world-building. Not every story needs a trope from each category, especially if the others are prominent or pack a strong punch on their own.

However, you might find that bringing in a separate framework trope category fills in the gaps of your narrative that you've been struggling with. By crafting a story premise using a main Character Trope that resonates with readers, a Relational Trope that fuels romantic tension, a Storyline Trope that draws characters together, and a captivating Setting where everything will unfold, you set the stage for a compelling narrative. While not every trope combination will be successful and some might have been explored before, remember that you, as the author, have the power to infuse your unique perspective and creative voice into the story, making it your own.

CHAPTER 4

HOW TO USE THIS BOOK

The Romance Writers Encyclopedia Series will aim to provide more than just a list of tropes. Our goal is to give you an in-depth breakdown of some of the most widely used romance Storyline Tropes. With each entry, we will introduce and define the trope so we are all speaking the same language. Then we'll dissect what it is that readers love about the trope, spoken and unspoken expectations of the trope, and common pitfalls. We'll talk about related tropes or framework tropes it is commonly paired with (so you can decide to play into that or twist it).

These books are intended to be used at every stage of planning, writing, and publishing your books. If used effectively, *The Storyline Trope Encyclopedia* will help you write a romance that readers will love, and it will also help you market that book to get it into the hands of readers who will devour it. In Part 3, we've broken down more than thirty of the most popular Storyline Tropes of romance fiction. In Part 4, we'll pick a few popular movies and break down the successful use of Storyline Tropes in each film.

CHAPTER 4

TO BRAINSTORM AND PLAN YOUR BOOKS

The Storyline Trope Encyclopedia will help spark ideas for you while plotting or planning the premise of your book.

Each section will give you ideas for how to fulfill reader expectations, breathe fresh life into a story, and maybe even combine tropes in new ways. The information in this book may help you decide what to write through our shared research into which tropes are the most popular, which are underserved, which tropes may be best utilized to help you set up a successful book or series with intentional choices.

TO EDIT YOUR BOOKS

While drafting or editing your book, the encyclopedia entries serve as an excellent source to double-check whether you are hitting the mark for the intended trope. With common plot devices, key moments, and pitfalls in easy-to-reference entries, you can use the encyclopedia to zero in on the reader expectations for each trope and make small adjustments to your manuscript that will have a big impact on the reader experience.

These changes don't always require an entire rewrite—you may be surprised what a few well-placed new lines of prose or dialogue can do to round out elements such as character or conflict!

TO MARKET YOUR BOOKS

Tropes (including Storyline Tropes) are one of the most powerful marketing tools available to authors today. Using the information in the encyclopedia about WHY readers love each trope will help you craft your marketing content, write an effective sales blurb, and hook readers before they even crack the cover. Elements such as title and subtitle, cover design, and keywords or browsing categories can get a major boost by capitalizing on the prominent tropes in your work.

But this isn't a trope list. This is an encyclopedia. So let's dive into specific information about Storyline Tropes.

Part Two
STORYLINE TROPES IN ROMANCE

CHAPTER 5

INTRODUCTION TO STORYLINE TROPES

If you remember our definition of a trope (any story element—including figures of speech, theme, setting, character, or plot devices—that is used many times by many different writers), then we can say that a Storyline Trope is any trope that directly influences the plot or storyline. It may involve common plot elements, story beats, or plot themes used many times by many different writers.

Storyline Tropes may include recurring and recognizable patterns which can be found in all mediums of storytelling (novels, movies, books, even video games). It's a shorthand way to quickly convey certain themes, conflicts, and key moments that a reader is likely to encounter when picking up a book involving a certain plot element, such as **Marriage of Convenience** or **Forced Proximity**.

Now, that obviously doesn't mean the author isn't writing an original story with compelling conflict and characters that draw readers in. Any use of a specific Storyline Trope will be highlighted to indicate that it is functioning as a unit of genre, reader expectations, and (in general) maintaining the established structure and pattern set forth by hundreds or thousands of other writers (i.e. intro, rising action, climax, resolution). However, each iteration of any Storyline Trope is bound to be unique in some way, for worse or for better.

Throwing your characters into a locked room for two-thirds of your novel may allow you to check the **Forced Proximity** box, but if you don't allow it to shape the conflict, the critical scenes and the key moments of your story, you'll be missing a crucial piece of the puzzle. It goes so much deeper than simply manipulating your scenes to include certain plot elements that readers love, which is why we've created this encyclopedia.

By informing your conflict, your Storyline Tropes have the opportunity to influence elements like scene-level setting, relational conflict, internal conflict, external forces, the impact of story beats, and maybe most importantly, theme. The hallmarks of each plot trope will act as a guide and a jumping off point for what readers expect from the high-tension or zany circumstances your characters find themselves in. Readers will be drawn to your stories because they know they can count on *that one moment* that will give them all the feels or make their heart drop into their stomachs.

Like the moment that your **Fake Relationship** lovers realize their relationship has shifted from simply being an act to a genuine connection based on mutual respect and blossoming desire.

You can let readers know to expect their specific Storyline Trope itch to be scratched by intentionally selecting marketing elements like the title, cover, and back copy (or Amazon description). While these tropes help audiences identify and anticipate plot points and conflict more easily, they can also lead to clichés or predictable storytelling if overused. The romance genre shares plenty of Storyline Tropes with other genres, but most of what we will discuss is unique or presented in a different light when it comes to love stories.

Regardless of how many stories a Storyline Trope may show up in, we'll discuss how they are shaped by the reader expectations of a romance novel and how they influence elements such as story beats and plot devices. The Storyline Tropes you will encounter in this book should especially influence the external conflict and story beats. They will affect some of the pacing, and the external forces inherent in each plot trope may directly affect internal or relationship conflict in the story as well. At their core, these tropes will reveal the path for characters to overcome the obstacles to a lasting love. Storyline Tropes provide a familiar framework that readers can engage with, allowing you as the writer to create a compelling narrative.

Here's how tropes can affect external conflict in a romance.

STORYLINE TROPES AND THE FOUNDATION OF YOUR STORY

This entire series of Trope Encyclopedias serves to show you, writer, that tropes are an excellent tool to utilize when laying the framework of your narrative, but they are not solid enough to carry it. Hear us when we say *tropes should serve your story*, not the other way around. As the author, your job is to take a Storyline Trope and create an interesting, original, and compelling narrative. Whether you plot, outline, or pants—your story is more than a carbon copy of every romance book with a similar premise.

While Storyline Tropes will guide your main plot (via the external conflict) in a specific direction, they will not pigeonhole your story. The setting, characters, and even subplots will go a long way to molding the rough structure provided by your Storyline Trope into a truly unique work of art. Layering tropes (even those that directly influence plot) will create complexity in your narrative and provide ample flexibility.

STORYLINE TROPE VS STORY VS PLOT

If you have read *Romance Character Tropes*, which is the first volume of this series, then you might remember our discussion about big C Characters (**Billionaires**, **Cowboys**, **Firefighters**) and little c characters (the specific character in your story with personality, quirks, backstory, wounds, and goals). We will make a similar distinction in this book between Storyline Tropes and story while also considering the influence of plot.

Before we dig into the difference between these elements, we first need to define both plot and story.

Plot is simply the sequence of events that tie together to form your narrative. It doesn't incorporate elements such as characters, settings, or conflict—all of which provide the context to your narrative to turn it into a *story*.

Story is where the character arc, the setting, the conflict arc, theme, and all the plot elements come together to create something with meaning. If plot is the *what* and *when* of your narrative, story is the *where* and *why* it happens.

While your Storyline Trope will directly impact plot elements such as the inciting incident and key moments, it will also *be affected* by the story. Depending on who your characters are, how their personal journey interacts with the plot, and how their individual character arcs come together to form the relationship arc, your Storyline Trope can take a million different directions. This is why using Storyline Tropes (or any type of trope, really) doesn't dilute your book down to a simple formula with no meaning or individuality.

Your Storyline Trope may be **Mistaken Identity**. But your *story* is about a down-on-her-luck single mother who is assumed to be the handsome prince's hired date when she shows up to the wrong entrance of the gala she is supposed to waitress.

A Storyline Trope is an empty shell of an idea waiting for you to bring it to life. The trope itself is a framework with basic stand-ins for the nuance and backstory and character details and context that will become your story.

Here are the basic elements you will want to add to a Storyline Trope to turn it into a story.

Characters: As you probably already know, you cannot write a story without characters. Don't get me wrong—depending on the story, these characters may not even need to be human. What they *do* need is personality, desires, and goals. The growth journey (aka character arc) is derived from the interaction between what happens in the story and the characters you create. Your readers will not care about *what* happens if they don't care about *who* it happens to.

Romance arc: The romance arc essentially boils down to the interaction between each individual character arc. As two unique personalities come together with their own goals and motivations, that collision forms the foundation of the romance arc, and it plays out as the characters change in their own right and grow toward each other. This increasing intimacy, alongside shifting values and priorities, is what melds their two paths into one.

Plot: This may start with the basic premise of your story—a guy falls in love with a girl who is way out of his league. The inciting incident and key moments may be determined depending on the Storyline Trope you choose, but it will take a multitude of scenes to take your characters through the conflict, through their personal growth journey, and to their happily ever after—together.

Setting: Setting grounds the reader in the story by providing context for place and time. It also contributes to the mood and tone of the story, allowing space for the readers to understand the character's personality and motivations in a multifaceted way.

Conflict: As your character's pursuit of their goals propels them through the events of the story, there must be obstacles in their path. External, internal, and relational conflict will all play an essential role in your story, so we will cover this extensively in the next chapter.

***

As you can see, a Storyline Trope is a wonderful framework on which to build your character arc, romance arc, plot, and conflict in the setting of your choice, but it isn't a story in and of itself. Utilized effectively, Storyline Tropes (and other tropes) can be used alongside any other literary device to enhance the power of your story and deliver an engaging experience for the reader.

CHAPTER 6

STORYLINE TROPES AND CONFLICT

THE ROLE OF CONFLICT

Conflict is one of the most important elements in any narrative. It is the key agent of change in stories of all genres, and it goes hand in hand with both plot structure and Storyline Tropes. Without sufficient conflict, even the most interesting story idea will fall flat—there will be no trigger for character development, no relationship arc, and nothing to compel your reader to finish the book.

A common expression of conflict is:

Goal + Obstacles = Conflict

The characters' pursuit of their goal is what drives the plot forward. Effective story goals should have a combination of some kind of external component and internal struggle. Your choice of Storyline Trope will often dictate the external conflict, but it may also influence the selection of your internal or relational conflict. The main conflict of your story will be an overarching thread or element throughout the narrative.

In *Beyond the Beats* by Jessica Barber, conflict is examined in Chapters 5 and 6. If you're looking for more information on how to deliver a cohesive plot in your story where character, conflict, and theme all work together, then we recommend studying further there. In this section, we will try to focus our discussion on the relevance of Storyline Tropes to your conflict. But please recognize that conflict is such an important part of your story, it cannot be ignored or oversimplified.

CONFLICT IS ONE OF THE MOST IMPORTANT ELEMENTS IN ANY NARRATIVE. IT IS THE KEY AGENT OF CHANGE IN STORIES OF ALL GENRES, AND IT GOES HAND IN HAND WITH BOTH PLOT STRUCTURE AND STORYLINE TROPES.

We do want to clarify terminology we will be using to separate the types of conflict in your story, so you can more easily identify how they are impacted by the Storyline (and other) Tropes. Types of conflict in your story include internal conflict, personal (or relational) conflict, and external conflict.

Internal conflict refers to the psychological struggle of the character. In this type of conflict, something—often trauma or some past wound—creates the obstacles that result in the ultimate resistance of values and principles. This struggle will stem from the character's beliefs, values, emotions, or desires and arises when a character must choose between competing priorities. The resolution of internal conflict will come about when the character undergoes a process of self-reflection, growth, and transformation, but first, they must grapple with their own beliefs and values.

Personal, or relational, conflict involves at least one antagonist character. This character may be a side character, but it may also be the love interest. This type of conflict involves disagreements, tensions, or misunderstandings between characters that can create obstacles to their goals or desires; whatever the case is, there must be a living, breathing person working in opposition to your protagonist's goals. Personal conflict should reveal the characters' motivations, values, and personalities, and the resolution should not be immediately clear or easy to achieve. This means that any conflict arising from a misunderstanding must not be of a nature that could be resolved with a simple conversation. Instead, the resolution of these conflicts will require your characters to be honest with themselves and others, compromise, or confront their underlying issues. This will lead to growth and development for the characters and will ultimately create the foundation of success in their relationship.

NOTE FROM YOUR STORY COACH

The stakes are whatever your character has to lose if they do not succeed at their goal or overcome the obstacles.

-JB

External conflict occurs when the threat to the protagonist's goals or desires comes from the character's world, society, or circumstances. The fear of being ostracized from one's world, a naturally occurring force, or an existential threat would all be considered external sources of conflict. The resolution of external conflict often involves the character taking action to overcome the obstacle or challenge in their path, including physical or mental struggles as well as personal growth and development, ultimately revealing the motivations and strengths of your protagonist. External conflict can be a powerful tool for driving the plot of a story, and it's what defines most of our Storyline Tropes.

By weaving several elements of conflict together, you will create depth and nuance to your story that keeps the reader turning one page after another. Storyline Tropes tend to deliver mainly the external conflict, but they also create opportunity for relational conflict between the characters and force internal conflict with the main character as they wrestle with their changing goal and overcome their great lie. By being intentional about the layering of conflict, authors can effectively raise the stakes of the novel.

When you have determined the specifics of each layer of conflict, you need to introduce complications with ever-increasing stakes. This is where Storyline Tropes tend to shine.

THE ROLE OF STORYLINE TROPES

> UTILIZING CONFLICT TO PUSH YOUR CHARACTERS TO GROW AND CHANGE EVEN FURTHER, YOU CAN HIGHLIGHT THE RESILIENCE AND DETERMINATION OF YOUR CHARACTER.

The Storyline Tropes you employ play a significant role in shaping the conflict of your romance story by providing the framework for character development and resolution of obstacles in addition to contributing to the overall romance arc. It is the external conflicts that arise over the course of your narrative plot that challenge your characters and force them out of their comfort zones to confront their flaws and weaknesses. Character development isn't a linear process, and challenges can be just as important as successes. So utilizing conflict to push your characters to grow and change even further, you can highlight the resilience and determination of your character. When we also take into account the storyline trope, past experiences, current circumstances, as well as settings and character values, you create an atmosphere rife for conflict and tension.

At the core of any conflict arc in a romance novel, you will have two people whose worlds have collided in such a way that they are now forced to reconcile their own internal and external goals with an irresistible pull to the union with their love interest. With regard to tropes, the challenges that your character faces and the circumstances they find themselves in will force them to confront their worldview and overcome their circumstance by either adjusting to or changing them. The circumstances that have led your character to a state of unfulfillment at the start of the novel will change by the resolution of the narrative, either *because of* or *through* the events dictated by your storyline trope.

In many stories, a character pursuing their goal *chooses* a specific storyline trope in hopes it will help them achieve it—perhaps a **Marriage of Convenience**, **Fake Relationship**, or **Hidden Motive**. In other stories, a storyline is thrust upon the character, and they must adjust to or overcome the obstacle of their circumstance. For instance, they may have to challenge the circumstances against a storyline like **Forbidden Love** or **Long-Distance Relationship**, but they will likely adjust to circumstances such as **Accidental Marriage** or **Instant Family**.

Regardless of whether your primary conflict is an internal struggle or the external force of a storyline trope, both will play off each other in such a way that makes them integral to the plot of your romance. Will the conflict push your characters together, or will it force them apart? Are your characters happy to be in such close proximity, or has this put a real damper on their plans to never associate with that person ever? We cover the effect of relational conflict more in the Relational Tropes volume of *The Romance Writer's Encyclopedia*, but it's very important to recognize. The external conflict from the Storyline Trope must be considered alongside the internal and relational conflict of a Relational Trope. It is the Storyline Trope that will provide the opportunity and the proximity for the internal and relational conflicts to occur.

A **Marriage of Convenience** between best friends shares common reader expectations, key moments, and pitfalls as a **Marriage of Convenience** between enemies. The Storyline is similar, but the overall story is very different because of the flavor of the relational and internal conflict.

Also, consider where you are in the plot structure (Are your characters nearing the midpoint or the dark moment?) and how that should influence their current dynamic. And how have the events of your story challenged your character in ways that have led to a gradual or dramatic shift in their perspective, relationships, and circumstances? We'll dive into this in the next chapter.

CHAPTER 7

STORYLINE TROPES AND STORY STRUCTURE (KEY MOMENTS)

As the Storyline Trope shapes the external conflict and character development, it will also influence the structure of your narrative. By that we mean that the Storyline Trope will impact the key moments of the story, as well as the other beats that help fully form the narrative. The external pressures bringing your characters together should serve as a major driving force of your plot, moving your characters toward these key moments of impact. It may be a singular pressure or an amalgamation of external forces, and it may directly affect the emotional arc of your characters, but it *will* guide the forward and backward motion of the story (especially during the second act).

We'll discuss the key moments of romance fiction, along with other important story beats that may be influenced by your choice of Storyline Tropes, but this is by no means an in-depth coverage of the subject. If you would like more information on key moments, see Chapter 12 of *Beyond the Beats* by Jessica Barber. If you are interested in gaining a better understanding of story beats, Jessica Brody's *Save the Cat Writes a Novel* and *Romancing the Beats* by Gwen Hayes are great resources for romance writers.

STORYLINE TROPES AND KEY MOMENTS

In *Beyond the Beats*, Jessica defines key moments as high-impact emotional scenes that anchor the romantic arc. If these moments are missing or fall flat, it could ruin the entire experience for your readers. Conversely, if these moments strike a chord with your readers, it could be the reason they rave about your writing. In the romance genre, these key moments are the hook and inciting incident, the declaration of love, the breakup, and the dark moment.

INCITING INCIDENT AND MEET CUTE

We consider the hook to be the element or elements that initiate the readers' investment in the story. When speaking about writing craft, we clarify this definition by referring to the narrative hook (in contrast to the marketing hook), in which the author utilizes certain storytelling elements to grab the reader's attention and entice them to keep reading. This happens during the opening scene and inciting incident in a romance novel, and it may or may not include the meet cute. Many Storyline Tropes, such as **Runaway Bride** or **Wager**, will dictate that the inciting incident coincides with the meet cute. When the storyline involves characters who already know each other, the inciting incident is typically a moment that challenges or upends the current state of their relationship. In either case, the inciting incident of your Storyline Trope serves to reveal the motivations and goals of your characters as well as the external obstacles that stand in the way of their idea of success. As you'll find in the trope entries, many of the Storyline Tropes will be introduced at the point of the inciting incident.

THE DECLARATION OF LOVE

The declaration of love is the second key moment in romance that typically occurs in act two, and for many Storyline Tropes, it is a major turning point in the story. This is the point where the **Fake Relationship** is truly acknowledged as not-so-fake-at-all. In **Hidden Motives** tropes, the declaration of love could come before the ruse is revealed, which means the feelings are real but there are still secrets between the characters. While your characters may not actually use the L-word, this moment should be wrought with vulnerability and a willingness from the characters to open up their hearts to each other. The majority of romance stories will probably place this scene just before the climax (at the end of the second act), but sometimes it comes as early as the midpoint.

This is a moment that cannot be overlooked in any story, but leaning into the motivations and circumstances of the characters will help it strike an even deeper chord with your reader.

THE BREAKUP

The third act breakup has become a divisive topic among romance readers and authors alike. Many champion the lack of a third act breakup in their stories, feeling that it depends on immaturity, poor conflict resolution, and misunderstandings. While this *is* a problem

> THE BREAKUP DOESN'T HAVE TO BE AN ACTUAL BREAKUP. THIS IS THE MOMENT WHERE THE GROWTH ARCS OF YOUR CHARACTERS FINALLY INTERTWINE, FORCING THEIR TRANSFORMATION TO COME TO FULL FRUITION BEFORE THEY HAVE EARNED THEIR HAPPILY EVER AFTER.

in many romance novels, it is not the point of the breakup scene. In fact, it doesn't even have to be an actual breakup.

The point of this key moment is for the obstacle to feel so insurmountable that we cannot see a way through it. The breakup can take many forms, such as a heated argument, a betrayal, a realization of irreconcilable differences, or external forces that pull the characters apart. It is the climax of the relational conflict, with the climax of the external conflict often acting as the catalyst. This could be due to the revelation of secrets, an impossible choice, or conflicting values. This is the moment where the slowly building growth arcs of your characters finally intertwine, first creating a massive collision, then forcing their transformation to come to full fruition before they have earned their happily ever after.

The key to a compelling third act breakup is to make it emotionally resonant and relevant to the overall themes and character development in your story—it should feel like a natural progression of the plot and characters' arcs. By giving your characters the opportunity to overcome a nearly impossible obstacle, you demonstrate to your reader that they really will go the distance, regardless of whatever adversity they face.

THE DARK MOMENT

If the breakup scene functions as a catalyst for fulfillment of the growth arc, the dark moment is where that transformation happens. It's the turning point when the character stops pursuing the thing they *think* they need and starts pursuing what they truly need.

The Storyline Trope of any story is almost always critical in pushing the characters to their dark moment. While the dark moment is a deeply internal struggle where the character must battle their wound and overcome the lie they believe, the external circumstances are what push them to the bottom of that pit. Whether that is terms of the **Wager** being revealed to the love interest they now genuinely care about or the **Community Project** they are working on together failing (or nearly failing) dramatically, the external conflict of the Storyline Trope will drive the characters to reevaluate their feelings for the love interest as well as realize their true goal.

As the author, you have the freedom to choose how the storyline propels your character through their growth arc. Perhaps they get everything they hoped for: Their Marriage of Convenience ends and they get the inheritance, which was their

THE EXTERNAL CONFLICT OF THE STORYLINE TROPE WILL DRIVE THE CHARACTERS TO REEVALUATE THEIR FEELINGS FOR THE LOVE INTEREST AS WELL AS REALIZE THEIR TRUE GOAL.

AS THE AUTHOR, YOU HAVE THE FREEDOM TO CHOOSE HOW THE STORYLINE PROPELS YOUR CHARACTER THROUGH THEIR GROWTH ARC.

entire goal at the beginning of the story. But the victory falls flat without the love interest at their side.

Or they may have everything they wanted ripped from their hands along with losing their chance at love.

STORYLINE TROPES AND OTHER STORY BEATS

In addition to impacting the key moments of your story, the Storyline Trope you choose may also shape other story beats and common scenes.

THE MESSY MIDDLE

Many writers struggle with the messy middle of the manuscript, or if you are familiar with *Save the Cat*, this is the Fun and Games beats. However, by staying focused on the Storyline Trope and leaning into the situations and moments created because of the trope itself (eg. the couple in a **Fake Relationship** is forced to act lovey-dovey in front of their boss), you can write scenes that fit the narrative, push your characters to examine their feelings about one another, and amp up the external conflict.

You may find suggestions for scenes that move your story forward in the Common Plot Devices section of each trope entry.

THE GRAND GESTURE

I (Jessica) don't typically include the grand gesture or happily ever after in the key moments discussion of the romance genre. This is

IN ORDER FOR THIS MOMENT TO RING TRUE WITH READERS, THE GRAND GESTURE MUST BE SINCERE, AND IT MUST BE MEANINGFUL TO BOTH LOVE INTERESTS.

because a strong grand gesture or happily ever after scene can't save a poorly constructed romance arc. Whereas the inciting incident or hook, the midpoint, and the dark moment all form the key framework scenes for anchoring your romance arc, the grand gesture and happily ever after can be viewed as more of the icing on the cake.

However you will see the grand gesture scene featured in the key moments section of our trope entries because several Storyline Tropes have very specific patterns for these moments. In the **Bet/Wager** trope, for example, the arrogance and pride of the character who has placed the bet must be utterly humbled in the grand gesture moment in order to atone for their heinous actions against the love interest.

In order for this moment to ring true with readers, the grand gesture must be sincere, and it must be meaningful to both love interests. Part of what gives the grand gesture meaning is the inherent sacrifice for at least one half of the couple. This sacrifice doesn't have to be anything material—in fact, it usually isn't. It may be a sacrifice of pride, a priority, or some great desire. What really makes the grand gesture stand out is when it involves your character doing something they would *never* do at the beginning of the story.

***

In each encyclopedia entry, we've tried to give you some guidance for how each specific Storyline Trope might impact these key moments, but don't let that inhibit your creativity. Your characters and the nuances of the situations (and especially the relational and internal conflicts of your story) will impact these moments as well.

However, readers do carry some expectations of these moments, depending on the trope, and we've done our best to inform you of those within the encyclopedia.

CHAPTER 8

GOING DEEPER WITH STORYLINE TROPES

We have already discussed how the association of conflict and plot depend largely on the character arc of your narrative, but as we zoom out from that, we find that these three elements can be combined masterfully to weave the common threads of theme throughout your story.

Character (Growth) + Plot + Conflict = Theme

As the plot unfolds, the growth of your character should be a natural consequence to encountering conflict, displayed through the actions and reactions of your character to the events of your plot. Throughout the course of your novel, the character will struggle to reach a goal. It is the repeated efforts of your character trying and failing to achieve this goal that constitutes the majority of your plot points.

The key agent of change throughout each of these points is conflict. Storyline Tropes should introduce conflict into the narrative that challenges your characters and forces them to confront their flaws and weaknesses to push them toward growth. Storyline Tropes will often reveal these weaknesses or misconceptions that that character lives with through the introduction and the inciting incident.

The series of events that the Storyline Trope sets off will provide the catalyst for the conflict and ultimately growth of the character. With each obstacle presented in the narrative, your character should become stronger and closer to the person they want to be. Each of the key moments we discuss in the trope entries will signify a change not only in the character's circumstances but also a turning point in their character arc.

A NOTE FROM YOUR STORY COACH

Theme refers to the central message of a story—but if we really want to connect with the reader, then theme goes a step further by giving a central message that connects with universal human experiences.

-JB

THEME TIES IT ALL TOGETHER

As the conflict forces your character to grow and change, the shift in their worldview should serve to illuminate the theme—but this doesn't happen by accident. At the core of any conflict arc in a romance novel, you will have two people whose worlds have collided in such a way that they are now forced to reconcile their own internal and external goals with an irresistible pull to the love interest. It takes intentional effort on the part of the author. This truth is most often revealed through the reactions and decisions of your characters, as well as their respective consequences. As your character comes closer to the person they are meant to be at the close of your novel, the theme of your narrative should become increasingly clear.

The external forces of your trope may also serve to illuminate the theme. The impact of your story's conflict on the characters (and on readers) will inherently reflect the theme when done well. To find this connection, ask yourself, *What if the external conflict presented by the Storyline Trope never happened to your character? What lessons would they have never learned? What would they have missed out on?*

If that specific catalyst for change presented by your chosen trope had never occurred, would something else have come along and caused the same transformation in your character? What lessons would have been lost instead of gained had your character never faced the circumstances of the external conflict?

The theme illuminates the reason that the events of your story, and your Storyline Trope, *matter* to your characters. And once they matter to the characters, you can make it matter to the reader as well. This is why story conflict that doesn't engage theme often results in stories that don't feel meaningful. In addition to layering significance over your narrative, using theme automatically raises the stakes of your story by connecting with the reader and garnering their investment.

If the external conflict impacts the character's motivations, successes, and failures, the consequences of your character's action are impacted *by* the external conflict. And this is where we find the intersection between external conflict and theme—*something* has to motivate your character to react to the trigger of the external conflict—and that *something* is typically where you'll find your theme.

STORYLINE TROPES AND READER WISH FULFILLMENT

Wish fulfillment has become something of a dirty phrase in literary circles—but we've already established that we're not afraid of the stigma by snooty literary types. The truth is, the act of reading itself is grounded in wish fulfillment. Readers choose genre, topic, writing style, etc., all based on what itch they are looking to scratch.

At the crux of reader wish fulfillment for most Storyline Tropes is the opportunity for readers to live through the characters' experience of events or circumstances that they will likely never experience themselves. Even those that are easily relatable (which is a great thing!) take things one step further if they are able to stir up new emotions and perspectives in the reader or if they can spark the reader's intellectual curiosity. Take, for example, the following Storyline Tropes and the incredible experience they draw the reader into.

Fish out of Water—Waking up one day and life is completely different; finding happiness in unexpected places.

Marriage of Convenience—Finding out that the person you never would have chosen for yourself is exactly the person you need.

From the reader wish fulfillment, you can often pull the theme of your narrative based on the experience of your character and the lesson or transformation that results from it. Take these examples:

Instant Family—Family is meant to be treasured, regardless of how that family is made or came to be.

This reader wish fulfillment highlights the theme of Family of Choice, whereby characters find family based on chosen bonds rather than biological relations.

Amnesia—Love is a soul-deep connection between two people who are inextricably intertwined.

This reader wish fulfillment highlights the theme that love is a connection beyond logic. Even when the Amnesia character's draw toward the love interest doesn't make sense to anyone else, they will prove to everyone that true love is worth the fight.

Recognizing the reader wish fulfillment of your specific story will be hugely important in crafting a story that meets the reader's expectations and satisfies the deeper longing they carry with them into the story. Then you utilize a commonly derived theme from your chosen storyline trope to weave this wish fulfillment into the narrative.

One of the biggest secrets to succeeding in the area of reader wish fulfillment is in nailing down the desires and fantasies of your target audience. Understand the preferences of your readers, their desires for content, and expectations. (As we've already noted, the content and even story expectations of steamy romance or erotica readers will differ greatly from the expectations and desires of clean or inspirational romance readers!)

The reader desires and wishes we refer to in the encyclopedia entries tap into fundamental human experiences, emotions, and desires. While this makes one of the driving forces of your novel relatable and compelling to a diverse audience, it is with your target audience where you find truly captivated readers.

CHAPTER 8

Some storylines are popular because we can have all been there—forced to work with that coworker who is constantly getting under our skin, **Fish out of Water,** and even **Disguise** or **Hidden Identity**. These storylines quickly draw the reader in, allowing them to "bond" with the reader over shared experiences, good or bad.

We gravitate toward other storylines because they seem so outrageous that we can't help but look away (see **Matchmaker Gone Wrong**, **Accidental Marriage**, and **Secret Baby**). These tropes feed the reader's desire for entertainment and drama, as well as curiosity to see characters grow through their mistakes and find redemption and love.

Other storylines endear us to the characters through the depth of their strength and willingness to fight against even the most insurmountable of obstacles. These tropes fulfill the reader's wish to see pain and adversity be used for something good in their lives or the lives of others. The **Star-Crossed Lovers** trope is a prime example in this category—regardless of how the story ends, we know beyond the shadow of a doubt that these characters are better off for having loved one another.

There are others, but as you are writing, be cognizant of what deeper desire your reader might have for choosing to go along on the adventures of your characters. Even readers who read across subgenres will have these desires, and these wish fulfillment strategies can be used to fulfill nearly any given reader desire, regardless of the chosen trope. If the story aligns with a specific wish fulfillment, lean into the insecurities in the inner dialogue of the main character and deliver the fulfilled wish with the resolution of the story and the culmination of the relationships.

Oftentimes, this is where the layering and mixing of tropes can add complexity and unexpected elements to your narrative and characters. With that being said, the themes we have pinpointed at the end of each encyclopedia entry are just the most obvious or common themes found in that storyline.

Let your characters be drawn so deeply into their own adventure that readers can't help but want to go along for the ride. This will inevitably be influenced by the uniqueness of your characters, as the specific challenges they face within the trope will keep the narrative fresh and engaging. It's the blend of relatability and novelty that creates the immersive experience for the reader and draws them into the very fiber of your narrative.

CHAPTER 9

SUCCESSFUL USE OF STORYLINE TROPES

AVOIDING PITFALLS

Storyline tropes can go wrong in romance novels when they're executed in a way that feels formulaic, unrealistic, or extreme. Some of the most common pitfalls of Storyline Tropes include: lack of character motivation, unrealistic circumstances, predictability, lack of consequences, character development, or resolution.

You can avoid these pitfalls by building on top of the framework and patterns provided by tropes to create compelling conflict, subverting tropes, and choosing Storyline Tropes for the love interests in such a way that it creates tension and pushes your main characters toward overcoming their obstacles and finding fulfillment. We'll look at each of the ways Storyline Tropes tend to fall flat.

Lack of character motivation: This problem is often the result of one-dimensional characters or unclear values or goals. This significantly hinders the depth and authenticity of the storyline.

When characters lack clear motivations, they become flat and fail to engage readers emotionally. In a romantic context, this pitfall might manifest as characters entering relationships without genuine reasons or pursuing love without underlying personal growth or development.

To address this issue, it's crucial to invest time in developing well-rounded characters with identifiable and relatable motivations. Explore their individual desires, fears, and aspirations, ensuring that their romantic involvement aligns with their personal journeys. Incorporate character growth and evolution throughout the storyline.

Predictability: When authors rely too heavily on tropes to carry their story or when tropes are never subverted or given any unique twists or creative elements, the story often feels overly predictable and formulaic. Readers may find themselves anticipating every key moment. This sense of predictability can diminish the emotional investment readers have in the characters' journeys, as the outcome becomes too apparent.

Instead, strive to innovate within the framework of tropes. Introduce unexpected turns, unconventional character traits, or unique settings that challenge or subvert typical expectations. Ultimately, striking a balance between familiarity of the storyline and innovation within the context of established tropes can help create a more engaging and satisfying romantic narrative.

Lack of consequences: When the plot unfolds without realistic repercussions for the characters' actions or choices, it diminishes the stakes and makes the narrative feel disconnected from the complexities of real life. Any Storyline Trope is likely to disrupt and significantly alter your character's life. It is crucial to explore the aftermath and consequences of these events. Failing to address the ripple effects of pivotal moments can result in a shallow portrayal of the characters' experiences and relationships.

Whether it's the revelation of a long-held secret, a major decision, or a significant sacrifice for love, the consequences should be woven into the narrative to provide depth and authenticity. Delve into the emotional and practical fallout of pivotal events. This drives character growth as they navigate the challenges and consequences of their choices.

Lack of growth: Character growth is essential for creating a compelling love story. Readers have difficulty empathizing with static, unengaging character arcs. Instead, they deeply connect with characters who evolve over the course of the story—overcoming obstacles, learning from experiences, and becoming more nuanced individuals.

Characters should confront and overcome internal and external obstacles, and their romantic relationships should contribute to their overall development. Whether it's overcoming personal insecurities, confronting past traumas, or evolving in response to the romantic relationship, characters need to exhibit a dynamic and transformative journey.

Lack of resolution: This pitfall occurs when significant storylines, conflicts, or character arcs are left unaddressed or unresolved by the end of the narrative. The absence of closure can lead to a sense of incompleteness, leaving readers with lingering questions and a sense of dissatisfaction.

To avoid this pitfall, it's crucial to tie up loose ends and provide a clear resolution to key elements of the story. This includes addressing the central romantic conflict, resolving character arcs, and offering a clear sense of closure for the overall external storyline. Readers invest time and emotion in the characters and their relationships, and a lack of resolution can leave them feeling cheated or disconnected from the story.

The resolution should feel earned and authentic, aligning with the tone and themes of the romance novel. This doesn't necessarily mean providing a perfect fairy-tale ending, but rather offering a conclusion that feels emotionally resonant and appropriate for the characters' journeys. A well-executed resolution contributes to reader satisfaction, making the entire romantic experience more fulfilling and memorable.

READERS INVEST TIME AND EMOTION IN THE CHARACTERS AND THEIR RELATIONSHIPS, AND A LACK OF RESOLUTION CAN LEAVE THEM FEELING CHEATED OR DISCONNECTED FROM THE STORY.

Happening* to *your characters* vs for *your characters: While you are bound to throw a whole host of obstacles and challenges into your character's path, the secret to avoiding contrived or convenient plots lies in how effectively you use the circumstances and conflicts you place at the center of your character's journey to actually grow them rather than stifle them.

If the events of your story don't serve to challenge your character's goals, motivations, and perspectives, they tend to feel convenient or formulaic. Give your characters enough agency to react and adapt to your story, rather than passively allowing everything to happen to them. While you may take immense pleasure in placing the characters at the mercy of your choices, your readers will derive significantly less joy from these events if they don't feel like a natural outgrowth of the story and the choices of your characters.

Without character growth, it's easy for the individual conflicts of your story to appear as though their only purpose is to increase the word count of your novel.

In order to avoid this pitfall, be sure that your character gets proactive about resolving their conflicts at some point in the novel—this may come as late as the dark moment (at the end of act two), but when they decide to confront their problem head-on rather than simply react to every crisis it brings, it gives the reader something to root for and solidifies the character's growth arc in the process.

SUBVERTING EXPECTATIONS AND KEEPING TROPES FRESH

We wish that we could give you a list of all the ways your Storyline Trope could be flipped on its head or refreshed to take it from trite to tantalizing—but the truth is, if we did that, not only would it rid your story of the individuality that only you can bring, but soon enough, none of those creative methods would feel fresh, because we'd all be using them to stir up our stories!

THE GOAL IS NOT TO COMPLETELY ABANDON THE TROPE BUT TO INFUSE IT WITH UNEXPECTED ELEMENTS AND DEPTH.

While some entries will include an idea to subvert reader expectations, most of them won't. The good news is that when you understand why these tropes are so beloved by readers and how they function, you'll be well-equipped to take and preserve all the yummy bits of your chosen trope and mix them in with unexpected theme, setting, or character traits that will leave your readers in awe.

For any trope, you can generally freshen things up by:

- adding complexity to the storyline by deviating from the typical path (within reason!). If your **Secret Romance** is discovered by even one character within the first act and used as leverage against your lovers, it will automatically up the ante and take the conflict of your story down an entirely different (and more intense) path.
- layering additional Storyline Tropes, such as combining the **Coming Home** trope with the **Fish out of Water** to flip the familiarity and comforts of home completely on their head
- switching up settings or time periods. A **Marriage of Convenience** in the 1600s is going to look entirely different from a modern **Marriage of Convenience**.
- subverting expectations (unexpected twists that defy the usual trajectory of the trope like an arranged marriage between the heirs to two feuding dynasties . . . what is that they say about keeping enemies closer than friends? *smirk*).
- exploring secondary conflicts (what conflicts can you explore that would be a natural outgrowth or consequence of the Storyline Trope that you've chosen?).
- embracing diversity (exploring different cultures can change the entire lens through which you tell your story, and stories with central characters of color are in high-demand—just be sure to enlist the help of a sensitivity reader).
- infusing humor and wit.
- creating complex or unexpected backstories that challenge the stereotypes associated with your trope.
- using the transformation arc of your character to highlight ways in which they have overcome challenges inherent to

their trope or rejected a long-held belief that stemmed from the nature of their trope.

Remember, the goal is not to completely abandon the trope but to infuse it with unexpected elements and depth. You can retain the core appeal of your Storyline Trope while freshening it up with your own creativity and unique author voice. This approach can make your novel stand out while still resonating with readers who enjoy the familiar comfort of well-loved tropes.

CHAPTER 10

STORYLINE TROPES AND "THE MARKET"

It's a common question in romance writing circles. How do I make my books more marketable? You'll find dozens of answers in the comments that all read the same: Add more tropes to your books!

While we are firm believers in tropes (obviously, we're writing this entire series of books about them), we also believe that tropifying your work isn't enough. Jessica writes all about this in her book *Beyond the Beats*. There is far more to a compelling and sellable romance than slapping a few tropes on the blurb and calling it a day.

However, it wouldn't have become advice if there wasn't a hint of truth in it. Tropes reign supreme in the romance genre.

All tropes are powerful for marketing, don't get us wrong, but Storyline Tropes in particular are a powerful way to hook your readers and capture their interest from the first chapter.

Some Storyline Tropes are definite reader favorites and can be very effective marketing tools. There are readers that specifically look for **Mail-Order Bride** stories, **Runaway Brides**, and **Fake**

Relationships. It can be incredibly powerful to lean into these tropes in your titles.

Other Storyline Tropes are powerful to use in your blurb or social media. They let the reader know that there is more going on in the story than two people meeting, going on a few dates, and having a happily ever after. Whether it is the **Renovation** of a historic bed-and-breakfast (with very different ideas of how that should happen), going on a **Road Trip** (complete with a navigationally-challenged partner who needs too many bathroom breaks), or someone pushing the injured athlete through rehab so he can return to the city and win the championship, undoubtedly leaving her behind when he goes (**Short-Term Fling**). These Storyline Tropes hint toward conflict, excitement, adventure, and purpose for the characters—and readers want to go along for the journey!

STORYLINE TROPES USED IN MARKETING MATERIALS HINT TOWARD CONFLICT, EXCITEMENT, ADVENTURE, AND PURPOSE FOR THE CHARACTERS—AND READERS WANT TO GO ALONG FOR THE JOURNEY!

While avid readers light up at the phrases **Marriage of Convenience**, **Forced Proximity**, and **Secret Baby**, other readers might not recognize the jargon we as authors are so familiar with. Think outside the box and use wording that is familiar and conveys the feeling and experience of the story.

STORYLINE TROPES WITH A BAD RAP

There are some Storyline Tropes that we know get a bad rap, but it's usually due to the trope not being executed well rather than an inherent flaw in the Storyline. For the most part, tropes that initially reflect poorly on the female main character are a hard sell. Readers really have to connect with the character to forgive them for whatever decision is setting the Storyline Trope in motion.

Examples include **Secret Baby**, **Hidden Identity**, **Hidden Motives**, as well as **Runaway Bride** and **Accidental Marriage**. Readers can be a bit hard on characters if the decisions are impulsive, deceptive, or socially unacceptable. But with clear motives, strong character arcs, and likable personalities, you can make sure readers are willing to give your character the benefit of the doubt and then reward them with a super satisfying growth and resolution.

A NOTE FROM YOUR MARKETING COACH

Our editor suggested we change this to not be gender specific in the description – so tropes that reflect poorly on the character. We've chosen to leave it as it stands now.

In my experience, romance readers (who are overwhelmingly women) are significantly more likely to be critical of the FMC's choices than the MMC. It's not really fair, but it is what it is. Approach your tropes armed with the assumption that readers will be harder on the woman.

-TGE

On the flip side, readers struggle with heroes who do dumb or insensitive things like make a **Bet** that they can seduce a woman. In this case, it's important to secure the reader's investment in the story by creating opportunity for them to connect with and empathize with the character right off the bat.

MOST POPULAR TROPES

Now, just because a trope has a bad rap doesn't mean it can't be a reader favorite. Readers may say they hate **Secret Baby** stories, but it doesn't mean they don't fly off the shelves. **Accidental Marriage** has two strikes against it for impulsive and/or irresponsible characters, but readers still want to see how the scenario plays out. All we're saying is that actions speak louder than words, and a good story (l*owercase s story, not Storyline*) trumps tropes every time.

Readers love nearly every trope that pits performance versus reality and leans into perception via deception—**Fake Relationships** and **Hidden Motives**, along with many ***Going to the Chapel*** tropes where the couple is forced to behave as though they are in love are the classic examples of this.

Other tropes are less dramatic but definitely enjoyed by readers who prefer an externally focused, non-deceptive, or drama-focused plot. Tropes like **Coming Home**, **Save the Town**, **Renovation**, and **Work/Community Project** are almost universally well-received, though they don't carry the marketing power of more drama-heavy tropes. Usually these are combined with other powerful marketing tropes to create an exciting hook that pulls the reader into a satisfying story. These are more common in **Small Town** settings but definitely work in other subgenres as well.

In historical romance, **Arranged Marriage**, **Marriage of Convenience**, and **Mail-Order Bride** stories have been popular for decades and will continue to be so.

UNDERSERVED TROPES

Knowing which tropes are underserved is a bit more challenging for Storyline Tropes than it was for Character Tropes, since they are not as obvious within most titles or covers. Reading blurbs (and a lot of books!) can help you see where gaps exist.

From your authors' perspective at the time of writing this book (early 2024), **Instant Family** stories (not **Single Parent**, but along the lines of **Unexpected Guardian**) are less common but loved by readers for all the "good dad" vibes on the reader-wish fulfillment scale.

Marriage Pacts, **Accidental Marriages**, and **Secret Relationships** are similarly well-received and less popular, so they can be a good option if you're looking to add a Storyline Trope that isn't done very often.

TITLES, KEYWORDS AND BLURBS

Remember, your Storyline will impact the external conflict of the story and create opportunities for internal and relational conflict to occur. Be sure to mention the existence of external conflict in your blurb, even if it is a couple well-placed words like "approaching deadline" or "left at the altar," or even "mistaken for his fake date."

CHAPTER 10

There are only a few tropes that trend toward being mentioned in the title of the book. **Marriage of Convenience/Mail-Order Bride** are big ones. **Runaway Bride**, **Secret Baby** and **Fake Relationship** are the other major ones. Don't be afraid to be creative when including the trope in the title though. There are only so many ways to title a book "The Duke's Convenient Marriage." One or two well-placed words can hint at the trope—"Convenient" being the obvious one for that trope, and "Inconvenient" being a fun twist on it.

Like we explained in *Romance Character Tropes*, tropifying your titles isn't strictly necessary, but it does help sales, since it is the first thing readers will learn about your book.

Faking it with the Quarterback

The Quarterback's Secret Baby

Secretly Dating the Quarterback

They're all obvious and tell you about the story, in this case communicating the Storyline Trope and the Character Trope in one fell swoop.

However, you could be just as effective with subtler words.

Remembering the Quarterback (**Amnesia**)

Contract with the Quarterback (**Fake Dating**, **Marriage Pact**, **Marriage of Convenience**)

A Match for the Quarterback (**Matchmaker**)

Or drop the Character Trope altogether:

Remember the Scars (**Amnesia**)

A Contract to Break (**Fake Dating**, **Marriage of Convenience**)

A Match Made Perfect (**Matchmaker**)

You can also include Storyline Tropes in your subtitle or keywords, if you deliver on the expectations of the trope and it is a major part of your story. Don't call it a **Forced Proximity** story if they simply see each other sort of frequently.

Anything in your title, keywords, blurb, or on your cover is a promise to the reader. Deliver on the promise, and you'll have them coming back for more!

Part Three

THE STORYLINE TROPE ENCYCLOPEDIA

CHAPTER 11

GOING TO THE CHAPEL

MARRIAGE TROPES

All of the Marriage Storyline Tropes center on the event of marriage between the two main characters of your romance novel. These are strong adhesion tropes (binding the characters together) with common themes of commitment, choice, and finding a balance between personal and societal expectations.

ACCIDENTAL MARRIAGE

ARRANGED MARRIAGE

MAIL-ORDER BRIDE

MARRIAGE OF CONVENIENCE

MARRIAGE PACT

ACCIDENTAL MARRIAGE

In this trope, characters find themselves in a spur of the moment, sometimes drunken, decision to marry. The hallmark of this trope is the "Vegas wedding" scenario, but it could also occur when characters find themselves accidentally married legally without any intention and sometimes any knowledge or memory of it happening. Perhaps they thought a cruise ship wedding wasn't binding or were married by proxy. As the story unfolds, the characters must face the consequences of their choice or work together to undo the marriage. They may have been strangers before the inciting incident or have a prior history; each scenario adds to the nuance of the conflict in the story.

WHY READERS LOVE IT

Think about how interested you would be if your best friend suddenly announced they'd gotten married by accident. You would want all the details and the drama, and most of all—are they going to stick it out? Readers love the delightful chaos and unexpected twists found within Accidental Marriage stories, so be sure to give it to them!

These narratives are imbued with a humorous charm, as the protagonists find themselves thrust into matrimony through a series of unforeseen events, often resulting in uproarious situations that defy logic and expectation. The element of surprise keeps readers on the edge of their seats, eagerly anticipating the next comedic mishap or unexpected turn of events.

Another thing readers love about these stories is the journey of falling in love with someone at their most imperfect and vulnerable state. In the midst of navigating the fallout of their accidental union, the protagonists are given the opportunity to see each other's flaws, quirks, and vulnerabilities, fostering a deeper connection that transcends initial impressions.

As the protagonists grapple with the reality of their accidental marriage, readers delight in witnessing the evolution of their relationship. Despite their initial desire to part ways, they are bound together by a common goal: generally, to extricate themselves from the confines of this marriage. This shared objective sparks moments of collaboration, problem-solving, and camaraderie.

As they work together and grow closer, the transition from accidental to intentional marriage is slow but oh-so-enjoyable. As the protagonists navigate the complexities of their newfound relationship, they are forced to confront their own feelings and desires, leading to moments of self-discovery and emotional growth. What began as an impulsive decision, set up, or hilarious misunderstanding evolves into a heartfelt exploration of love and commitment.

READER EXPECTATIONS

Readers may not see the buildup to the accidental marriage on the page, but you should reveal enough about the characters and their situation that we can understand how they got there. Readers will be hungry for glimpses into the characters' lives and circumstances that led to this unexpected twist of fate. The characters should have major elements of shock or confusion and even anger upon discovering what's happened.

It's also crucial that readers see the characters marry on the page, or at the very least, we expect the story to pick up in the immediate aftermath. In fact, depending on how your characters came to be married, the tension of working to undo an event that the characters have no recollection of can be a powerful force to drive the plot forward.

Central to the appeal of Accidental Marriage stories is the nuanced exploration of character development and emotional depth. Readers expect to witness the protagonists grappling with the unintended consequences of their actions, navigating through a range of emotions as they come to terms with their newfound marital status. Whether it's the gradual acceptance of responsibility or the unexpected shift from creating distance to clinging to each other, readers crave a journey to true intimacy that unfolds at a deliberate and measured pace. The slower progression allows for a deeper exploration of the characters' vulnerabilities, fears, and desires, fostering a sense of authenticity and connection that resonates with readers on a profound level.

This trope really shines in the gradual development of genuine feelings. Although the two characters' lives were thrown together in a chaotic way, as they sort through the mess, they will grow closer and closer until they choose to stay together in a deliberate and meaningful way.

Side characters and family also tend to play a big role in this trope, whether it is hiding the relationship status from them or being forced to play it up as real because of Mom's excitement at the news. Lean into the consequences of the characters' accidental marriage on their other relationships.

POTENTIAL PITFALLS

As the characters navigate the impact on their relationships, they should be forced to confront the reality of their very unstable marriage relationship.

Heavy-handed comedy: Don't rely too heavily on the humor element. You don't want to get so stuck in the comedic premise that you miss the heart. Even in a romantic comedy, you'll want a good balance of heartfelt connection between the characters to go along with the funny scenes and banter.

Lack of romance arc: Somewhere along the journey through this narrative, your characters need to move from distant to emotionally intimate. Even if they originally agree to address the accidental marriage by getting to know each other with the open-ended possibility of forever, the romance arc should develop naturally and not be a static part of the story as the characters simply move through the plot.

Immature characters: The circumstances that land a character in the throes of an accidental marriage are not always made from the most thoughtful and responsible choices. While we can expect a lot of mishaps to lead up to the culmination of the accidental wedding, don't make your characters' personalities or actions too cringeworthy if you want readers to make it past the first chapter.

FREQUENTLY PAIRED TROPES

Adding layers to an Accidental Marriage story often begins with the question of who is the unexpected partner. It's complicated to wake up married to a stranger. But it's even more complicated to wake up married to your enemy (Enemies to Lovers), your boss (Boss/Employee), or your ex (Second Chance). Get creative with the scenario and see what additional fun you can add to your character's accidental escapades.

Depending on the circumstances, your characters will often lean into a Fake Relationship (acting as though the marriage is real in front of others), or a Secret Relationship (desperately trying to hide the fact that they are married).

In many cases, this trope carries similarities to the Amnesia trope. Perhaps one character vividly remembers the marriage night while the other has no recollection. Or maybe neither of them remember, but they will walk through the mystery of figuring out exactly what happened together as they try to undo it.

COMMON PLOT DEVICES

Impulsive characters: One or both protagonists are often depicted as impulsive individuals who act on whims or without thinking through the consequences. Their impulsive nature leads them into situations where a sudden and unexpected marriage occurs, setting the stage for the ensuing comedic and romantic developments.

Accidental marriage of convenience: Sometimes external circumstances such as legal or financial pressures push the protagonists to consider changing their accidental marriage into a temporary marriage arrangement. This provides a believable reason for the characters to stay together a bit longer than strictly necessary.

Mom's thrilled for you: In many Accidental Marriage stories, parental involvement adds an extra layer of complication and humor. Protagonists will grapple with their parents' overenthusiastic support or disapproval of their unexpected union. Whether it's the mother who eagerly starts planning a big reception or the father who is vehemently opposed to the marriage, parental reactions add both tension and comedic relief to the storyline.

Misunderstandings and miscommunication: Central to the Accidental Marriage trope are misunderstandings and miscommunications that happen in any marriage, but especially with characters who didn't know each other or plan to get married. These misunderstandings often serve as catalysts for character growth and relationship development.

KEY MOMENTS

Inciting incident: The heart of the Accidental Marriage trope lies in the inciting incident—the moment when the unexpected marriage occurs. This pivotal event thrusts the protagonists into a whirlwind of confusion, disbelief, and often comedic chaos—together. Whether it's a spontaneous Vegas wedding, a drunken escapade in a foreign country, or a paperwork mix-up at the courthouse, the marriage itself serves as the catalyst for the rest of the story, setting the stage for a series of humorous and romantic developments. This event might not even be shown on the page, especially if the story opens on "the morning after," but details of the incident can and *should* be revealed later.

Call to action: Following the shock and confusion of the accidental marriage, the protagonists face a crucial decision: whether to stick it out or to do everything in their power to annul or dissolve the marriage. This call to action sets the stage for at least one character's goal during the rest of the story. Whether it's embarking on a quest to find a loophole in the law, seeking advice from well-meaning friends and family, or attempting to confront the circumstances that led to their accidental union, the protagonists are faced with the challenge of determining the fate of their marriage.

Resolution: An Accidental Marriage story must culminate in a poignant moment of commitment where the protagonists decide their future together. Since their first vows were accidental, this commitment must be the opposite: deliberate and informed. It's the juxtaposition of these two experiences that brings the relationship arc to completion.

POTENTIAL THEMES

Embracing the unexpected
Love in spite of imperfections
Second chances
Personal responsibility
Team vs. individual

ARRANGED MARRIAGE

In an Arranged Marriage, characters find themselves bound together in matrimony through a predetermined agreement made by family members, friends, or societal conventions. Unlike love marriages, which are based on the individuals' mutual affection and choice, arranged marriages are orchestrated by external forces, often with the aim of securing financial stability, political alliances, or preserving cultural traditions. But because this is a romance novel, their happily ever after will show these two sharing a genuine love by the end of the book.

Despite their initial reluctance toward or even refusal to agree to the arranged union, the protagonists gradually discover common ground, shared values, and emotional connection as they navigate the challenges and joys of married life. Through moments of vulnerability, compromise, and personal growth, they embark on a journey of self-discovery and mutual respect, ultimately finding love and fulfillment in each other's arms.

WHY READERS LOVE IT

Because many Arranged Marriage stories are speculative or historical, one aspect that captivates readers is the opportunity to immerse themselves in Historical or Fantasy settings, where intricate world-building and vivid descriptions transport them to a different time and place. Through richly detailed narratives, readers can explore the nuances of customs, traditions, and societal norms, adding depth and authenticity to the reading experience. The novelty and uniqueness of arranged marriages, particularly in the modern Western world, piques readers' interest and fascination.

Readers also enjoy the mutual journey of uncovering the hidden layers of each partner. As the protagonists navigate the arranged union, they slowly unravel the mysteries and secrets that lie beneath the surface of their new partner. Readers are captivated by the gradual revelation of character traits, fears, and desires, as the protagonists peel back the layers of pretense and discover the true essence of their partner.

The trope of Arranged Marriage shares striking similarities with the Forced Proximity trope, adding an extra layer of tension and intimacy to the narrative. Readers are sucked in by the dynamic interplay between the protagonists as they find themselves thrust together in close quarters, forced to confront their differences and forge a connection amidst the confines of their arranged union.

Readers are drawn to Arranged Marriage stories for their Slow Burn elements, characterized by the gradual development of love and intimacy between the protagonists. Despite the initial reluctance or unexpected nature of their romantic connection, readers revel in the anticipation and longing that accompanies the slow unfolding of their relationship. For those who appreciate the Slow Burn trope, the gradual progression of feelings and the emotional depth it brings are immensely satisfying.

READER EXPECTATIONS

The initial reluctance or unwillingness to marry the chosen match is the hallmark of this trope. Both parties may not express this with the same vehemence, but as the relationship develops, the question of whether the relationship has blossomed out of nothing more than obligation is likely to serve as a significant setback to true acceptance of the marriage.

The initial reluctance, doubt, or fear over the arrangement sets the stage for moving both the character arc and the romance arc in a positive direction. However, the external pressures, expectations, or even personal differences will serve as obstacles aplenty to keeping the love birds apart for most of the book and challenging the positive trajectory of their emotional and romantic journeys.

Because the Arranged Marriage trope has something of a Forced Proximity element, your story should provide plenty of opportunity for your characters to foster genuine connection and understanding. So don't shy away from throwing your characters together and doing it often, even when dealing with settings such as Royalty or Regency that may change the nature of a typical marriage arrangement. If your characters are never on the page together, it will be incredibly difficult for readers to believe that they've had enough time to fall in love.

POTENTIAL PITFALLS

Cultural insensitivity: Given that some of these stories will involve different cultures or religions as the basis for the arranged marriage, it is important for authors to respect and accurately represent the culture rather than resorting to stereotypes or misconceptions. Utilize sensitivity readers for any culture (even speculative cultures that are loosely inspired by real-life people groups).

Lack of agency: In Arranged Marriage stories, protagonists may sometimes lack agency in their own destinies, particularly if the narrative focuses solely on fulfilling societal or familial expectations rather than allowing the characters to make meaningful choices. Readers may find it disheartening or frustrating when characters are passive participants in their own lives, rather than active agents who shape their own destinies. To avoid this pitfall, authors should ensure that protagonists have agency and autonomy, allowing them to make decisions that reflect their desires, values, and personal growth throughout the story.

Consent: Arranged Marriage stories often grapple with the theme of consent, as characters may find themselves bound to a marital union without their explicit agreement or understanding. Readers may be uncomfortable with narratives that romanticize or gloss over the lack of consent inherent in arranged marriages, particularly if the protagonists' autonomy and choices are disregarded in favor of cultural or familial expectations. Authors should strive to depict nuanced portrayals of consent in arranged marriages, exploring the complexities of power dynamics, agency, and personal autonomy within the context of the narrative.

Lack of chemistry: Even in clean fiction, keep in mind that these characters are already married. While intimate relationships may be a sensitive subject for the characters, it is bound to crop up as a symbol of true and lasting commitment—of the characters giving themselves over fully and opening up their heart and souls to their spouse. In order to maximize the impact of this moment (even if it never happens on the page), be sure to highlight the chemistry between your characters. Whether it's an irresistible draw, a feeling of being fully known and accepted, a physical spark, or just being a downright entertaining match, give the reader a reason to believe that this couple will last the long haul.

COMMON PLOT DEVICES

Cultural clash: The protagonists come from different cultural backgrounds, leading to clashes in beliefs, customs, and traditions. This plot device adds depth to the narrative as characters navigate the complexities of their arranged union while grappling with cultural differences.

Buried secrets: Because getting to be intimately acquainted is not necessarily a prerequisite for these marriages, it is common for characters to go through the process of uncovering shocking or buried secrets. Whether they are about the protagonist, their family, or their new spouse, these secrets color the external, internal, and relational conflict.

Honor marriage: This is a plot device where a couple is forced to (or chooses to) marry due to the "honor" of the woman being threatened, usually by an overnight interlude or being found in a compromising situation. Note that in clean romance, the characters will not be having sex during their overnight, and the act of staying the night together is usually unintentional. In contemporary romance, this plot device may also be used in a shotgun wedding scenario, where the father of the heroine compels the hero to marry her after premarital sex results in a pregnancy.

Trash to treasure: In many Arranged Marriage stories, one of the protagonists (usually the woman) is regarded as lesser, unimportant, or undesirable by her own family—making it easy for them to trade her away in an arrangement that benefits them. But her new partner (inexplicably, in her mind) considers her a treasure and desires to love her fiercely, forcing her to face her own internal wounds and great lie to embrace the romance.

Keep up appearances: To avoid the consequences of their arranged marriage or to fulfill certain obligations, the protagonists may need to pretend to be in love in public. This plot device often leads to genuine feelings developing over time and forces them to cross stages of physical intimacy (hand-to-body, hand-to-face, mouth-to-mouth) that they might not otherwise have breached, propelling them down the path of emotional intimacy at the same time.

FREQUENTLY PAIRED TROPES

Royalty and Regency tropes easily lend themselves to the Arranged Marriage trope, with the likelihood of politically arranged marriages or alliances being a common motive.

These stories are also commonly Fantasy or Sci-Fi settings, where the author is given freedom to create entire species, cultures, and worlds where Arranged Marriage seems more realistic.

Since the reluctance or outright refusal to marry is a key element of Arranged Marriage, it's common to see this trope paired with Enemies to Lovers in a situation where the characters are determined to avoid marriage in the true sense.

The Arranged Marriage trope often intertwines with Hidden Motives, adding layers of intrigue and suspense to the narrative. In these stories, one or both characters enter into the arranged union with ulterior motives, sometimes including the ultimate demise of the character they are marrying.

These stories also often feature protagonists who find themselves thrust into unfamiliar or uncomfortable situations, making them ripe for the Fish out of Water trope, such as the princess being married off to the neighboring kingdom's prince to forge an alliance and finding herself in an entirely different world than the one she grew up in.

KEY MOMENTS

Inciting incident: The story may start at the arrangement of the marriage, just before the marriage, or in the moment. Whatever the case is, your reader needs to understand what the impetus or external force of the marriage arrangement is—why are these two people being brought together in marriage? Make sure that your reader also gets an idea of how the characters feel about the arrangement.

Call to action: By the end of the first act, your character must face the choice of committing to marriage or seeking a way out. In a story where the character has no real aspirations of not being married (such as for societal reasons), we want to see them choose to make an intentional effort in the success of the marriage, even if romantic love is not a part of their plan.

Turning point: At least one of your characters has truly fallen in love at the turning point, and they have developed a comfortable marriage relationship or routine—however, at this turning point, all of the external factors and obligations that lead the couple into the marriage come back to cast a shadow over their developing feelings. This typically comes at the end of act two and may even be the dark night moment, but in either case, it should cause a significant amount of doubt, fear, and insecurity in the characters.

POTENTIAL THEMES

Duty vs. desire
Identity
Loyalty
Sacrifice
Autonomy

MAIL-ORDER BRIDE

While the following entry on Marriage of Convenience will be extremely relevant to this trope, the Mail-Order Bride does have a few specific things that differentiate it from other Marriage of Convenience storylines. These arrangements are usually (but not always) intended to be permanent and are far more prevalent in historical romance, when the mail-order bride concept was a reality.

Mail-Order Bride stories typically center around a woman who, for reasons such as financial hardship, limited opportunities, or a desire for adventure, agrees to marry a man sight unseen, usually from a distant locale. The other main character needs a wife (or husband, for an interesting gender swap) for practical reasons, typically to share the burden of parenthood, homesteading, or other vocation, such as mission work or leading a church. These stories are often set in the historical American West or other frontier regions, where men outnumbered women and societal norms facilitated the practice of arranging marriages through correspondence, though modern settings can be a fun twist on the trope. The character, or sometimes someone close to them, places an ad for a partner. Whether that is in the paper or online or using a service depends on the setting and time period of the story.

Once the bride arrives, she must navigate the complexities of a new environment, forge connections with her husband and the community, and ultimately decide if she can find happiness in her new life. While the other person is seeking a partner to help achieve their goal, the motivation for the respondent is often a matter of escape or survival. Whatever made them seek a mail-order marriage in the first place may or may not come into play later in the story, but either way, they will be relocating and absorbing the goals of their new spouse as their own.

Despite the initial arrangement being based on practical considerations, Mail-Order Bride stories explore themes of love, resilience, and the pursuit of dreams amidst the backdrop of rugged landscapes and frontier life. As they spend time together and work together to achieve success in the now-mutual goal, the characters grow in respect for each other, develop a friendship, and eventually a deep, lasting love.

WHY READERS LOVE IT

See Marriage of Convenience.

In addition to the things mentioned in that entry, the rarity of the Mail-Order Bride storyline in modern culture makes it a fun escape for readers. The story allows them to live an adventure they will likely never face. A story about a character leaving everything behind and starting over, making the best of circumstances with a complete stranger, is incredibly compelling. Mail-Order Bride stories tend to feature strong, resilient heroines who are not afraid of hard work.

Whereas many Marriage of Convenience stories tend to pull characters into a practical arrangement while fighting the development of true love, the characters in a Mail-Order Bride scenario often desire a true marriage. The focus instead becomes the uncertainty of whether two complete strangers can form that kind of lasting bond after they've already tied their lives together forever.

READER EXPECTATIONS

See Marriage of Convenience.

While a Mail-Order Bride typically accepts the arrangement due to lack of other options, the character herself is full of grit, hardworking, and tenacious. While they might come to their new life without any of the skills required to help their partner achieve the goal of running the farm or building a church, they earn the respect of their partner with their determination.

More often than not, a Mail-Order Bride story is a Fish out of Water story and should meet the expectations of that storyline. Sometimes, the mail-order bride is a candidate selected specifically because of skills they bring, but they will still be relocating and should face obstacles connecting with side characters, unfamiliar environmental factors, or cultural differences. Think of the governess who is used to teaching high society children in the city and becomes the bride and a mother of three unruly children on a farm on the Kansas plains, where her new husband views reading as a rather unnecessary skill.

These characters have a genuine desire to work together, as their situation necessitates it. They both enter into the marriage seeking mutual respect and looking to work together toward a common goal. While this may seem like the recipe for the perfect marriage, keep in mind that the expectation of these characters may be (and likely will be) entirely different from their reality. It's the unexpected aspects of each character's personality, temperament, skills, and even physical traits that tend to serve as a catalyst for tension and internal or relational conflict. Your rough and tumble rancher may have been perfectly ready to accept a working partner and life companion, but if the woman who shows up is too dad-gum beautiful to keep his hands (and his lips) off her, it sure may throw a wrench into his deadline of getting the ranch up and running before winter sets in.

POTENTIAL PITFALLS

Lack of conflict: These characters can't simply painlessly waltz into their new life together. The challenges they face should be significant, whether they are external conflicts they overcome together, internal conflicts as they each wrestle with the ramifications of their romantic entanglement on their character, or relational conflict as they get to know and love one another.

Low stakes: If the characters' motivations or the reasons behind the marriage feel forced, artificial, or downright stupid, readers will struggle to connect with the story. Strive to make the characters' actions authentic and consistent with their goals or internal conflict, ensuring that readers can understand and empathize with their choices.

Lack of chemistry: Even in clean fiction, keep in mind that these characters are already married. While intimate relationships may be a sensitive subject for the characters, it is bound to crop up as a symbol of true and lasting commitment—of the characters giving themselves over fully and opening up their hearts and souls to their spouse. In order to maximize the impact of this moment (even if it never happens on the page), be sure to highlight the chemistry between these characters. Whether it's an irresistible draw, a feeling of being fully known and accepted, a physical spark, or just being a downright entertaining match, give the reader a reason to believe that this couple will last the long haul.

COMMON PLOT DEVICES

Meddling side characters: Well-meaning friends, nosy neighbors, or concerned family members may interfere in the protagonist's life, offering unsolicited advice, orchestrating unexpected encounters, placing the advertisement for the main character, or even attempting to sabotage the new marriage. Their meddling actions add layers of humor, tension, and drama to the narrative, influencing the characters' decisions and shaping the course of their relationships.

Bad first impressions: When the Mail-Order Bride arrives at her intended husband's doorstep, a bad first impression can set the tone for their relationship. Whether it's a misunderstanding, a clash of personalities, or a series of awkward encounters, initial tensions and miscommunications often arise, leading to uncertainty and apprehension on both sides. To a lesser degree, this may even be a case of the bride or groom not matching up to the expectation or picture that the characters have formed in their minds prior to meeting. Overcoming these bad first impressions becomes a central challenge for the protagonists as they strive to find common ground, build trust, and forge a connection amidst the uncertainty of their arranged marriage.

Surprise bride: In some Mail-Order Bride stories, the groom-to-be is taken by surprise when his intended bride arrives unexpectedly, usually because some well-meaning friend took it upon themselves to find him a bride. This plot device adds an element of shock to the narrative, as the groom grapples with the sudden arrival of a stranger who is meant to be his wife. The unexpected nature of the situation may lead to initial resistance or reluctance on the groom's part as he struggles with the reality of his new bride's arrival or even attempts to send her back where she came from.

Finding an ally: Upon arriving in a new and unfamiliar environment, the Mail-Order Bride often finds herself in need of a friend or ally to help navigate the challenges of her new life. Whether it's a kind-hearted neighbor, a sympathetic townsperson, or a fellow newcomer, finding an ally becomes crucial for the character's emotional support and integration into the community. This plot device highlights themes of camaraderie, compassion, and the importance of human connection amidst the isolation and uncertainty of their new life.

FREQUENTLY PAIRED TROPES

Mail-Order Bride stories have a very strong "adhesive" force for the protagonists, so they are commonly paired with strong tropes that repel the characters, such as Hate to Love, where initial animosity between the prospective bride and groom evolves into genuine affection. The groom is often featured as a Tough Guy, especially in Western or Cowboy romances, as a character who does not wear his heart on his sleeve and may reluctantly agree to the arrangement with no illusions of finding genuine love.

Forced Proximity, such as a blizzard on the plains, is often used to force the characters together even further, in case they find it too easy to ignore one another with the wide open spaces that are common in the Rural and Small Town settings.

If the Mail-Order Bride is running from something, the hero may take on the role of Protector, standing by the bride's side and protecting her when her past comes to call.

KEY MOMENTS

Inciting incident: Like a Marriage of Convenience, this is usually the moment when our characters are given the push they need to seek out a marriage partner. This scene may only focus on the spouse seeking the arrangement, or it may also include a scene where the new bride makes arrangements to travel to her husband. It may also coincide with the meet cute.

Meet cute: The meet cute of a Mail-Order Bride story is critically important. These characters are almost always strangers, and this is the moment where they make their first impressions, setting the stage for the tone of the marriage relationship. If the characters don't hit it off, or make an unfavorable impression, that probably doesn't bode well for the marriage. Even if the first meeting leaves your characters with nothing but excitement, we as the readers know there's only one way to go from there—down. (Until they fall in love for real, of course.)

Turning point: One or both characters realizes the depth of their romantic feelings and desires to take the relationship a step further emotionally or physically. This leads to a moment of vulnerability and openness, typically leading to a declaration of love by one or both characters.

Dark moment: Typically this is tied to whatever the character's motivations were for getting married. Things may backfire and the marriage prove to be insufficient, secret motivations may be revealed, or characters may go back on their word. They likely question whether the other character truly returns their feelings or if the connection is one-sided and their spouse was simply making the best of the time they were forced to spend together.

POTENTIAL THEMES

Partnership vs. self-reliance
Choosing joy
Overcoming loss
Courage
Self-discovery

MARRIAGE OF CONVENIENCE

The Marriage of Convenience trope is a popular and enduring one in the romance genre, and it's a personal favorite of your authors. In this storyline, two characters enter into a marriage for practical or pragmatic reasons rather than for genuine love. The motivations behind such marriages typically involve social, financial, or legal considerations. The individuals involved may not have any pre-existing romantic feelings for each other, but the marriage is seen as a mutually beneficial arrangement.

Common scenarios include getting married to secure an inheritance, gain social status, provision of a home or safety, or fulfilling a contractual obligation. The characters in a Marriage of Convenience may intend to end the marriage after a predetermined time, or they may be committing to a lifetime without love, planning to be partners and perhaps friends. However, through the course of being legally married, the characters grow closer, typically through shared obstacles, close proximity, and the ever-blurring lines between the business and the pleasure of the relationship.

WHY READERS LOVE IT

The characters in these stories may be complete strangers or they may have a history (romantic or otherwise), but in either case, readers love the journey from a contract marriage with no feelings involved to a genuine connection. While this arrangement is initiated by practicality rather than passion, there is no shortage of romantic sparks in these stories—which continue to build until they are an unbridled inferno. Tender and passionate scenes, moments of vulnerability, and small displays of affection are the bread and butter of this trope.

This trope is especially fun for readers because there are so many opportunities for physical intimacy to jump forward. For example, in historical romances, the propriety during a typical courtship forbids much unchaperoned time together, but the married couple would have all the access and proximity they can handle. In any subgenre, the characters in a Marriage of Convenience are often living together, and even if they keep separate bedrooms, will be exposed to unguarded versions of their new partner—decompressing after a long day, sick or injured, or even fresh out of the shower (eep!).

For some readers, the trope allows them to indulge in a romantic fantasy. The idea that love can bloom in unexpected circumstances and that two people can find happiness despite a nontraditional beginning. At the heart of this trope is the idea that love is an action, a choice, rather than a fleeting emotion.

READER EXPECTATIONS

Characters may enter into a contract marriage as a matter of permanence or as a temporary arrangement. In Christian romance, the marriage is nearly always seen as a permanent commitment, as readers may frown on a view that marriage would be treated as anything other than forever. But in other subgenres, the setup of a temporary marriage that becomes forever is very accepted. The turning point of the narrative will differ slightly based on what the original understanding of the relationship was.

Despite the initial motivations being driven by external factors, readers expect to see a genuine emotional connection develop between the characters. The romance should feel authentic and serve as a catalyst for growth, but it should happen gradually, not all at once. This is a key expectation of the trope. As characters encounter obstacles to their initial goals and motivations, these priorities and perspectives tend to shift, drawing the characters closer together.

Readers want to see all the awkward encounters that result from two strangers suddenly sharing space and life. They often want the wedding itself (is it an elaborate production? Or a private, emotionless courthouse wedding?). And they definitely want the wedding night, even if it is closed door. Or your characters may choose to abstain from intercourse, but that likely depends on the arrangement terms and character arcs. Whatever it looks like, the readers want to experience the discomfort of determining just what each character expects from that night, especially if they were not careful to lay out those kinds of terms ahead of time.

POTENTIAL PITFALLS

Lack of character development: If the characters don't undergo meaningful development throughout the story, readers may find it challenging to connect with or care about their journey. Shallow characterizations can make the emotional arc of the romance less engaging.

Low stakes: If the characters' motivations or the reasons behind the marriage feel forced, artificial, or downright stupid, readers will struggle to connect with the story. Strive to make the characters' actions authentic and consistent with their goals or internal conflict, ensuring that readers can understand and empathize with their choices.

Instant marriage: The hallmark of this trope is the gradual buildup to a genuine love and connection. A rushed or unrealistic progression of the romantic relationship may leave readers unconvinced by the characters' feelings.

Contrived conflict: Introducing unnecessary or contrived conflicts solely to prolong the story is bound to frustrate your readers. Ensure that conflicts arise naturally from the characters' personalities, circumstances, and genuine misunderstandings and avoid relying on artificial obstacles that don't contribute to the overall narrative.

Overemphasis on external conflict: While external threats and challenges are common in these romances, an overemphasis on external conflict at the expense of internal emotional growth can leave the story feeling extremely unbalanced.

COMMON PLOT DEVICES

Fake relationship: In some cases, the marriage must be believed by others to be a genuine relationship, such as in politics or the military. When this occurs, characters must pretend to be in love for the sake of others, maintaining the appearance of a loving couple while dealing with their own internal conflicts.

External threats to the arrangement: External forces, such as legal issues, blackmail, or interference from others, can threaten the stability of the marriage, forcing the characters to confront challenges together.

Terms and stipulations: Characters will frequently create a set of rules of policies to govern the union in order to avoid uncomfortable or unwanted situations.

Crisis moments: Critical moments or crises, such as a threat to one of the character's well-being or a significant life event, often serve as catalysts for emotional revelations and the deepening of the romantic connection. This may be achieved on a lesser scale through physical separation, when the absence of the love interest deepens the desire of the characters for a genuine connection.

Honor marriage: This is a plot device where a couple is forced to (or chooses to) marry due to the "honor" of the woman being threatened, usually by an overnight interlude or being found in a compromising situation. Note that in clean romance, the characters will not be having sex during their overnight, and the act of staying the night together is usually unintentional. Note that when the circumstances leading to an honor marriage are coerced by a third party, this plot device follows the Arranged Marriage trope more closely.

FREQUENTLY PAIRED TROPES

While an Enemies to Lovers story is somewhat hard to pull off with this trope, it hasn't stopped authors from doing it often. Other strong repelling tropes do well here also, working against the relationship where the marriage is pushing the characters together. Examples include Hidden Motives, Opposites Attract, and Forbidden Romance.

When a Forbidden Romance is at play, characters may manipulate the situation to force a marriage where the union would otherwise never be permitted, through an Honor Marriage. In this case, it shifts the dynamics of the Forbidden Romance trope slightly—rather than finding a way to be together amidst opposition, these characters must prove the worth of their love amidst disapproval.

The Friends to Lovers trope presents its own challenges in the pacing of the romance arc, but it is another commonly used pairing with the Marriage of Convenience. This trope is used often in Western romance and Regency romance, among other historical settings. Given the rushed circumstances of these marriages, this trope often leads to a Love Triangle situation or an Imaginary Love Triangle.

This trope also plays well with Character Tropes where the stakes for reputation are high—Billionaire, Politician, Celebrity, and Royalty are common examples.

KEY MOMENTS

Inciting incident: The need for marriage is established by one or both characters. The motivation for the marriage must be strong. Characters don't get married lightly, even in historical or speculative settings.

Call to action: Characters agree to marriage, set the terms, and possibly tie the knot.

Turning point: The characters acknowledge that the marriage and feelings are no longer simply an arrangement of convenience, but that their love is real. If the marriage was supposed to be temporary, then they now admit they don't want it to end. If the marriage was supposed to be loveless, then they must now recognize that the feelings they have are real, though they often don't publicly admit them.

Dark moment: Typically this is tied to whatever the character's motivations were for getting married. Things may backfire and the marriage prove to be insufficient, secret motivations may be revealed, or characters may go back on their word. They likely question whether the other character truly returns their feelings or if the connection is one-sided and their spouse was simply making the best of the time they were forced to spend together.

Grand gesture: Characters must choose to stay together, not for the practical benefits to be gained from the marriage, but for the sake of loving each other. This scene typically involves an act of sacrifice or compromise.

POTENTIAL THEMES

Partnership
Vulnerability
Love as a choice
Love as an action
Mutual respect

MARRIAGE PACT

In the Marriage Pact trope, two characters who have previously known each other are revealed to have agreed to marry if they haven't found anyone else by a certain age or milestone. While these stories may involve scenes of the pact, the focus is on what happens *after* one or both parties come around to make good on the promise.

Often these characters haven't seen each other for years, or even a couple decades, but it's the common history that ultimately ties them together and leads them to accept the terms of the marriage pact made so long ago. It should be noted that marriage vows might not actually take place until the end of the book after the characters have reconnected; the marriage pact acting as the impetus for a tentative consideration of a relationship instead of immediately jumping in to honor the pact. In other stories, the marriage might happen relatively early in the narrative, making the narrative take on flavors of the Marriage of Convenience or Arranged Marriage tropes.

The pact is usually a promise made in middle or high school, but sometimes it is even later, with the agreement made during college or early adulthood. One or both protagonists find themselves dissatisfied with their current situation when the pact deadline approaches, pushing them to reconsider claiming what they now likely feel is a bit of a ridiculous idea.

WHY READERS LOVE IT

Despite the initial impracticality of the pact, readers are drawn to the characters' vulnerability and longing for love, rooting for them to defy the odds and find happiness together. Whether it's the reluctant romantic who begrudgingly agrees to honor the pact or the steadfast believer in fate who remains hopeful despite years of separation, readers can't help but empathize with characters who are willing to take a leap of faith in pursuit of love.

Themes of love, commitment, and friendship permeate Marriage Pact romances, resonating with readers who crave stories that explore the complexities of human relationships. As the protagonists navigate the terms of their agreement and confront their pasts, they grapple with questions of loyalty, trust, and the true meaning of love. The gradual progression from contractual obligation to heartfelt connection adds depth and emotional resonance to the narrative, leaving readers eagerly turning pages to see how the characters' journey unfolds.

Like any contractual marriage or relationship, readers revel in the switch from tentative to genuine connection in Marriage Pact romances. The protagonists' initial reluctance or skepticism gives way to moments of vulnerability, intimacy, and ultimately, love, as they rediscover each other and themselves along the way.

There is an element of "almost realistic" when it comes to these romances, as we remember being young girls with close guy friends, usually twinged with a hint of Unrequited Love on one. What would we do if our friend from so many years ago finally showed up and asked us to honor an agreement?

READER EXPECTATIONS

While the initial pact may be featured as a scene in the book, the focus is on the present-day events as the protagonists navigate the implications of their promise. Readers anticipate a backstory that delves into the events that led the characters to make the pact in the first place. This backstory often involves a strong friendship or shared history between the characters, laying the foundation for the emotional stakes of the narrative.

As your lovers confront the present-day circumstances that compel them to make good on their promise, readers expect a collision of past and present, driving the story forward as they navigate their agreement and confront their feelings for each other.

Readers anticipate moments of vulnerability, intimacy, and conflict as the characters grapple with the implications of their pact and the burgeoning attraction between them. Whatever drove the characters to make good on the marriage pact will come back around, emphasizing that the marriage is not a magic wand to solve all their problems. Just as with any contractual relationship, readers expect that the characters will face challenges that test their commitment and resolve. The journey toward love and fulfillment is not without its trials, but ultimately, readers hope for a satisfying resolution that reaffirms the transformative power of love.

POTENTIAL PITFALLS

Lack of character arc: Without a compelling character arc, the story may feel stagnant or lacking in emotional depth. The growth arc is key in these stories, acting as the bridge from the past to the present, paving the way for a happily ever after.

Lack of chemistry: Even in a story centered around a contractual marriage, readers need to be drawn into the undeniable connection between the characters. Without palpable chemistry, the romance may feel forced or contrived, failing to evoke the emotional investment and satisfaction that readers crave in a romantic narrative.

Strictly enforcing the pact: The idea that someone is legally bound to honor a contract they made when they were young, especially if it's imposed in a coercive or manipulative manner, can be off-putting to readers. Such forceful claims may come across as unrealistic or unsympathetic, undermining the authenticity of the protagonists' relationship development. Unless the character is normally a jerk (presumably for good reason), it is best to avoid.

COMMON PLOT DEVICES

Flashbacks: Revisiting the moment of the pact or another time in the past provides context for the relationship, revealing key moments that shaped their connection and motivations for entering into the marriage pact. Sometimes this is taken as far as a nonlinear timeline, where entire scenes from the past are revealed throughout the narrative.

Secrets revealed: Long-buried secrets serve as a powerful plot device that drives the narrative forward and deepens the emotional stakes for the characters. Exposing hidden truths, past traumas, or unresolved conflicts about their past relationship, family members, or other events, these revelations lead to moments of tension, vulnerability, and growth.

Interfering family members: Whether it's well-meaning parents, overbearing siblings, or even just meddling townspeople, these characters often have their own agendas and opinions about what the character's relationship should look like. Their interference may manifest as attempts to sabotage the relationship, impose their own expectations, or uncover hidden secrets that threaten to derail the protagonists' happiness.

Supporting cast: Because of the unique scenario presented by the potential fulfillment of the pact, characters often find themselves turning to a best friend or other supporting character to help them process and determine their course. Alternatively, the character may hide the fact that the marriage pact was the impetus for the relationship, perhaps embarrassed that they have gone along with it.

FREQUENTLY PAIRED TROPES

The Friends to Lovers trope is the hallmark of Marriage Pact stories, for obvious reasons. It is also commonly paired with Unrequited Love or even Second Chance romance, where characters ended a relationship with the understanding that they'd come back together if still single at a certain time.

Other frequently paired tropes include tropes that play on the fact that time has passed for the characters, such as Coming Home and Secret Baby, or that they carry other baggage from former relationships such as Single Parent, Jilted, or Runaway Bride.

KEY MOMENTS

Inciting incident: One character decides to pursue the pact for a specific reason. This usually occurs just before or at the time of whatever the predetermined milestone or event is, triggering the character's realization that the opportunity to fulfill the marriage pact has arrived. This will often lead into a meet cute reunification scene where the character confronts the other participant in the marriage pact and asks them to consider following through.

Call to action: The characters are faced with the decision to fulfill the marriage pact or walk away from the opportunity. Readers must have some clarity over what has driven the characters to take such drastic measures.

Dark moment: At the end of the second act, your characters will be led into a moment of emotional or physical separation or withdrawal. Because these stories involve characters who are brought together due to the seeming unavailability of anyone else to fill the role of spouse, this moment often involves feelings of inadequacy, unworthiness, or otherwise blaming themselves for their unsuccessful love life.

Grand gesture: Characters must choose to stay together, not out of desperation or obligation, but because they truly love each other. This scene typically involves an act that demonstrates these characters love each other for who they are and not who others expect them to be.

POTENTIAL THEMES

Friendship
Societal or familial expectation
Vulnerability
Living without regret
Trust

CHAPTER 12

NOT GOING TO THE CHAPEL

BROKEN ENGAGEMENT TROPES

These Storyline Tropes are launched by the end of a previous commitment, with common themes of forgiveness, trust, and looking to the future over the past. The Jilted and Runaway Bride tropes tend to heavily feature emotional baggage, with pain stemming from past experiences, traumas, or unresolved issues that impact one or both characters' ability to trust, open up, or commit to a relationship. These stories are all about breaking down emotional barriers and insecurities in order to pave the way for a genuine and vulnerable love connection.

JILTED

RUNAWAY BRIDE/GROOM

JILTED

In this trope, one of the lovers is left at the altar or in the days/weeks leading up to the wedding. In either case, they are typically blindsided by the event. This is also used when the betrothed discovers infidelity just before the wedding, resulting in a broken engagement and broken heart. Even if they were the one to call things off, it was because of the betrayal (or jilting) of the other character. Typically this trope portrays the female character left at the altar, but there are plenty of examples of the groom being the one left as well.

The deserting lover may have cold feet, second thoughts, simply be a jerk, or there may be some unexpected obstacle that prevents the wedding from taking place. The key elements of the trope—heartbreak, self-discovery, and the potential for new love—remain relevant regardless of the gender of the character involved.

WHY READERS LOVE IT

This trope is used to evoke empathy from the readers and set the stage for personal growth and self-discovery for the Jilted bride or groom. The jilting at the altar creates a high-stakes emotional situation, and readers are hooked by the intense feelings of heartbreak, betrayal, and vulnerability experienced by the Jilted character. It should be a starting point for a character's journey toward independence, strength, and finding true love.

Readers love the display of resilience and strength in these characters as they overcome their circumstances and pain. As the Jilted character finds a path to new love, whether the result of a more suitable partner or personal growth, readers are swept up in the sense of hope and redemption.

This is a trope where secondary characters can shine in providing support, comfort, advice, and even comedic relief during the Jilted character's journey of healing. Whether the character turns to a quirky best friend, a loving sibling, or their work wife, the impact of side characters will help the new romantic interest not simply feel like an opportunistic therapist, though their support will obviously be important to the Jilted character as well.

When well-executed, the Jilted trope can explore the complexities of relationships and the unpredictability of life. Readers appreciate stories that feel genuine and authentic, even if the initial setup may seem like a classic romance trope. Most readers can, in fact, relate to the pain of heartbreak and the challenges of moving on from a failed relationship, making the character's struggle relatable and fostering empathy.

READER EXPECTATIONS

While the Jilted character may experience some initial relief at the end of the relationship which, in their heart, they likely knew was doomed, readers will expect an emotional and impactful depiction of the heartbreak. Whether they knew the relationship wasn't great before they were jilted or they must accept that fact as they heal, they will inevitably mourn the loss of the relationship or the life they were building. There may be a grieving period where the character comes to terms with the end of the relationship, or the process may be more subtle, buried in the subtext of the narrative.

The character should have plenty of opportunity to face reminders and memories of their lost love or obstacles to moving on (such as having to deal with the fallout of a canceled wedding or having to retell the story over and over). As they face these situations, they should slowly evolve, learn from the experience, and become stronger with each painful encounter—although this should come with at least a couple of setbacks, where they fall back into old patterns, insecurities, or heartbreak.

While the Jilted trope is sometimes combined with the Relational Trope of Love On The Rocks, the romantic interest of the Jilted character is typically a new romantic opportunity, whether it's with a character introduced after the inciting incident or someone who was always there—this is because the promise of a new beginning is a key element of this trope.

Regardless of who the new love interest is or how well they know the character, readers expect the emotional baggage of the Jilted character to serve as a significant obstacle to building new connections. This may involve forgiving the person who left them, letting go of bitterness or resentment, or recognizing that there are people willing to commit and stay. In some cases, the very nature of being left causes these characters to put up so many walls that in the future, they are the ones most likely to run from commitment—an effort to leave a situation before they suffer the heartbreak that they have come to believe is inevitable.

The Jilted character is often forced to confront the person who abandoned them, whether the deserter is trying to win them back, conspicuously seen with a new love interest, or pushing your main character to forgive them and minimizing the hurt of their actions for some other reason. When the protagonist can truly feel as though the former love has no bearing on their future, they've conquered that ghost of their past—a key step to truly being able to move on with their new life and new love.

POTENTIAL PITFALLS

Dependency on miscommunication: Some iterations of the trope rely on miscommunication or lack of communication between characters, which can frustrate readers who prefer conflict to arise from more substantive issues.

Rebound love: In certain versions of the trope, the Jilted character's entire storyline may revolve around finding a new romantic partner. Some readers may find this limiting or wish for a more independent and self-driven narrative for the protagonist. Part of the character's journey should likely be the realization that they didn't need their original partner in order to be happy. But if they "need" a new partner to do so now, their growth was incomplete.

You will also want to use caution when developing the new relationship, so that it does not feel as if your Jilted character has unceremoniously moved from one lover to the next.

Perceived lack of agency: As with any Storyline Trope where the situation was thrust upon the character, it can start a chain of events where the character is only reacting to situations that happen *to them*, instead of the character making intentional *choices* in pursuit of their goal. Be sure your character is in the driver's seat at least most of the time once the jilting happens.

COMMON PLOT DEVICES

Symbolic objects or locations: Symbolic objects or specific locations tied to the relationship may play a crucial role in the storyline, serving as reminders of the past or catalysts for change.

Matchmaking friends or family members: Well-meaning friends or family members may try to play matchmaker, either to help the Jilted character move on or to reunite them with the person who left. Even if this is not a true use of the Matchmaker trope, it may either propel the Jilted character to move on or act as a stumbling block, causing them to retreat further into their heartbreak and build their walls higher.

Secrets and revelations: Uncovering hidden secrets or revealing long-buried truths can propel the plot forward. This may involve secrets about the jilting, the reasons behind it, or other significant aspects of the characters' pasts.

FREQUENTLY PAIRED TROPES

There are several other Storyline Tropes that are commonly paired with Jilted. Consider a character who enters into a Fake Relationship or a Marriage of Convenience in order to move on from the jilting.

The Jilted character may initially clash with or dislike someone who later becomes a romantic interest in a pairing with the Enemies to Lovers or Opposites Attract tropes. Whether it's a result of the Jilted character's protective walls, past experiences, or simply a clash of personalities, there will be much to overcome in the way of emotional barriers to the relationship.

After the initial heartbreak, your character may return to the comforts and familiarity of the Coming Home trope, where they may rekindle an old relationship and delve into unresolved feelings. This can also be achieved by pairing with the Friends to More or Best Friends to More trope, where a constant support becomes crucial to the healing of the Jilted character and ultimately crosses the line from friendship to romance.

The Jilting storyline may involve a secret pregnancy or child that was unknown to one of the characters. The revelation of a Secret Baby can complicate relationships and heighten the intensity of the heartbreak.

KEY MOMENTS

Inciting incident: The inciting event is the jilting itself, whether it involves the groom not showing up, calling off the wedding, or revealing last-minute doubts. This may also be a moment where the Jilted character uncovers a shocking secret such as infidelity or hidden motivations that lead to the wedding being canceled *immediately* before the wedding day.

Call to action: At this point, the Jilted character should resolve to rebuild their life, getting just a glimpse of the healing to come. They may even still be intent on regaining the affections of the deserting lover at this point, but in either case, they have chosen to find purpose and are willing to put in the work toward reaching their goal—whether it's reconciliation or moving on.

Turning point: The story should include a moment of confrontation or closure between the Jilted character and the person who left them, giving the Jilted character an opportunity to resolve lingering issues, or even discover that the breakup was a blessing in disguise.

POTENTIAL THEMES

Forgiveness
Identity
Healing
Learning to trust
Finding happiness after tragedy

RUNAWAY BRIDE/GROOM

The Runaway Bride trope involves one character, typically the female, who gets cold feet or experiences doubt about their upcoming marriage. This doubt must lead them to physically flee their intended, sometimes before the day of the ceremony or even on the day of. This storyline is usually wrought with emotional tension and conflict.

Your character may fear commitment, struggle with unresolved issues from the past, discover a world-shattering secret, or realize they are in love with someone else. This sets the stage for the character's growth and reconciliation.

Note that if their fleeing the marriage was due to a betrayal by their intended spouse, the story would fall under the Jilted Bride trope. In this case, despite your character being the one to walk away, it was due to the emotional scars of being hurt by their partner as opposed to choosing to run for another reason.

This trope is commonly reversed with the groom being the one to run, known as Runaway Groom. In both of these cases, it is the act of abandoning their commitment that introduced the conflict. Themes of commitment, identity, and lasting love are common elements in these stories.

WHY READERS LOVE IT

Readers love that this trope introduces immediate conflict and romantic tension, but it is also typically portrayed with a humorous tilt. The woman fleeing in a wedding dress is the hallmark of this trope, and for good reason. For better or for worse, there is something inherently awkward and uncomfortable about a woman wearing her wedding dress anywhere outside of the wedding. What happens in the immediate aftermath and chaos of the moment when the character decides to flee sets the course for the remainder of the story.

The circumstances that cause the character to run are often jarring and emotionally charged, immediately creating a connection between the reader and the Runaway. While the reader may not agree with the way the character chose to handle it, they become quickly invested in the story, pulling them down the path of the reader's growth journey. It's that transformation that ultimately satisfies readers by the end of the book, with the choice to flee acting only as a catalyst for later growth.

These stories are often infused with the idea of the Jilted character getting a second chance at love, and readers love to see the themes of redemption and forgiveness. In many cases, there are also elements of Fated Mates or Meant to Be, as it becomes clear that without having made the choice to leave their partner at the beginning of the book, they never would have found the one they are meant to be with.

READER EXPECTATIONS

As noted, the inciting incident is often presented with a comedic or shock-inducing twist, and this sets the tone for the entire novel. While you can and should still have plenty of drama and genuine emotional growth present in your narrative, readers will be jarred if you shift from a comedic opening to a somber tone in the rest of the story. In fact, this is one of the main contrasts between the Runaway Bride and the Jilted Bride.

In order to believe your Runaway lover has gone from literally running away from love to a happily ever after by the end of the book, readers will expect to see a significant growth arc. Your character must not only confront their choice to run (more on that in the key moments), but they must deal with whatever the root cause of that choice was. In most cases, that means dealing with their great lie or deep-seated wound.

The scene or chapter leading up to the runaway scene shines best when authors are able to infuse a sort of *fight or flight* response in the character. This shouldn't be an easy moment, and it's one that your reader expects the character to struggle with. In many cases, this choice will be seen as a disappointment to those they care about or a shattering of social expectations. After all, their world is essentially falling apart, and the choice to leave a wedding after typically months of elaborate planning and expenses is not taken lightly. This is a gut-wrenching decision, which makes the comedic aftermath remarkably successful at pulling the character from their despair and the reader into whatever the tone of the book will be going forward.

It's worth noting that this trope almost never ends with the Runaway character ending up with the intended they have left at the beginning of the book. While the bride or groom often has to face that individual, it is typically a moment of closure or an opportunity for the character to face their mistakes and move onto something better, rather than going back to the relationship that so clearly was not the right fit.

POTENTIAL PITFALLS

Lack of consequences: As discussed in the Reader Expectations section, your character must deal with the consequence and fallout of their choice to leave in such a way. If not, the happy ending with a new love interest doesn't feel earned, and the reader will likely feel short-changed. This is why the growth arc of the Runaway character is vitally important to these stories.

Low stakes: If the character's motivations or the reasons for leaving feel forced, artificial, or downright stupid, readers will struggle to connect with the story and the character. Strive to make the characters' actions authentic and consistent with their goals or internal conflict, ensuring that readers can understand and empathize with their choices.

Contrived conflict: Introducing unnecessary or contrived conflicts solely to prolong the story is bound to frustrate your readers. Ensure that conflicts arise naturally from the characters' personalities, circumstances, and genuine misunderstandings and avoid relying on artificial obstacles that don't contribute to the overall narrative. While these stories are inherently *dramatic*, striking a balance between tension and realism is crucial for maintaining reader engagement.

Unlikable/morally gray characters: This is a tricky trope to place an unlikable character. Sometimes the new love interest can also land in this territory. When that happens, readers tend to find themselves uninvested and struggling to care about the characters or any budding romance.

COMMON PLOT DEVICES

Revelation of secrets: The choice to run away is often prompted by the discovery of something shocking or devastating to the Runaway character. It could be a hidden aspect of the runaway's past, a concealed truth about the relationship, or a revelation about another character that influences the decision to run away.

The lover's pursuit: The other main character, usually the one left at the altar, often embarks on a pursuit or search to find the Runaway partner. This adds a sense of urgency to the story as the character attempts to evade them before eventually confronting them to overcome their past.

The supportive friend: The Runaway often has at least one ally or friend group that supports their decision to end the relationship and helps the character find their footing as they try to navigate the fallout. Sometimes this supportive "friend" becomes the love interest.

Can't let you go: The ex will often come back to pursue the Runaway, whether out of malice or genuine grief for the relationship. When this happens, it is typically a catalyst for the completion of the growth arc. Your character must confront the consequences of their actions while acknowledging the reasons they chose to leave in the first place.

FREQUENTLY PAIRED TROPES

This trope is ever-present in historical romance, especially in the Regency and Western settings. In these stories, there is often a measure of threat from the intended that the Runaway Bride has fled from, and the hero steps in to protect her.

This trope is often combined with a Friends to More trope, where the Runaway character seeks refuge in the arms of the familiar, only to find that they can't keep things just friendly anymore.

Another common pairing for this trope is the Fake Relationship trope, where the new love interest helps the Runaway Bride save face by acting as their new fiancé(e), date or even spouse.

KEY MOMENTS

Inciting incident: At the outset of the story, the character discovers a reason to leave or faces a moment of overwhelming doubt. This is typically an emotional scene, but because this is an inherently comedic trope, the Runaway usually falls into absolute chaos.

Call to action: The escape. This is most often on the wedding day *in the wedding dress*. The dramatic and public departure from the wedding ceremony is a crucial moment in these stories. This may happen just before the ceremony, during, or even immediately afterward (in which case, an annulment of the marriage will likely be necessary).

Turning point: The Runaway must confront their choice to leave, deal with the consequences of their actions, or address the root cause of their doubts about the previous relationship. Without doing so, it becomes clear that they will never find true happiness in their new love relationship.

Grand gesture: Before these characters can have their happily ever after, the Runaway must demonstrate their commitment to stay, even when things get difficult or scary. It's this vulnerability and courage to face "the hard things" that proves the depth of their love and earns the couple their happy ending.

POTENTIAL THEMES

Learning to be vulnerable
Commitment
Redemption
Lasting love
Letting go of expectations

CHAPTER 13

ALL IN THE FAMILY

FAMILY TROPES

The Family Storyline Tropes center on family ties, with the character's family relationships significantly shaping the trajectory of their growth arc and subsequently affecting the storyline. These stories share common themes of acceptance, self-discovery, and finding home. In each of the Family Storylines, characters learn that they become the best version of themselves when they choose to embrace the most important bonds in their life.

COMING HOME/RETURN TO HOMETOWN

INSTANT FAMILY

SECRET BABY

COMING HOME/RETURN TO HOMETOWN

The Coming Home/Return to Hometown trope revolves around a protagonist returning to their hometown (shocking, we know) after an extended absence, often sparking a journey of self-discovery, reconciliation, and rediscovery of roots. Whether returning after years away, following a personal crisis, or for some other purpose such as attending a family event or inheriting property, the protagonist finds themself immersed in the familiar yet changed landscape of their hometown. The character may be coming home to stay or believe that the stay is only temporary, with their goals and priorities mostly focused on the life waiting for them when they leave (yet again).

Your character may find themselves reveling in the familiar places and people of their hometown. Or perhaps your character is so different from the person they used to be that they are now a Fish out of Water in their own hometown (see the case study on Sweet Home Alabama in the first episode of our future podcast).

As they navigate the familiar streets and faces of their hometown, old sparks may reignite, leading to a rekindling of romance. Alternatively, they may find that they view someone they knew in a completely different light, or there may now be someone in town who wasn't there before.

In any case, the common thread is that the protagonist undergoes a process of reflection and growth, ultimately finding closure, forging new connections, and rediscovering the essence of home. At the heart of this trope is the idea of the character returning to their roots, setting the stage for personal growth and reconnecting with their past (including past relationships), with a touch of nostalgia.

WHY READERS LOVE IT

The statistics on Americans who never move away from the place they grew up is over thirty-five percent, and if you zoom that out to include people who never leave their home state, it's nearly half of the population. Regardless of how many people spend their lives talking about *getting out of here for someplace better*, statistics are clear: the pull toward home is strong for most people. These stories tug at those very heartstrings.

The experience of nostalgia is universally relatable. We love reunification with loved ones, even if it happens reluctantly, enjoying old comforts, and finding peace somewhere familiar. We all have unresolved things in our pasts, and within the Coming Home trope, we get to watch characters walk through the (sometimes agonizing) conversations that should have happened years ago.

The idea of returning home—whether it's in triumph or disgrace—for the sake of obligation or nostalgia is one that has clearly maintained an enduring hold on the imaginations of readers. Readers are drawn to the bittersweet journey of returning to a place filled with memories, where the past collides with the present and the character grapples with confronting unresolved emotions and relationships. Whether it's the familiarity of small-town life, the warmth of community bonds, or the chance to rediscover one's roots, Return to Hometown stories offer readers a poignant exploration of the ties that bind us to the places we call home.

READER EXPECTATIONS

For many of these characters, the rediscovery of self comes about as they realize that home isn't just a place that they've grown beyond, but it's the place where they've left the best pieces of themselves behind.

In this trope, the history of the person and place is critically important. Why did your character leave? How did everyone else react to that? Have they been in touch at all over the years?

Opportunities for renewed or rekindled relationships, especially romantic ones, are complicated by the secrets and baggage that characters are forced to confront upon their return home. Whatever your character has been able to forget about while they were gone is likely to slam back into their periphery in the worst way. Interaction with the community or past acquaintances is bound to come into play with these stories, typically giving the characters space to reflect on past decisions and their impact, leading to self-awareness and a shift in the character arc.

As the character reconnects with their roots, they may find themselves surrounded by a supportive network of friends and family members who play a role in their romantic journey. Whether it's meddling relatives, childhood friends, or wise mentors, these secondary characters add depth and richness to the story, offering guidance, support, and sometimes a gentle nudge in the right direction when it comes to matters of the heart.

On the other hand, the character may find nothing but animosity or burned bridges from their past. In either case, the protagonist must wrestle with the choices of their past and confront misunderstandings and mistakes to move forward.

The vast majority of these stories involve a Small Town homecoming, but that's not to say that there isn't room for big city or even suburban Return to Hometown stories. Though the Small Town setting is uniquely qualified to give the nostalgia and personal connection that comes from familiar faces and places, you can achieve the same effect by zooming in on a community within a community in Urban settings—such as a church group, a neighborhood or even a school community.

POTENTIAL PITFALLS

Successful city heroine leaves it all behind for small town man: This isn't an automatic pitfall, but it *has* become something of a cliché. But keep in mind, this is the very resolution of the millennial classic *Sweet Home Alabama*, and we *dare* you not to finish this quote: *Why you wanna marry me, anyhow?*

While keeping the conflict shallow or contrived and coupling that with one-dimensional characters can put your Return to Hometown story solidly in the cliché zone, this is easily avoided by fleshing out your character arcs, romance arcs, conflict, and even layering tropes for a fresh take on an old tune. Your story may still end with the Successful City Heroine Leaving It All Behind for Small Town Man, but if the romance and conflict arc deliver enough depth, the reader will be rooting for that predictable ending anyway.

Lack of realism: In some cases, readers might find the narrative too idealistic or unrealistic, especially if the reunion or reconciliation feel forced or overly romanticized. Lean into the conflicts (external, internal, and especially relational) to ensure the story reads as realistic and the happy ending is truly satisfying.

Lack of consequences: When your protagonist left—perhaps unexpectedly, keeping secrets or burning bridges in the process—there was fallout to that decision that they weren't around to witness. Coming home should force them to belatedly face the consequences of their leaving or their extended absence.

COMMON PLOT DEVICES

Inheritance or legacy: The protagonist's return is linked to inheriting a family estate, business, or responsibility, driving the plot forward as they navigate claiming or ridding themselves of the inheritance.

Family reunions or events: The storyline revolves around a significant family event like a reunion, wedding, or celebration, bringing characters together and creating opportunity for conflict in many forms.

Community projects: Upon returning home, characters often find themselves volunteering for or being roped into a community project or event that sets the stage for a change in perspective and forces time spent with the love interest

Temporary visit: This plot device puts an assumed end date for the character's return, adding resistance to any potential romantic connection as they focus on the impending return to their "real life" elsewhere.

FREQUENTLY PAIRED TROPES

This Storyline Trope is often paired with the character returning home for a fresh start. Regardless of the character's reasons for leaving, the safety of home and a well-established support system in a moment of crisis or uncertainty can entice even the most reluctant characters. Because crisis can be a convincing pull back home, tropes such as the Widow, Jilted, and Single Parent are often combined with Coming Home.

Family responsibility is another commonly used reason for returning home, and using tropes like Save the Town/Farm/Family Business and Caregiver can tug at the heartstrings of your character's family obligation and bring them home, even if it's only temporary.

Because the character is returning someplace they've lived previously, this is very often paired with a Second Chance romance. It absolutely still works, but "character moves home and falls for their old flame" can be a little flat. Consider adding an additional storyline layer like a Secret Baby or Jilted Lover or a Relational Trope such as Love Triangle or Enemies to Lovers.

KEY MOMENTS

Inciting incident: The event that triggers the character to return home happens right at the outset of the story. Readers may not know what led the character to leave home in the first place, or how they feel about returning there, but it should quickly become clear that whatever aspects of their past they were able to hide from or ignore while they were away will suddenly come front and center.

Turning point: Whatever tension or conflict served as the catalyst for your character's departure from their hometown will come back into the picture—this time as a catalyst for growth, rather than a cause for them running. Be sure that the reader has some understanding of how the character's time away has uniquely prepared them to face this same problem with different results.

Happily ever after: With the help and/or support of the love interest, your character chooses to embrace their roots for all that it is—good *and* bad. Once your Hometown character has reconciled with their past, it paves the way for their happy future with a new love, either in their hometown or with the people in the community playing a significant role in their future.

POTENTIAL THEMES

Reputation
Taking responsibility for mistakes
Family or community roots
Shifting goals/dreams
Personal growth

INSTANT FAMILY

The Instant Family trope involves a storyline where characters find themselves suddenly in a family or family-like situation without the opportunity to plan or establish expectations. This can occur through various means such as adoption, guardianship due to death, or any other means of the sudden introduction of a relative into the character's lives. The focus of this trope is on the characters' journey to adapt to their new family situation and how that impacts relationships, daily life, and their own personal development.

This trope unfolds as one or both partners become responsible for raising children unexpectedly, finding support as they navigate the responsibilities and complexities of parenthood or guardianship. The emotional turmoil of the situation is often amplified when grief, sacrifice, or past trauma are present.

Stories with a single parent may share some similarities to this storyline, as one character suddenly finds themselves in the role of co-parent due to the developing romance with the single parent, but the Single Parent entry in *The Character Trope Encyclopedia* will more closely detail what readers are looking for in that scenario. The Instant Family trope is more about characters suddenly being thrust into the role of guardianship or parenthood, either independently or together.

WHY READERS LOVE IT

The journey of forming an Instant Family often includes heartwarming moments, such as bonding between characters, shared experiences, and the development of a strong family bond.

Readers enjoy these positive and uplifting aspects of the trope. Themes such as loyalty, sacrifice, and chosen family resonate with readers and pull them into the emotional and romantic arc.

Readers appreciate seeing the representation of unconventional family structures. It often fosters both relatability and empathy in the reader, giving the story a very realistic feel. The balance of creating a convincing family dynamic while recognizing the challenges of a nontraditional home situation can be tricky, but it is incredibly rewarding for characters and readers alike.

Some of the best moments of these books come with the heartwarming encounters that showcase the characters bonding with the children and "learning the ropes" of parenthood. These moments help to build a sense of family and often provide the opportunity for humor, even in a story with heavy themes. Scenes where the new parents and the child aren't on the same page, have unmatched expectations, or different understandings of how things should be done can create comedy while also paving the way for character growth.

Readers without a family of their own (but who long for one) are drawn into the fantasy of suddenly being cast into the role of parent. Seeing the characters embrace a new part of their life and finding that it fulfills them in a way they never expected is an emotional and rewarding experience for these readers.

READER EXPECTATIONS

Dealing with the sudden responsibility of parenthood or caring for others should lead to significant character development. One or both of the romantic partners may initially be reluctant or unprepared for the responsibilities involved, leading to tension, conflict, and ultimately character growth.

Readers anticipate the development and strengthening of the romantic relationship as the characters navigate the challenges of family life together. The romance should evolve in tandem with the characters' growth as parents or guardians.

Let's be real . . . parenting is NOT easy. Readers expect to see the characters facing and overcoming the challenges of parenting, whether dealing with behavior issues, handling unexpected situations, or adjusting to the demands of family life.

The unexpected nature of the situation should wreak absolute havoc on the life of your characters. External pressures, conflict, busy schedules, judgments from others, interference from other family members—the possibilities for intrusions on the daily life and routines of your character are truly limitless. If you don't have children, ask any mom to shed some light on the realities of raising a family. I guarantee you she could write a graduate-level thesis on the interruptions to the first hour of her day, let alone over a lifetime. Oh, wait, no she can't—she's too exhausted (and so are your characters, by the way)!

POTENTIAL PITFALLS

Unrealistic scenarios: Some readers may find the premise of characters suddenly becoming parents or guardians in improbable or unrealistic ways to be a stretch. The abrupt introduction of children or family situations without proper development may strain believability.

Forced romantic relationships: In some instances, the Instant Family trope may be used to force characters into romantic relationships solely because of shared parental responsibilities. To avoid this, give the couple plenty of time and space to develop the romantic relationship organically, and don't forget to add the chemistry!

Perfect, precocious kids: While it may be tempting to depict children as adorable and exceptionally mature for their age, it is essential to strike a balance and present them as authentic characters with their own flaws and age-appropriate behaviors. Readers may find it unrealistic or off-putting if the children behave in ways that are not developmentally appropriate for their age. Ensuring that the kids' actions, dialogue, and emotional responses align with their age and stage of development will create a more genuine and relatable portrayal of family dynamics in the romance.

Disappearing child(ren): Even though this character is new to parenting, don't let your hero or heroine completely forget about their child once the love interest comes along; the romance will become the forefront of your novel, but that doesn't mean that the children disappear. It may be a challenge to find time alone due to parenting schedules, and the new guardian may worry how the blossoming relationship will affect already shaky family dynamics. They may daydream about how the love interest will fit into their lives. Whatever the case, much of your main character's journey will be finding the balance between personal and family life, so don't let the kids fall to the wayside as the protagonist become more invested in their love life.

COMMON PLOT DEVICES

Legal battles: Custody battles or disputes with biological parents or some other party who wishes to lay claim to guardianship can introduce conflict and tension into the story, forcing the protagonists to confront both the external and internal challenges to their newfound family structure.

Never wanted kids: What better way to shake up the world of a character who sees no use for family or children than by throwing a few in their lap? The character growth spurred on by their (often reluctant) embrace of their new role is dramatic and rewarding.

Facing their own trauma: The Unexpected Guardian often feels ill-equipped to raise a family due to their own past experience or trauma. In this case, reconciliation between estranged parents or family members can be a powerful plot device. Even if the character doesn't have an individual to reconcile with, if they are able to finally process the trauma of their past, it should have a positive impact on the characters' relationships and provide opportunities for healing and growth.

Buried secrets: The revelation of family secrets, such as hidden relationships, undisclosed parentage, or undisclosed pasts, can introduce dramatic twists and impact the dynamics of the instant family. Often the person who hid these secrets is no longer around (hence the reason their children are in the care of your character) and the character is faced with reconciling the hidden information without the ability to confront the other party.

Adjustment period: Addressing challenges related to children's integration into school or social environments is often used to highlight the characters' efforts to provide a stable and supportive environment for the family, as well as to introduce doubts and challenges.

Family events: Milestone events and celebrations, such as birthdays, holidays, or achievements of the children, provide opportunities for the characters to come together, bond, and create lasting memories as a family.

FREQUENTLY PAIRED TROPES

Your characters are neither prepared nor accustomed to the reality of caring for a family, making the Fish out of Water trope a clear choice for combining with this trope. Characters are likely to find themselves in uncomfortable and unanticipated situations while navigating everyday challenges.

When paired with Second Chances, characters may be reunited after a painful history and choose to work together for the sake of the kids. This may also be used with an old flame coming into the Unexpected Guardian's life during a moment of upheaval and serving as a source of support and stability.

The Secret Baby trope may be used here, especially in conjunction with Second Chances, in which a father discovers a child (of any age) whose pregnancy or birth he had no knowledge of. In this case, the male character most likely makes the commitment to be a part of the child's life, bringing them back into the life of the mother and often rekindling old flames.

In addition to the Instant Family trope, the story may also involve the Single Parent trope, where one of the protagonists is already a parent before entering into the romantic relationship.

KEY MOMENTS

Inciting incident: The moment when characters discover they are unexpectedly responsible for a child(ren) or the existence of a child. This is followed by a moment of shock, disbelief, and reevaluation of the characters' lives.

Call to action: Your character may be initially resistant, but by the end of the first act, they should have accepted their situation and they should be ready and willing to step up for the sake of the children entrusted to them.

Turning point: These characters tend to be guarded and/or cautious in forming romantic connections, for the sake of the children in their care. The romantic turning point will come when they choose to truly let the romantic interest into their life and their heart, possibly culminating in an outright confession of love.

POTENTIAL THEMES

Resilience
Teamwork vs. self-reliance
Family
Embracing the unexpected
Grief and joy

SECRET BABY

The Secret Baby has long been a staple in the genre, and despite the fact that it has taken plenty of heat over the years, it is unlikely to be jettisoned anytime soon. Typically the female protagonist becomes pregnant sometime before the events of the story and keeps the pregnancy or the existence of the child a secret from the love interest (often the father). The reasons behind keeping the baby a secret can vary. It might be due to fear of rejection, a belief that the other person is not ready for parenthood, or external factors such as societal expectations, safety, or family pressure. Whether concealed out of fear, necessity, or a desire to protect the child, the Secret Baby serves as a catalyst for conflict, revelation, and ultimately reconciliation between the protagonists.

While the reader knows about the existence of the baby, or at least has a VERY strong hunch, the love interest will not know until much later in the story. This creates a sense of anticipation in the reader and dramatic irony that naturally complicates the romantic relationship and conflict as the parent who was unaware of the child's existence discovers the truth, leading to a rollercoaster of emotions.

In some Secret Baby stories, the love interest is not the father of the child. In these stories, they must come to terms with either the existence of a child in the life of the person they are falling for, or—if they knew about the child—the specific parentage of the child is the revelation and often one that has personal ramifications for the love interest.

Secret Baby stories often explore themes of love, forgiveness, and second chances, as the protagonists navigate the complexities of parenthood and strive to build a future together despite the obstacles in their path. Additionally, the presence of the child introduces a new dynamic to the relationship, as the protagonists must learn to co-parent and overcome their differences for the sake of their child's well-being.

WHY READERS LOVE IT

The revelation of a secret baby introduces a significant element of drama and tension to the story. Readers are eager to see how the characters will react and how the revelation will impact their relationship. The longer the omission goes on, the more the tension ratchets up, with everyone collectively holding their breath and waiting for the other shoe to drop.

Secret Baby stories are a playground for a wide range of emotions in the story, including heartbreak, regret, and eventually, hope. Because of the shared history and the gravity of the secret being kept, the emotions run high and the story draws the reader in.

Readers love to watch people (men, in particular) step up and take responsibility, committing to be a parent and embracing all the messy inconvenience that requires. As the father or love interest steps into the role of fatherhood, readers enjoy watching the couple learn to work together for the sake of the child and find that happy family feel of everyday moments together.

Like with the Single Parent trope, much of the connection for the reader comes from watching the characters find love despite their past mistakes or emotional baggage.

READER EXPECTATIONS

The initial concealment of the pregnancy is a crucial aspect of the trope. This could also be twisted to include concealment of the parentage of a child, if not necessarily their outright existence.

Readers anticipate that the character learning about the baby will experience shock and disbelief. This initial reaction adds to the tension and sets the stage for the emotional journey that follows. It also emphasizes the depth of the deceit if the love interest has no idea the revelation was coming. This revelation scene is charged with emotion and drama, and it tends to be a turning point in the narrative.

If the love interest is the father of the child, they must come to terms with their newfound parenthood and grapple with the consequences of past actions. The character must confront their unresolved feelings and reassess their priorities in life as they decide what kind of role they will play in the child's life.

Any love interest must deal with the emotional fallout of the secret and ultimately work toward a resolution for the sake of their child and their relationship.

Character growth is crucial for love interests to move forward in the relationship; readers don't want characters who are unwilling to change and grow when a child is in the mix. The character who kept the secret must go through a redemption arc, seeking forgiveness and making amends for their actions. They may justify their choice, and readers may even sympathize with it, but they need to feel the weight of the consequence as well as work to rebuild trust and reconcile relationships. The other character must also grow through the story, overcoming their own insecurities or flaws that might prevent them from committing fully to a future as a parent and partner.

POTENTIAL PITFALLS

Weak justification: If the character keeping the secret doesn't have a convincing reason for doing so, readers may find it hard to empathize with their actions. It is important to establish believable and sympathetic motivations for keeping the baby a secret. There are very few motivations for which readers could forgive characters for such enormous lies, but anytime characters act in the best interest (or the perceived best interest) of a child, readers will likely give them the benefit of the doubt.

Lack of consequences: Failing to address the emotional fallout and conflicts stemming from the secret can leave readers unsatisfied. This was a major secret to keep, and the resolution must reconcile the gravity of the deception. The resolution should be earned and aligned with the character's growth and the challenges they've faced.

Foundation of lies: Some readers will struggle to root for a romantic relationship that has been built upon a lie that to many will seem almost unforgivable. The narrative should acknowledge that the character responsible for the deception has significantly breached the trust of the love interest. Even if a relationship can be built on a foundation of lies, it will not stand there long. The deception must be addressed, and the character who was deceived will likely struggle with trusting the other enough to move forward.

Suspected it all along: If the father has too many suspicions ahead of the reveal, it lowers the emotional impact of that moment.

Readers are smart, so don't feel like you have to spoon-feed them genetic or behavioral similarities to clue them into the parentage too early or often. The female character knows the truth, and that's enough. If your narrative includes more than one POV, lean into the shock of the moment by telling that scene from the person discovering the secret.

Contrived conflict: Some stories may rely too heavily on the secret baby revelation as the primary source of drama without developing other aspects of the story. This can make the plot feel contrived and formulaic. The character's internal and relational conflict should be impacted by the trope as well as their overall character arc and romance arc.

FREQUENTLY PAIRED TROPES

While this trope is not always a Second Chance romance, many times it is paired with that trope, where characters are given the opportunity to rekindle or rebuild their past relationship after the revelation of the secret. If the love interest wasn't the father or the connection that ended in pregnancy was a one-night stand, then the Second Chance romance trope doesn't necessarily apply. However, especially in clean and Christian romance, readers don't love characters who have sex without emotional connection, and the characters are more likely to have had at least some sort of relationship prior to bringing a baby into existence.

This trope is often paired with the Return to Hometown trope, either with the mother returning home, secret baby in tow, or the father returning to town to discover he has a child he left behind unknowingly.

Other common pairings are tropes where the initial relationship was a Forbidden Romance or otherwise off-limits (such as Sibling's Best Friend or Best Friend's Ex.) This leads into additional motivation for the character to hide the pregnancy, fearing even more backlash from the family, friends, or community based on the identity of the father.

Characters may have a contentious relationship initially, based on how the relationship ended, leaning into an Animosity trope like Enemies to Lovers or Hate to Love. The secret baby revelation forces them to confront their feelings and transform their dynamic.

Honor Marriage is another common added trope for Secret Baby, especially in historicals. In these stories, the love interest (not the father) steps up to marry the pregnant woman to protect her reputation or provide for her. This can be especially powerful if the man feels obligated because of his own ties to the father (perhaps his brother or friend who abandoned the woman).

Amnesia may be used as a microtrope to add a fun layer to these stories, where one character may have forgotten the events leading to the pregnancy (perhaps a drunken one-night stand), adding an extra layer of tension and an even greater level of shock when the parentage is revealed.

COMMON PLOT DEVICES

Co-parenting: Discussions about parenting styles, custody arrangements, and the characters learning to work together for the well-being of their child are a common way to show development of emotional intimacy. This likely includes scenes depicting shared responsibilities and the challenges of raising a child together as well as disagreements in parenting philosophies or the newly revealed parent feeling dismissed or undermined by the other.

Saved from the father: In this case, the love interest is not actually the father but assumes a fatherly role and takes charge of the protection of the woman and her child. This scenario typically means that there is some external risk to the child from the biological parent and it comes to head in the climax of the external conflict.

Lies or lies of omission: As the main character tries to hide the baby or the parentage, their web of lies or omissions becomes more and more unstable, leading to the eventual discovery of the baby. This also increases the hurt and betrayal felt by the other character when they realize how committed the other was to keeping the truth from them. If the character comes to town and quickly discovers the child, the deception was more passive and somewhat easier to forgive.

KEY MOMENTS

Inciting incident: While the truth may not all come out, your characters are brought back into proximity during the inciting incident so that the inevitable fallout of the Secret Baby becomes front and center in the mind of the mother. In this moment, your character is likely to be faced with the choice to either reveal the truth sooner rather than later, or they will choose to double down on their decision to conceal the existence of the baby.

Turning point: A dramatic confrontation or confession scene where the truth comes to light about the existence of a child or the parentage of the child. This should be emotionally charged, as the character learning about the secret baby experiences shock, disbelief, and often anger at the revelation.

Midpoint: By the midpoint, your characters should reach a point where they are willing and ready to work together for the sake of the child, even if the idea of romance is still off the table. Once they commit to interacting and dealing with each other for the foreseeable future, the focus of the story shifts to fighting their attraction or learning to balance their romantic feelings with doing what is right for the child.

POTENTIAL THEMES

Family
Forgiveness
Mutual trust
Priorities and personal growth
Finding purpose

CHAPTER 14

SECRETS DON'T MAKE FRIENDS

DECEPTION TROPES

These Storyline Tropes involve at least one character withholding information from each other or from those around them. While writers should tread carefully with starting a relationship on a bed of lies in order to not turn readers off to the narrative, there is an inherent thrill for these readers being the ones who are in on the secret. These stories highlight common themes of trust, forgiveness, and loyalty.

FAKE RELATIONSHIP

HIDDEN IDENTITY/DISGUISE

HIDDEN MOTIVES/BET

MISTAKEN IDENTITY

REVENGE

SECRET RELATIONSHIP

TWIN SWITCH

FAKE RELATIONSHIP

This trope involves the characters entering into a fake relationship for various reasons, such as avoiding unwanted attention, impressing others, or fulfilling a specific goal. The fake relationship serves as a convenient facade, allowing the protagonists to navigate social expectations, evade scrutiny, or manipulate external circumstances to their advantage. Despite not having genuine romantic feelings for each other at the start of the relationship, as the story unfolds, the characters will start to develop real feelings for each other, leading to a genuine romantic relationship.

The Fake Relationship trope is all about a growing tension between appearances and reality. Despite their initial reluctance or reservations, the characters find themselves drawn to each other in unexpected ways, leading to genuine feelings and romantic entanglements that blur the lines between fiction and reality. As they maintain the facade, the characters struggle to reconcile their staged relationship with their growing attraction and desire for each other.

WHY READERS LOVE IT

The allure of this trope is all about the imbalance the fake relationship creates. These characters are caught in a cycle of convincing others that their relationship is real and convincing themselves that it is not. They are compelled to do all the things a couple must do when falling in love *publicly*, and as that begins to creep into their private interactions, it becomes harder and harder to deny the truth of their burgeoning feelings—obviously to the delight of readers.

FAKE RELATIONSHIP

The Fake Relationship trope often leads to humorous situations and misunderstandings as characters try to maintain the facade. Pretending in front of family, coworkers, and friends, may lead to inconsistent stories, awkward kisses, and other public displays of false affection. Until the line between pretend and real begins to blur, and those public displays suddenly feel all too real or are done without the excuse of an audience. All this while the characters cling to whatever lie is preventing them from embracing the relationship until the end of the story.

The tension and misunderstandings that arise from the fake relationship creates a compelling romance arc and storyline. The Fake Relationship trope often allows for emotional depth and exploration of the characters' vulnerabilities. Until the turning point, and then sometimes again in the dark moment, characters will likely struggle with the fear that their feelings are one-sided, with the other character not as emotionally invested as they are.

The reader knows that isn't true, and watching the characters realize it has readers cheering for the growth of each character and the happy ending. Whether it's the witty banter, sizzling chemistry, delightful subtext, or tender moments of vulnerability, Fake Relationship stories captivate readers with their irresistible charm and undeniable appeal, making them a perennial favorite in the world of romance fiction.

The ultimate payoff in a Fake Relationship story is the moment when the characters acknowledge and act on their genuine romantic feelings. Readers are swept up in the moment as they confront their own feelings and the consequences of their actions.

READER EXPECTATIONS

Initial justification of deception usually begins with the characters entering into a fake relationship for a clear and specific reason. Readers expect to be given the motivation behind the decision to fake the relationship. Whether it's to ward off unwanted attention, fulfill a contractual obligation, or meet a specific goal, the characters' reasons for pretending to be a couple should be well-established. Especially in Christian romance, readers are sometimes uncomfortable with any intentional deception, and a strong motive helps alleviate that discomfort.

Readers prefer to see that at least one of the characters is totally unaccustomed to lying like this. The imbalance this creates in the character automatically creates discomfort and tension in the narrative and ratchets up the stakes for your character—if they are going to act so out of character, then the payoff better be worth it. And they definitely can't go screwing it up by falling in love.

This trope shares some similarities with Forced Proximity, as the characters are forced to spend a significant amount of time together due to circumstances, intensifying the fake relationship and creating opportunities for genuine emotions to develop. Because time spent together is often with an audience, the characters experience what the relationship *could* be like—if they were to give in to it. These moments of bliss help the characters move toward admitting true feelings.

Despite the initial lack of genuine romantic feelings, readers look for chemistry and tension between the characters. The dynamic should hint at the potential for real emotions to develop over time. When the characters do spend time alone, their level of emotional intimacy will increase, but it will also do so as they see sides of their fake partner during interactions with family and others. This growth should be gradual, with the characters slowly realizing their true feelings for each other. Both characters typically experience internal conflicts as they grapple with their evolving emotions. Readers expect to see the characters confront their own vulnerabilities and insecurities as they move from pretending to acknowledging genuine feelings.

External challenges, such as the discovery of the fake relationship by others or unforeseen obstacles, often heighten the stakes. Readers anticipate some form of external conflict that threatens the relationship and adds drama to the story. Near-misses or suspicions from side characters about the true nature of the relationship help add to the constant tension of maintaining any deception for very long.

To provide a sense of completeness, readers look for closure regarding the initial deception. This likely involves addressing the reasons for the fake relationship and resolving any lingering consequences.

POTENTIAL PITFALLS

Foundation of lies: Some readers feel that the fact of establishing a relationship on a bed of lies sullies the authenticity of the romance that develops later. To avoid falling into this, or at the very least to steer readers away from these complaints, give your characters reasonable motives that the reader can empathize with.

Artificial/convenient conflict: Some readers feel that the conflict in Fake Relationship stories can feel forced or artificial. The misunderstandings and obstacles that arise from the fake relationship may be seen as manufactured, detracting from the authenticity of the characters' emotional journey. This trope truly creates enough tension and conflict on its own, so lean into that and let the obstacles arise naturally. Ask yourself two questions:

What are the consequences of breaking the fake dating agreement (keeping it fake)?

Why can't these characters be together right now?

Poor communication: Readers may become frustrated with characters who fail to communicate openly about their feelings or continue to uphold the fake relationship when it seems unnecessary. This is why it's important to establish stakes for breaking the agreement—what will happen if the character admits the relationship has become real to them?

Unrealistic resolution: Readers may find the resolution of the fake relationship—where characters transition from pretending to being genuinely in love—too convenient or unrealistic. Avoid focusing too much on external conflicts and not enough on the deep emotional connection between the characters.

FREQUENTLY PAIRED TROPES

Whether your characters are Enemies or the best of Friends, either use of the trope will involve an adamant refusal of romantic feelings. The Fake Relationship trope has strong adhesion properties, so it is commonly paired with tropes that offer repelling forces, such as Animosity, Emotional Baggage tropes (Single Parent, Widow), or Jilted.

FAKE RELATIONSHIP

The progression from a fake relationship to genuine feelings is a great pairing for a Slow Burn romance. Readers appreciate the anticipation and buildup as the characters move from initial deception to realizing their true emotions for each other.

The Fake Relationship may be part of an Arranged Marriage scenario where the characters must convince others of their love before they can pursue their own paths.

One or both characters may be a Celebrity or Royalty (or really, any *Money, Money* trope from Volume 1 of this series), and the fake relationship is used to manage public image or meet certain expectations.

COMMON PLOT DEVICES

Contracts: One of the most common elements of the Fake Relationship trope is the creation of a formal or informal contract outlining the terms of the boundaries of their relationship. This sets the stage for both comedic and dramatic moments as they navigate the stipulations. This is the classic *You have to promise not to fall in love with me* arrangement. Characters are likely to find themselves bending or breaking these rules as their feelings evolve.

(Imaginary) love triangle: Introducing jealousy, either real or feigned, is used to create tension and push the characters to confront their emotions. It's a classic element that adds complexity and tends to force the hand of one or both pretend lovers. When there is a genuine second love interest, this leads to moments of rivalry, self-discovery, and ultimately, a choice between the fake partner and a real romantic possibility. *Hint*: When it comes to the Fake

Relationship trope, the fake partner is usually chosen and the relationship is established in truth.

The fake relationship ends in a fake breakup: To intensify the emotional stakes, the characters may decide to stage a fake breakup, only to discover the true depth of their feelings in the aftermath. This ending of the fake relationship symbolically allows for the beginning of the real relationship.

Meddling mother: In this plot device, much of the motivation for the Fake Relationship is to appease the matchmaking, disapproval, or relentless badgering of a mother or other party who is unreasonably concerned with their child's relationship status. Resolution of this plot device typically involves the mother finding out the relationship is fake and, recognizing the lengths they've forced their child to go to, eventually stepping back.

KEY MOMENTS

Inciting incident: This typically comes in the form of giving one or both characters a reason to seek a fake relationship as the solution to their problem. They may not see a fake relationship as the solution until the fake partner presents themselves, but they recognize at this point that they have to figure a way out of their problem.

Call to action: Characters either enter into the relationship at this point or they are given an opportunity to showcase their false romance. This is usually in the form of some public or family event, whether it's a wedding, a party, or some other social gathering. This amplifies the pressure to convincingly play their roles and sets the stage for the rest of the story.

Turning point: By the point of climax, characters must face the truth of their genuine feelings. This may or may not include a declaration of love moment, but it should be emotionally charged and highlight the stakes of what your characters stand to lose by failing to keep up their end of the bargain—*not to fall in love.*

Dark moment: The dark moment typically forces at least one character's hand to act on their true love. By this point, the facade of the fake relationship has crumbled or run its course, and the characters are forced to make the choice to either walk away or try to let the relationship stand on its own merits rather than a charade. Because these characters have already seen how real things can feel when the relationship is supposedly nothing more than an act, they must find a way to prove to one another that their connection is genuine and meaningful.

POTENTIAL THEMES

Authenticity
Letting go of the past
Family ties
Vulnerability
Not caring what others think

HIDDEN IDENTITY/ DISGUISE

The Hidden Identity or Disguise trope involves one or both of the main characters concealing their true identity or assuming a disguise. This storyline often leads to misunderstandings, secrets, and unexpected revelations. If the disguise is used specifically for the purpose of growing close to the love interest, this trope will lean heavily on the Hidden Motives trope. As a standalone trope, this Hidden Identity is usually in place for other reasons, and the character is in their fake persona when their world collides with the other protagonist.

Characters may adopt false names, professions, or personas for various reasons, such as protecting themselves, pursuing a goal, or escaping their past. Truly, this is an incredibly versatile trope, as there are so many scenarios where hidden identities could come into play. These tropes work especially well in historical fiction, but there are a multitude of examples in contemporary fiction as well.

WHY READERS LOVE IT

Readers who enjoy romantic suspense appreciate the touch of intrigue and mystery that this trope brings to the narrative. Even for readers who are not looking for these elements, the tension and anticipation built into the reveal of the Hidden character's true identity is likely to sweep them into the story all the same.

The Disguise trope creates a unique form of romantic tension as characters navigate the challenges of keeping their true identities hidden. This often comes along with the buildup of emotions and physical tension between them, making the eventual reveal more impactful.

Depending on how the disguise is implemented, there will likely be opportunities for humor, wit, and comedy that readers love. Misunderstandings and awkward situations arising from the disguise are the hallmark of the trope in non-suspense iterations. Comical attempts to maintain their disguise lend this trope to romantic comedy as well.

These readers probably spend the entire book waiting for the moment when the truth comes out. The point where the character reveals their deepest secrets (and in this case, true identity), desperately hoping to be loved and accepted anyway, creates a powerful moment. The moment of trusting the other person enough to let them into their shame, fears, or troubles must come after a true and deep connection has been established if it's going to stand firm. And the deeper in love these characters fall, the closer the reader knows they are coming to the moment of truth (to their absolute delight).

READER EXPECTATIONS

The reader is likely in on the secret of the hidden identity, or else it's been made clear to them through the narrative that something isn't quite right. In either case, they will expect a clear and compelling reason for the character's choice to adopt a hidden identity. Give them insight as to motivations and goals of the character if you want this (relatively outlandish) behavior to be believable. Let's face it, most of us don't go around pretending to be someone else.

Readers expect obstacles and conflicts to arise from the deception—it will drive the plot of the narrative, after all. These could be external challenges or internal struggles faced by the characters as they grapple with the consequences of their hidden identities. Sometimes the secret is a huge deal to begin with, sometimes it starts off slow and snowballs into something bigger, and sometimes the character never intends to hide anything (until they do). There's always some measure of unpredictability to the narrative, necessitating a delicate balance of keeping the reader on their toes without going beyond the limits of what is acceptable or believable.

The deeper the connection formed between your characters, the more raw it is when the truth is revealed. With huge stakes at risk, the reader should experience the character's own struggle of being drawn to the love interest while battling with the temptation or pressure to reveal their secrets. Of course, you can't let them reveal it too soon—that would be too easy, and not nearly painful enough.

The character may reveal the truth themself, they may get caught in a trap, or they may be forced by circumstances into stripping their disguise. This tension keeps the reader gripped and builds anticipation toward the end of the second act (when all should be revealed).

There is an undeniable measure of vulnerability that comes along with the Hidden character revealing their true identity. Will they be accepted without their disguise? Did their love interest fall for them or who they were pretending to be? Can they ever atone for the lies and secrecy? This creates a complete roller coaster of emotions as readers puts themselves in the shoes of the most vulnerable character (the disguised lover), as well as the character being lied to.

POTENTIAL PITFALLS

Rushed reveals: Building up to the revelation of hidden identities is crucial for creating tension and engagement. If the reveal happens too early or too late without adequate buildup, it can diminish the impact and emotional resonance of the moment.

Foundation of lies: Some readers feel that the fact of establishing a relationship on a bed of lies sullies the authenticity of the romance that develops later. To avoid falling into this, or at the very least to steer readers away from these complaints, give your characters reasonable motives that the reader can empathize with.

Contrived conflict: Introducing unnecessary or contrived conflicts solely to prolong the story is bound to frustrate your readers. Instead, lean into the conflicts that may naturally arise from the reasons behind your character's hidden identity and the ones created from their deception.

Lack of consequences: The deception is bound to have significant consequences on the relationship, even if the love interest can recognize it was for a good reason. Be sure to address the emotional impact and fallout of the character's hidden identity rather than glossing over these aspects.

FREQUENTLY PAIRED TROPES

When paired with the Law Enforcement trope, this trope could be called Love Undercover. Typically the LEO goes undercover on an assignment where they encounter the love interest. The high stakes of their undercover position make it nearly impossible for them to reveal the truth of their identity, even as the romance blossoms into true love.

This trope may also be paired with the Fake Relationship trope, where the relationship is used to further disguise the truth of the character's hidden identity. In this case, the romantic partner may or may not know the true identity of the Hidden character.

When paired with the Royalty trope, the story may be considered Secret Royalty. These stories capitalize on elements of class difference or social expectations, creating challenges for the romantic relationship through the course of maintaining the deception or in the aftermath of the reveal.

COMMON PLOT DEVICES

Disguise as a means of escape: Characters may adopt disguises as a means of escaping a challenging or dangerous situation. This is especially common when the story contains an element of suspense.

She's the man: In this version of the trope, the hidden identity involves the female main character pretending to be a man. This can mean interacting with the other protagonist both in disguise and in their true form before the revelation that they are one and the same, or the non-disguised character fighting their feelings because they believe the disguised character shouldn't be more than a (guy) friend. This plot device is not typically gender-swapped, but it has been done, as in the 80s classic *Tootsie*.

Blackmail or coercion: The character may be forced into adopting a disguise due to blackmail, coercion, or external threats. Another opportunity to involve blackmail may appear when a secondary character discovers the Hidden character's true identity.

Masked events or balls: The setting of masked events, masquerade balls, or other social gatherings where characters wear disguises provides opportunities for romantic encounters and mistaken identities.

Revelation through external circumstances: The character's true identity may be revealed due to external circumstances, such as a sudden emergency. In this case, the deceptive character typically hasn't yet come to terms with owning up to the disguise, forcing them ahead in the character arc journey and likely leading to a deeper dark moment as they process what they otherwise would have come to terms with before the reveal.

KEY MOMENTS

Inciting incident: This is the moment that the disguise is adopted or the hidden identity is otherwise revealed to the reader. The character may already be in disguise at the start of the book, so the inciting incident may be explained rather than witnessed. Whatever is forcing the character to assume a hidden identity is the inciting incident, as it will drive the plot forward and introduce the conflict of the story.

Meet cute: The Hidden character must be in their disguise at the time that they meet or encounter the love interest. This sets the stage for all the deception that follows the character. If the character's real intersects with the love interests as well, they may have two meet cutes, where they interact with the love interest as both their fake persona and their true self.

Turning point: True identity revealed. This moment typically occurs during the dark moment or during the act two breakup. This scene should be emotionally charged, and it will directly impact the romance arc.

Grand gesture: Because one or both of the characters have been hiding their true self from the other for the majority of this story, the resolution and/or grand gesture needs to address the complete declaration of the truth of their love and the truth of their identity, admitting that the two were never separate and that their feelings were genuine, even if their identity was not.

POTENTIAL THEMES

Honesty
Trust
Being fully known and accepted
Forgiveness
Facing consequences

HIDDEN MOTIVES/BET

The Hidden Motives trope and the Bet (sometimes called Wager) trope are both terms-and-conditions-based stories. The key to the Storyline Trope is that one character is somehow incentivized to develop a relationship (or at the very least, maintain proximity) to the other and then unintentionally falls for their "target."

The Bet trope involves one romantic partner agreeing to a bet with a third party to seduce or otherwise initiate a romantic relationship with a target character. Sometimes the target is chosen and included in the terms of the bet; other times the character is given the flexibility to choose their own target.

The Hidden Motives trope is not as straightforward, but it involves a character who is intentionally not transparent about their reasons for entering into a friendship or romance. This motive may be revenge, blackmail from a third party, a confidence scheme, promotion or professional advancement, or any motivation that feeds the character's perceived need at the beginning of the story.

As their deception plays out, the characters develop genuine feelings and then must overcome all the lies that rest at the foundation of their relationship in order to move forward and find their happily ever after.

WHY READERS LOVE IT

Although this trope appears to victimize the romantic interest, these stories actually tend to choose strong and resilient characters as the target. The moment of revelation—the *I heard this, is it true?*—moment is used to demonstrate the backbone of these characters.

The character must recover from the betrayal of someone they now care about, then we get to see them decide to take a risk in trusting a person who has done them wrong. It's these second chances and journeys of forgiveness and trust that keep readers coming back to these stories.

As much as readers love to hate reading the moment when the deception is revealed, they enjoy the buildup to it just as much. The conflict and tension that comes along with waiting for the other shoe to drop keeps readers turning the page, simultaneously being swept up in the budding romance and waiting for the floor to fall out from under the lovebirds.

Readers enjoy witty banter, meaningful conversations, and emotionally charged exchanges that contribute to the development of the romantic relationship. The fact that a genuine connection is completely unexpected by at least one party seriously increases the entertainment value for readers and adds a layer of tension throughout the majority of the narrative. Opportunities for near-misses, subtext, and half-truths add to the emotional rollercoaster of the reader as they wait for the truth to be fully revealed.

While bets are rarely made with honorable intentions, the joke ends up coming back on the character who took the bet. After all, they were the one to pick a target who is so gosh darn lovable that they couldn't help but be pulled into a genuine connection, ultimately making them realize what an absolute jerk they are and what an incredible opportunity they've sullied with their immature actions.

For a Hidden Motives story, the deceptive character is similarly humbled, usually setting aside whatever goal motivated them to deceive the love interest in the first place—facing the wrath of their blackmailer, setting aside their revenge mission, or sacrificing their career advancement if it would be victimizing their love. This shift in priorities from the beginning to the end of the story is where the magic of these stories.

READER EXPECTATIONS

Despite the initial motivations being driven by external factors, readers expect to see a genuine emotional connection develop between the characters. The romance should feel authentic and serve as a catalyst for growth. A well-executed Hidden Motives or Bet trope includes believable conflicts and obstacles that arise naturally from the characters' motivations and circumstances. These challenges should test the strength of the developing relationship. The consequences of winning or losing the bet should be significant to the character entering into the agreement. One of the easiest ways to turn readers off to these stories is failing to have clear stakes that add tension and urgency to the story.

When it comes to the Bet trope, the Bet character will typically agree to the terms of the wager, but they won't always initiate it. It's a bit easier for readers to forgive a character who was roped into a poor choice by their friends, but harder if they were the one callous enough to suggest it.

As for Hidden Motives, the reasons for perpetuating the deception must be strong, and the reader should be able to empathize with the character. Whether they didn't have much of a choice (blackmail or financial desperation) or were so committed to their own goal that they compromised their values (revenge, promotion, etc.), the reader needs to be able to eventually overlook their decision to lie to the other character so they can root for the romance.

As the romance develops and becomes more intimate, pressure increases on the offending lover to face the consequences of their choice. The plot at this point often shifts to revolve around their efforts to conceal the truth from coming out, break the agreement, or atone for their mistakes without having to actually own up to them—until the revelation of the deceit.

Once the truth comes out—whether through a confession, a side character's interventions, an overheard conversation, a discovered object, fulfillment of the Bet or Hidden Motive goal, or some other method—readers expect the deceit to be addressed in order to reach a satisfying resolution to the central conflict that feels earned and meaningful.

POTENTIAL PITFALLS

Lack of consequences: The forgiveness of the betrayal should not come too easily for the victimized character, and there should be some consequence for not fulfilling the terms of the bet or covert mission. The offending character should be willing to face the consequences, and generally, they should not simply disappear to aid in the happy ending.

Low stakes: If the characters' motivations or the reasons behind the deception feel forced, artificial, or downright stupid, readers will struggle to connect with the story. Strive to make the characters' actions authentic and consistent with their goals or internal conflict, ensuring that readers can understand and empathize with their choices.

Foundation of lies: Some readers will struggle to root for a romantic relationship that has been built upon a lie. The narrative should acknowledge that the character responsible for the deception has significantly breached the trust of the love interest. Even if a relationship can be built on a foundation of lies, it will not stand there long. The deception must be addressed, and the character who was deceived will likely struggle with trusting the other enough to move forward.

Unrevealed to reader: Because a major key to making this trope work is the internal conflict of the deceptive character as the relationship progresses, if their motives remain hidden to the reader through too much of the story, then their character arc feels incomplete or rushed. The exact details of their motive do not have to necessarily be revealed, but there should be plenty of clues to the reader that this character has something they aren't sharing *as they wrestle with it*.

Unlikable/morally gray characters: This is a tricky trope to place an unlikable character in, especially when they are the one agreeing to the bet or hidden motives. The reader is already bound to take issue with this character without you giving them any extra reasons. Sometimes the target character can also land in this territory. When that happens, readers tend to find themselves uninvested and struggling to care about the characters or any budding romance.

FREQUENTLY PAIRED TROPES

The Ugly Duckling microtrope (often combined with the Genius/Bookworm trope) is a common pairing for this trope, with a wager placed on the character's ability to transform the character into someone desirable. Because of the rather juvenile tendency for bets of this sort, they are most frequently paired with Academy/High School settings.

The *Money, Money* tropes (Celebrity, Billionaire, Athlete, Royalty, etc.) are ripe targets for someone with Hidden Motives, as are characters with power or influence like Politicians.

This trope can be very successfully paired with other tropes that give excuses for close proximity and access to the character being deceived, such as Child's Caregiver, Boss/Employee, or Marriage of Convenience.

COMMON PLOT DEVICES

The unlikely or impossible challenge: To win the bet or achieve their hidden motive, the character must do something that seems impossible. Depending on the character and the timing of the challenge, it could feed the character's sense of competition and fuel them to succeed, or it may add to their feeling of helplessness and make them reconsider the terms of their arrangement.

Unexpected moments of intimacy: Despite their initial motives or intentions, the characters find themselves drawn to each other in moments of vulnerability, authenticity, and connection. These moments of intimacy often catch the characters off guard, challenging their preconceived notions and sparking feelings of attraction, desire, and longing. Whether it's a heartfelt conversation, a shared experience, or a passionate encounter, these unexpected moments deepen the emotional bond between the protagonists and pave the way for genuine love and romance to blossom

Time constraints: The character is faced with the pressure of limited time to fulfill their bet or hidden motive. Whether it's a looming deadline, a countdown to a major event, or a race against time as their deception approaches its expiration date for another reason, the presence of time constraints heightens the stakes and drives the narrative forward with a sense of urgency and tension. The characters race against the clock to fulfill their objectives while navigating the complexities of their burgeoning relationship. The deceptive character is forced to confront their priorities, make difficult choices, and ultimately seize the moment to pursue love and happiness before it's too late.

Miscommunication/misunderstanding: These stories often rely on a failure of characters to communicate their true feelings, a misinterpretation of intentions, or a lack of clarity about the terms of the bet or hidden motive, leading to emotional turmoil. These misunderstandings create obstacles for the protagonists to overcome as they address the betrayal and work toward resolution. In fact, much of the time, the deceptive character is happily vague or ambiguous in their answers.

Escalation of the bet or terms of the agreement: The initial wager or terms of the agreement often escalate midstory, raising the stakes and intensifying the conflict between the protagonists. Whether it's increasing the monetary value of the bet, adding additional conditions, or raising the stakes of blackmail, the escalation of the bet or terms of the agreement adds layers of tension and complexity to the story. Often this escalation occurs after a false victory, when the deceitful character has determined to call off their hidden agenda. After the stakes are raised, they feel as though they have no choice but to continue in the charade.

KEY MOMENTS

Inciting incident: This key moment at the beginning of the story is when the Bet is made or motives are established, typically before the characters meet.

Turning point: As the character realizes the depth of their feelings for their target, their motivations shift from winning the bet or achieving their goals to trying to keep the truth of their initial motivations concealed. They may attempt to break the agreement, or they may simply hope to solidify their commitment to the target in the hopes of earning forgiveness.

Dark moment: This is the moment the truth comes out and the character has to face the consequences of their bet or lies.

Grand gesture: Because these tropes see at least one character making a fool (or at least attempting to) of the love interest or inflicting a giant hit to the pride of a character who trusted someone only to be betrayed, the grand gesture moment requires an act of absolute and truly swoon-worthy humility or sacrifice.

POTENTIAL THEMES

Second chances
Forgiveness
Honesty
Reputation
Sacrifice for love

MISTAKEN IDENTITY

While the Hidden Identity or Disguise trope relies on intentional choice for the character to disguise their identity in pursuit of their external goals, the Mistaken Identity trope involves a character unintentionally *falling into* a false identity when they are mistaken for someone else. Typically they are not in a true disguise at all but are mistaken to be someone (or something) other than themselves. The key to this trope is that at some point the character *does* make the choice to keep up this false identity for any number of reasons. This storyline often leads to misunderstandings, secrets, and unexpected revelations.

As with Hidden Identity, this trope works especially well in historical fiction, but there are a multitude of examples in contemporary fiction as well. It is worth noting that in true contemporary romance, your characters will have the inclination to dig up as much as possible on the Mistaken Identity characters using avenues such as social media and online searches.

WHY READERS LOVE IT

Many of the reasons for readers' love of Hidden Identity hold true for Mistaken Identity. The anticipation of the revelation of truth, and its fallout, create a sense of tension that keeps building from the moment of the inciting incident. The additional component of the false identity being assumed unintentionally or under unexpected circumstances creates not only tension, but affords plenty of opportunity for humor. Misunderstandings and awkward situations arising from the mistaken identity delight readers.

A hallmark of this trope is when the deceptive character almost admits the misunderstanding multiple times through the narrative. Inevitably, however, those attempts to confess are interrupted or otherwise prevented or delayed, forcing the deception to continue longer. And the longer the truth remains hidden, the harder it is for everything to be brought into the light. At which point the Mistaken Identity character may not see a way out of their situation.

As the character navigates the challenges of keeping their true identity hidden, they are often forced out of their comfort zone. This often comes along with significant character growth and change of perspective, both of which readers appreciate.

As with Hidden Identity, these readers spend most of the book waiting for the moment when the truth comes out. The point where the character reveals their deepest secrets (and in this case, true identity), desperately hoping to be loved and accepted anyway, creates a powerful moment. The moment of trusting the other person enough to let them into their shame, fears, or troubles must come after a true and deep connection has been established if it's going to stand firm. And the deeper in love these characters fall, the closer the reader knows they are coming to the moment of truth (to their absolute delight).

READER EXPECTATIONS

See Hidden Identity.

The inciting incident of these stories typically involves a fair bit of confusion and miscommunication. When the Mistaken Identity character is misidentified, they will initially scramble trying to figure out the situation. By the end of that scene, they may decide that the false identity is advantageous for them and go with it, or they may remain confused for the entirety of the scene.

The circumstances of the mistaken identity should be both believable and compelling. It should make sense to readers that the character could be mistaken for someone else, for example, never having met the intended individual. The character who decides to take up the ruse should also have a compelling reason for doing so—readers need to understand what's at stake for the character if they choose to tell the truth right away.

Readers expect obstacles and conflicts to arise from the deception. These should include the external challenges AND the internal struggles faced by the Mistaken Identity character as they grapple with the consequences of their false identity. The secret may be a huge deal to begin with, or it may start off slow and snowball into something bigger. Often this comes in the form of a third party discovering the deception and forcing the character to perpetrate the ruse longer to satisfy the antagonist's motives, twisting what started as an innocent misunderstanding into a darker hidden motive. Once the truth is revealed, the characters are likely to question the authenticity of their feelings and whether their relationship can overcome the deception that brought them together.

POTENTIAL PITFALLS

Rushed reveals: Building up to the revelation of mistaken identities is crucial for creating tension and engagement. If the reveal happens too early or too late without adequate buildup, it can diminish the impact and emotional resonance of the moment.

Foundation of lies: Readers who dislike stories centered around deception and misunderstandings may struggle to empathize with characters who perpetuate a false identity. Some readers will struggle to root for a romantic relationship that has been built upon a lie that, to many, will seem almost unforgivable. The narrative should acknowledge that the character responsible for the deception has significantly breached the trust of the love interest. Even if a relationship can be built on a foundation of lies, it will not stand there long. The deception must be addressed, and the character who was deceived will likely struggle with trusting the other enough to move forward.

Contrived conflict: Introducing unnecessary or contrived conflicts solely to prolong the story is bound to frustrate your readers. Ensure that conflicts arise naturally from the characters' personalities, circumstances, and genuine misunderstandings, and avoid relying on artificial obstacles that don't contribute to the overall narrative.

Lack of consequences: The deception is bound to have significant consequences on the relationship, even if the love interest can recognize it was for a good reason. Be sure to address the emotional impact and fallout of the character's mistaken identity rather than glossing over these aspects.

FREQUENTLY PAIRED TROPES

Characters are often placed into an unfamiliar environment or social circle due to the mistaken identity. Characters may also swap identities intentionally after a mistaken mix-up, specifically when dealing with a Twin Swap or identity swap type story.

After the initial mix-up, the Mistaken Identity may create a situation of Forbidden Love where the romance is totally off-limits, adding stakes to the relationship and intensifying the drama.

This trope is often used in settings where a person can be swept into the scenario without having been seen before, like Boss/Employee, Nanny, Matchmaker, or a Fake Relationship or Marriage of Convenience where a third party or formal interview is involved in the selection. This is another reason it is commonly paired with *Money, Money* tropes. Suspicion cast on the Mistaken Identity character is often an obstacle to their forgiveness, with the rich or famous character assuming that there was a hidden motive, even though it was an innocent misunderstanding.

COMMON PLOT DEVICES

Doppelgänger: The Mistaken Identity character may look like or similar to the individual they are mistaken for.

Parallel lives: Characters may lead parallel lives that intersect in unexpected ways, leading to mistaken assumptions about each other's identities and backgrounds. This plot device lends itself to exciting near misses as the character interacts with the people and places from their real life while trying to maintain the facade of the mistaken identity.

Revelation through external circumstances: The character's true identity may be revealed due to external circumstances, such as a sudden emergency, leading to unexpected and dramatic moments.

Steamrolled into the identity: This plot device is often used as a way to make the character's willingness to embrace the identity they are mistaken for more palatable to the reader. In this scenario, the character is steamrolled into the role by a pushy and often fast-talking side character or sometimes the love interest themself. By the time your character can get a word in edgewise, they are firmly rooted in their mistaken identity, and extricating themselves from the situation becomes difficult.

KEY MOMENTS

Inciting incident: Typically in the inciting incident, the character is introduced under the mistaken identity—it may coincide with the meet cute if the character is introduced directly to the love interest, or they may just be introduced to someone within the love interest's social circle. This scene is likely somewhat chaotic externally, internally, or both, and the character is likely trying to figure out how and when to set the record straight.

Call to action: By the end of the first act, your character has made the deliberate decision to continue the ruse of their false identity. Readers should have a solid understanding of what the character expects to gain by fully committing to this deception.

Turning point: True identity revealed. The moment typically occurs during the dark moment or during the act two breakup. The discovery may happen gradually, as the love interest uncovers inconsistencies or discrepancies in the Mistaken character's story, or it can occur suddenly, through a revelation or confession. This scene should be emotionally charged, and it will directly impact the romance arc. Because the Mistaken character did not initially set out with the intention of deceiving the love interest, they may not be ready yet to take full responsibility for their actions, increasing the tension and hurt of the moment.

Grand gesture: Once the truth comes to light, the protagonist must confront the consequences of their actions and own their mistake in hurting the love interest through their deception. They must recognize that the cost of their deception includes a loss of trust and the forfeiture to hold claim over any romantic connection the two shared. Ultimately, the love interest will see the sincerity of the Mistaken character's regret and the authenticity of their love and choose to forgive them.

POTENTIAL THEMES

Trust and honesty
Communication
Authenticity
Forgiveness
Integrity—doing the right thing even when it is the hardest choice

REVENGE

The Revenge trope is a specific iteration of the Hidden Motive trope, so be sure to study that entry as well, as we'll only cover items specific to Revenge in this entry, though many other aspects of the Hidden Motive trope still apply. The Revenge trope involves one of the main characters coming into the life of their love interest while exacting revenge, usually on someone close to the love interest. This typically leads to power struggles, unexpected romantic entanglements, and ultimately betrayal once the truth of the character's motives are revealed. The character seeking revenge is usually doing so due to a perceived wrong or betrayal to themselves or a family member, typically a parent.

This trope may be more popular in dark romance, but it can definitely be used in other subgenres. While these stories don't usually include the love interest as the actual target of revenge in clean or inspirational romance, their proximity to the target often creates feelings of animosity toward them when they meet.

WHY READERS LOVE IT

This trope isn't everyone's cup of tea, but those who do love it are quickly drawn into the tension and drama inherent in the storyline. These stories are pretty emotionally charged and really shine when there is a depth to the Revenge character's deep-seated wound that will tug at readers heart strings, even if they don't approve of the character's choice to exact revenge.

One of the elements that makes these stories so rewarding is the redemption arc of the Revenge character as they learn that causing pain to others will not heal their own pain. As the romance grows under the weight of their secret, the character must face their choices and confront their own flaws, weaknesses, and ugliness—usually discovering they are no better than the person whom they've come to seek revenge on. This growth arc is immensely satisfying for readers, especially if the character is one they are able to connect to right off the bat.

The ultimate choice the Revenge character must make between the object of their revenge and the love interest serves as the pinnacle of their growth arc.

READER EXPECTATIONS

One of the most important factors in the success of Revenge stories is that the reader must understand the motivations and reasons behind the character's choice to seek revenge. If the reader can't empathize with it, then the entire thing comes off as quite malicious and your Revenge character will most likely come off as unlikable to your audience. Your character seeking revenge should be multidimensional with layers of vulnerability, strength, tenderness, and flaws that make them relatable and compelling.

This storyline tends to send the reader off on a bit of an emotional roller coaster. The high points are passionate and the low points can be absolutely gutting. This intensity of emotion compels the Revenge character to confront their choices and evaluate their priorities—in other words, the intensity of pain that has caused them to seek harm (whether bodily, emotionally or socially) to someone must be equally matched by the intensity of the romantic connection.

POTENTIAL PITFALLS

Low stakes: The reasons for your character's choice to seek revenge must be compelling, but the stakes of not succeeding with their revenge plan must be equally high. Will your character's actions land them in jail? Will they lose their home or their livelihood? Will it put someone's life at risk?

***Manipulation*:** If the power dynamics between characters are skewed or if one character's quest for revenge involves manipulation or coercion, readers may feel uncomfortable or find it difficult to root for the romantic relationship.

Lack of growth: Stories that fail to explore themes of redemption, forgiveness, and growth may leave readers feeling unsatisfied, especially if characters don't undergo meaningful development or if conflicts are resolved too easily without addressing underlying issues.

FREQUENTLY PAIRED TROPES

The Revenge trope is almost always paired with the Enemies to Lovers trope—at least a one-sided version of it. The character exacting revenge views the love interest as either the party they must take revenge upon, or at least an extension of that offending party. This can also mean pairing the trope with a Forbidden Love trope, as the other people in the Revenge character's world would not approve of the match.

While the Revenge storyline brings the characters into the same orbit, if the Revenge character intentionally pursues a Fake Relationship with the other main character, it adds even more betrayal and nuance to the story, and *all the angst*, as the character determined to keep the relationship fake realizes that their feelings are very real.

Often, the character attempting revenge must hide their true identity to avoid their motives being revealed. This combination of Revenge and Hidden Identity raises the stakes of the deception and challenges the characters' ability to keep everything close to the vest.

COMMON PLOT DEVICES

Flashbacks: Flashbacks are used to provide insight into the characters' pasts, revealing the events or betrayals that led to their desire for revenge and adding depth to their motivations.

Moral ambiguity: Characters' actions and motivations are often morally ambiguous, blurring the lines between right and wrong and adding depth to the ethical dilemmas they face in their quest for revenge.

Deadline/ticking time bomb: Characters must complete their revenge plan by a certain date or event. This plot device adds urgency to the narrative and challenges the character to consider the weight of their objective in comparison to the depth of their connection with the love interest.

KEY MOMENTS

Inciting incident: Introduce the character or situation against which the protagonist seeks revenge. This could involve a confrontation, discovery, or event that sets the revenge plot in motion. Readers also typically want to understand the reasons for the revenge plan as well.

Meet cute: Early in the journey, your characters will encounter their first significant obstacle. This may be a disagreement, unexpected obstacle or delay (often paired with the first detour), or a misunderstanding. This usually hits as a no way beat where characters have begun to get comfortable with each other and are suddenly pulled out of that rapport by the reintroduction of very overt conflict.

Call to action: By the end of the first act, your character has committed to taking revenge. They may have strategized and planned their revenge already, forming alliances and anticipating obstacles they might encounter along the way.

Turning point: As the romantic connection between your characters grows, the Revenge character should be grappling increasingly with feelings of guilt or remorse as they confront the impact of their quest for revenge on themselves and those they have come to care about.

Dark moment: This is almost always tied to the moment the truth comes out and the character who has been deceived since the beginning of the relationship feels utterly betrayed. In addition, this causes some feelings of disloyalty or misplaced trust as they attempt to reconcile the fact that the person they have fallen in love with has actively sought to cause harm to someone they care deeply about.

POTENTIAL THEMES

Redemption
Forgiveness
Vulnerability
Healing
Betrayal

SECRET RELATIONSHIP

In the Secret Relationship trope, your characters will either begin or maintain a hidden romance from most people or everyone they know. Sometimes your characters will let a select few individuals in on the secret, but often they are keeping their blossoming romance from absolutely everyone.

This secrecy may arise because of societal expectations, personal conflicts, or external obstacles. The plot tends to revolve around the challenges and consequences of maintaining a hidden relationship, affecting both the external conflict as well as the romantic arc. While this trope often goes hand in hand with a Forbidden Relationship, it doesn't have to. If the consequences of the relationship are one-sided (like a Rockstar avoiding the scrutiny of paparazzi on the relationship), the secrecy is temporary (like a Celebrity who needs to appear single until he gets an endorsement deal or prove he is taking his role seriously), or the characters are otherwise motivated to keep things on the DL (down low)—the Secret Relationship trope stands alone.

Ultimately, these stories tend to illuminate the problems with a relationship carried out in the dark, including dishonesty, insecurities, and "one-foot-out-the-door" feelings.

WHY READERS LOVE IT

The initial premise of a secret relationship automatically raises the stakes of the story and introduces tension for the development of compelling conflict. Sneaking around, carefully choosing their words with others, and especially subtext and stolen glances (or even moments!) when they are together in public and trying not to let the cat out of the bag give the reader delicious moments of intimacy and have them holding their breath. There is a delicate balance of fostering the growth of the romance and keeping it under wraps. With every relationship victory, the secret gets harder to keep and the stakes are raised.

Readers are drawn to the idea of characters being willing to defy societal norms, expectations, or bending the rules in order to get their happily ever after. While your lovers may initially keep the secret of the romance because they are not confident in its lasting value, readers are captivated by the moment when characters recognize that their love is worth fighting for and they are ready to shout it from the rooftops.

This balancing act also lends itself to something of an emotional rollercoaster for both the characters and the readers. Characters experience emotional whiplash as the person they interact with in private is cold and distant in public. They may be faced with their secret lover flirting with someone else to maintain appearances, or really anything that causes them to doubt the legitimacy of their relationship and the commitment of the other.

These moments of deep longing to publicly embrace their relationship pave the way for the eventual reveal and keep the reader invested. Characters are forced to face fears, insecurities, and the expectations of others as they navigate the inevitability of the romance coming to light. Despite any misgivings readers may have about starting a relationship on a foundation of lies, when done well, the overcoming of self makes the union of their happily ever after feel well-earned. This fulfilling resolution reinforces the ideal of true love overcoming any obstacle.

READER EXPECTATIONS

The beginning of the relationship may happen at the meet cute or it may happen off the page. In either case, it is likely that the relationship was established in secrecy, otherwise the lovers may have allowed others to believe that they had previously split while carrying on in secret. By the end of act one, it's likely that your reader will have a clear idea as to why secrecy is necessary. The story itself can provide clues, even if you don't outright state the reasons. For example, a wealthy, overbearing father who treats those below his station with no respect can give readers enough information to understand why his daughter wouldn't reveal a romance with a working-class man.

Initial justification of the deception usually begins as a temporary solution. Sometimes characters assume the relationship is temporary and insignificant, and other times they simply haven't found a way around the obstacles to their relationship and see hiding it as the only option. As with other deception-based romance premises, readers need a clear motivation behind the decision to enter into a secret romance. Whether it's to ward off unwanted attention, fulfill a contractual obligation, or meet a specific goal, the characters' reasons for pretending not to be a couple should be well-established.

As previously mentioned, this trope will directly influence the external conflict of your romance. Disapproving family members, societal constraints, and even workplace policies are all common sources for conflict when employing these tropes—but don't feel limited.

When the secret comes out, readers expect at least a touch of drama or chaos. It doesn't need to read like an after-school special, but we should be able to rely on some genuine consequences, even if they're only emotional in nature. And trust us, you won't get away with keeping this secret all the way through to the happily ever after—a love that must *remain* hidden is no happily ever after at all.

The revelation itself serves as a turning point, both in the external and internal conflict arcs. The reveal of the relationship may be voluntary, chosen by one or both parties. It may also be accidental, with the couple being discovered by others and forcing their hand. Either way, the revelation has consequences, and the characters now have to pay the piper.

The nature of a secret relationship should naturally limit your characters' opportunity for genuine connection and interaction. Any dates are likely private affairs at home or somewhere they won't be seen together, which can play into the insecurity of a character without their own motive for secrecy. Just be sure that the time they *do* get together is well spent.

Placing too much focus on the secret itself rather than the emotional connection will feel one-dimensional and likely bore readers. Secret Relationship is a repelling trope, keeping the characters at some amount of distance until it is revealed, so the intimacy must overcome that inherent distance placed by the trope.

While the initial sneaking around and clandestine meetings can make the reader feel like they're in on some special secret, that excitement dies down really quickly as your characters have to face the real-world consequences of their choices. Be sure to use these consequences to challenge your characters' perspective or priorities.

POTENTIAL PITFALLS

Inconsistent characters: The reason or motivation your characters claim for keeping their relationship hidden must align with their values, priorities, and behavior. A hidden relationship where characters are blatantly acting romantic but insisting there's nothing there tends to fall flat, as does a secret relationship with no apparent motivation for maintaining secrecy.

Lack of consequences: Readers expect to see the consequences of deception at some point during these stories. If your characters never have to face challenges to keeping their romance hidden from others or they never face consequences when the truth comes out, the entire premise feels silly at best and malicious at worst. At the very least, their friends and family will feel betrayed by the secret being kept, even if they don't disapprove of the relationship at its core.

Lack of character growth: A character who wasn't willing to have the relationship in the open at the beginning of the story must be willing to profess their love openly by the end due to the shifting priorities and internal growth caused by the relationship and external conflict. Without this internal growth, the external actions of the character feel unbelievable, too convenient, or unjustified.

Forced drama: Although your Secret Romance will naturally require some obstacles to come between the characters, you quickly run the risk of turning readers off if the forces keeping them apart don't feel organic or integral to the story. Be cautious of overdramatizing obstacles that feel too obscure, unrelatable, or that don't actually justify the risk of keeping the secret.

FREQUENTLY PAIRED TROPES

Forbidden Love is a clear high-stakes motivation for hiding a romance, and it is frequently paired with the Secret Relationship trope. A softer approach to a true Forbidden Romance is often employed as a Workplace Romance. These two pairings heavily influence the motivation and goals of your character to keep the relationship a secret. The Workplace Romance doesn't stay hidden if your character doesn't care deeply and work hard to advance or maintain respect in their career; nor does the Forbidden Love tend to stay hidden if your characters are bucking the values or priorities of the family or society that has forbidden such a romance.

Because of the public scrutiny in the profession, Secret Relationship is commonly paired with *Money, Money* tropes. Or it is paired with other "off-limits" Relational Tropes like Sibling's Best Friend, Age Gap, Boss/Employee, Student/Teacher, etc., where the backlash of revealing the relationship could have relational or professional implications.

COMMON PLOT DEVICES

They won't approve: Personal and familial motivations tend to create the most emotionally charged obstacles to the relationship, as the tension that arises with threat of disapproval from those who matter most to the character increases the potential consequences of discovery.

Blackmail or leverage: The discovery of the relationship by an adversarial character is often used to create leverage against or manipulate the behavior of one or both lovers. This introduction of an actual personification of threat gives the reader someone to be mad at other than the dumb people keeping their relationship secret.

Miscommunication or misunderstanding: Secrets tend to run amok when this trope is employed, creating ample opportunity for missed communication or miscommunication. Missed opportunities to relay a vital message to their lover or the inability to correct an assumption due to a limited amount of available time together (namely when other people aren't around) sets the stage for further complications in the relationship.

KEY MOMENTS

Inciting incident: At the outset of your story, readers should be made aware that a secret relationship exists and they should understand that there are *reasons* it must be kept secret, though they may not know exactly what those reasons are. In order to avoid totally frustrating readers with confusion, most of these stories which choose not to reveal all at the outset get around that risk by revealing *either* the reason for secrecy without revealing the consequences, or by revealing very specific consequences for having their secret come out without revealing the source of the conflict.

Fun and games: During the first half of act two, we'll want to see at least one significant moment of near-discovery—but don't be afraid to give your characters more than one close call. These near-discoveries add suspense and tension that all builds up to the moment of truth (literally).

Turning point: Since the plot of these stories revolves around the challenges to avoiding discovery, the climax naturally occurs when the secret finally comes out. This scene should be emotionally charged. However you choose for the truth to come out, it should have a major impact. After all, the entire story has been leading to this moment. We should see the consequences (disapproval, reprimand, job loss, paparazzi harassment, etc.) in full force, likely driving the characters to split up or (at the very least) pull back from the relationship and reconsider their commitment to each other.

Grand gesture: Before your characters reach their happy ending, they must resolve the external conflict that has kept them separated up until this point. If it's societal expectations, this is where they publicly declare their refusal to accept those expectations. If it's an actual threat, that threat must be eliminated or otherwise removed from the picture. Whatever the resolution looks like, before the story comes to a close, the reader needs to see the path forward for a future without this major obstacle.

POTENTIAL THEMES

Honesty
Not caring what people think
Authenticity
Trust
Consequences

TWIN SWITCH

The Twin Switch or Twin Swap trope is a classic romcom trope in which identical twins (or doppelgänger strangers) switch places and fall in love with someone who is unaware of the switch, and usually someone their twin would never fall for. The switch may be intentional or it may be accidental at first, but there comes a point by the end of the first act where the Twin commits to the ruse—because of this element, this trope does share some similarities with the Mistaken Identity or Hidden Identity tropes.

Although it's more complicated to do in a novel format, when used in movies, this trope often portrays dual love stories where *both* twins find love. This scenario adds an extra layer of complexity to the story as both twins navigate their feelings for someone who believes they are someone else.

WHY READERS LOVE IT

See Mistaken Identity.

This trope is pretty zany, especially when the swap involves two characters who didn't previously know each other and have no idea why they share a face—but they go with it for the chance to walk in someone else's shoes. Readers are usually more willing to suspend disbelief in these stories for the sake of a fun romp.

Since most of the time the Twin characters are polar opposites or live totally different lives, these stories have some Fish out of Water elements that really highlight the comedy and awkwardness inherent with this trope. The incongruity of these characters inevitably leads to the Twin Switch character making choices that will significantly complicate or disrupt the life of their twin when they resume their rightful place. This is bound to create opportunities for humor, but it also raises the stakes of the conflict and creates a constant tension that pulls the narrative along.

READER EXPECTATIONS

As in any false identity story, readers want to understand why characters have chosen this path and what the stakes are if they are found out or don't find what they're looking for. The switch should be enticing for at least one twin, and the other twin may not even be aware that someone has assumed their identity in their absence.

It's worth noting that although your character may not actually switch places until the end of the first act, readers expect to see at least one scene or moment on the page where the Twin Switch character has already interacted with their love-interest-to-be. This may involve a situation where the love interest mistakes the character for their twin, leading straight into the chaos and confusion that will color the tone for the rest of the narrative.

By the end of the story, readers will expect to see the truth revealed and the deception handled directly, with the Twin Switch character(s) having to deal with the consequences of their actions.

POTENTIAL PITFALLS

***Lack of differentiation*:** Failing to sufficiently differentiate between the twins can confuse readers and make it challenging to invest in the characters' individual journeys. Be sure to give each twin a distinct voice and personality, a task made even more difficult as they are pretending to be the other.

Lack of growth: If the focus is solely on the Twin Swap gimmick without delving into the characters' motivations, emotions, and personal growth, readers may find the story lacking and fail to engage. Lean into themes such as identity, trust, and even adventure that can connect the events of the plot to the character growth.

Foundation of lies: Readers who dislike stories centered around deception and misunderstandings may struggle to empathize with characters who perpetuate a false identity. Some readers will struggle to root for a romantic relationship that has been built upon a lie that, to many, will seem almost unforgivable.

The narrative should acknowledge that the character responsible for the deception has significantly breached the trust of the love interest. Even if a relationship can be built on a foundation of lies, it will not stand there long. The deception must be addressed, and the character who was deceived will likely struggle with trusting the other enough to move forward.

FREQUENTLY PAIRED TROPES

Twin Switch stories are often paired with Character Tropes that involve one twin being in the spotlight regularly, such as Royalty or Celebrity. This serves as motivation for the character to desire a chance to be "normal," but also raises the stakes for avoiding discovery and creates high-pressure situations where the ruse must be maintained.

These stories often have a Forbidden Romance flavor, as the Twin Switch character struggles with the reality that they cannot fall in love with someone who is part of their twin's life, not their own, especially if that person is someone off-limits or otherwise detestable by their twin.

COMMON PLOT DEVICES

Training montage: When the Twin characters haven't previously known each other or come from different worlds, there is often a scene or series of scenes where they take a crash course on the others' life and learn to emulate each other. This is specific to intentional twin swaps.

Coincidences and near misses: Incorporating coincidences and near misses where characters almost discover the twins' secret but narrowly avoid it

You can't fool me: Someone who knows one or both twins too well to be fooled by the ruse catches on and either challenges the Twin Switch character(s) to confess or attempts to reveal the truth before too much damage is done.

Healing the rift: In cases where the twins know each other, there is often a rift or resentment present in the relationship that is addressed by the switching of places. By literally walking a mile in each other's shoes, they recognize that each has their own struggles and difficulties that they face and learn to appreciate each others' strengths.

KEY MOMENTS

Inciting incident: Depending on how the characters are related and whether the switch is intentional, the Twins will either meet for the first time or one twin will find themselves mistaken for their lookalike.

Call to action: By the end of the first act, your character has committed to switching places. This may mean they have coordinated the switch with their twin or they may just be taking advantage of their twin's absence. In either case, they have typically strategized and thought through the challenges of their choices, but they are committed to seeing it through. Make sure that your readers understand the motivation behind the Twin's choice to switch places.

Turning point: The climactic moment when the twin swap is inevitably revealed, either through a series of misunderstandings, a deliberate confession, or an unexpected turn of events. This scene typically results in emotional turmoil and upheaval as characters confront the truth and reckon with the consequences of their actions. This may be paired with the dark moment, but typically it is more closely tied to the break up beat.

Dark moment: This scene often involves the external conflict that compelled the twins to switch places coming back to the forefront. If your character's deception has not already been revealed, it will be revealed now in the most damaging fashion. This scene often involves the fact that the Twin Switch character has crossed a line that they can not easily come back from, placing their character, the love interest, and the other twin in a very precarious position.

POTENTIAL THEMES

Identity
Trust
Loyalty/betrayal
Individuality
Adventure

CHAPTER 15

STUCK WITH YOU

FORCED PROXIMITY TROPES

In all Forced Proximity situations, characters are either physically forced into close quarters or forced to interact on a regular basis. As shallow attachments become more permanent, it leads to heightened intimacy and the development of romantic tension.

The Forced Proximity may be due to external circumstances or events such as being stranded by the elements (see Stranded), or otherwise being forced to coexist in some way. They could be locked in a building overnight, go on a road trip, or have temporary or long-term Shared Living Arrangements. Any circumstance that leads to them spending a lot of time together can be a Forced Proximity story, if you lean into expectations and keys to the trope. We'll first evaluate the broader Forced Proximity trope, then isolate specific iterations of the trope.

This trope is often used as a plot device in stories, playing a small role in the overall narrative, but don't think it isn't a powerful enough trope to stand on its own. Whether your characters are stuck together for three days out of their month-long story or for the entirety of the novel, if you understand the purpose and expectations of the Forced Proximity trope, you can meet them whether it is a plot device or the primary Storyline Trope.

We cannot emphasize enough how much the sheer amount of time spent together matters. But it isn't the only important thing about the trope that matters. If you read the introduction to this book (and didn't skip straight to the entries!) then this might sound familiar. But throwing your characters in a locked room for two-thirds of your novel may allow you to check the Forced Proximity box, but if you don't allow it to shape the conflict, the scene-level interactions, and the key moments of your story, you'll be missing a crucial piece of the puzzle.

It goes so much deeper than simply manipulating your scenes to include certain plot elements that readers love. But, boy, do readers love this trope. Let's examine why. We'll do the same for each variation of the trope in the subentries of the Forced Proximity category that follow.

WHY READERS LOVE IT

One of the aspects readers appreciate about Forced Proximity tropes is the (unwanted) interaction that comes about during the scenario. The characters are fighting with everything they have to not cross whatever boundaries exist between them, but they only have so much willpower. This is why readers are hungry for Forced Proximity stories, so be sure to deliver it.

In their time together, the characters discover the hidden depths of the person they are with. Aspects of their lives and personalities that may otherwise never be revealed eventually come out because the time allows or forces it. This also leads to moments of vulnerability and unexpected connection between the characters.

Through the adversity inherent in these tropes, characters are forced to grow and adapt—perhaps to overcome fears, but definitely to change perspectives and reevaluate priorities.

Readers absolutely love to see these characters working together, and they love to see how overcoming external challenges draws them closer to each other emotionally. As the bond deepens, cooperation naturally leads to mutual support and even an urge to protect and nurture one another. Whether the characters started the novel as friends, enemies, or strangers, the transition of their relationship is pushed along by the time spent together and the interactions they have in that time. These stories are absolutely strongest when we get to see the couple working as a partnership—especially in the most unlikely pairs. Individuals from different backgrounds, personalities, or motivations may seem unlikely to ever cross paths under normal circumstances, but, as they say—all's fair in love and war.

READER EXPECTATIONS

It is important to establish a clear reason for the Forced Proximity, and it's critical that this circumstance is not something characters can reasonably find their way out of. This lays the foundation of the initial conflict and tension between characters, especially when the reader has already been given a clear understanding of each character's motivations and goals—even better if those goals are in opposition to one another.

These romances may develop gradually or the characters may form a quick attachment, depending on the intensity of the situation. Either way, writers should build anticipation by creating moments of connection, and the obstacles the characters face should bring them closer, as previously discussed. The conflicts you introduce should be chosen intentionally in order to test their goals and the status of the characters' relationship. There may be old or unresolved conflicts that arise due to the extended time together in a shared space or other conflicts that are finally addressed because they are together for so long.

Keep in mind, this trope is called Forced Proximity, not Happenstance Proximity. Even if your characters are attracted to each other or they would ordinarily be happy about spending time together, they should be uncomfortable (if not outright horrified) with the idea of being stuck together.

Because most of the action of these stories takes place in a single setting, it is important to create a vivid and immersive experience for the reader. Whether it's a small town, workplace, cellar, or a phone booth, the setting should enhance the overall atmosphere of the story. It's not uncommon to use supporting characters to a similar effect. Just because the characters are in Forced Proximity doesn't have to mean they are there by themselves or cut off from the outside world, unless the setup demands it (like Stranded). Use side characters wisely to draw out aspects of your characters, provide comedic relief, or raise the stakes of the romance.

Authors should use the Forced Proximity setting to foster emotional intimacy between characters through moments of vulnerability and shared experiences. The proximity and extensive time together intensifies emotions and accelerates the development of relationships, which can mean these relationships solidify in just a matter of days or weeks, depending on the circumstances.

POTENTIAL PITFALLS

Weak arcs: Because the settings of these stories are often limited, some writers have a difficult time developing strong character arcs and conflict arcs within the confines of their isolation. While most of these characters will initially buck against the circumstances which lead to Forced Proximity, once they realize that things are out of their control, this opens the door for true growth. Lean into the moments of vulnerability that Forced Proximity circumstances inherently bring out in your characters in order to highlight this growth and enhance the intimacy between love interests.

Normal proximity: Being in the same room as someone once a week isn't Forced Proximity. While a plot like this can be good adhesion and force interactions for your characters, it isn't enough to satisfy the readers of these stories. The amount of time and relatively small space in a Forced Proximity should be enough to wear down the willpower of the characters to resist their growing chemistry and break down walls between them.

Unrealistic or contrived circumstances: If the Forced Proximity situation feels contrived or unrealistic, readers may find it difficult to suspend disbelief. A natural and organic setup is crucial to maintaining reader engagement.

Rushed romance: Sometimes the focus of the narrative rests so heavily on the external circumstances that the culmination of the romance feels fabricated and falls flat. Forcing the romantic relationship to develop too quickly or without sufficient emotional groundwork can make the story feel rushed and unsatisfying. In addition, readers may be turned off if the romantic elements feel forced or unrealistic given the severity of the circumstances. The relationship should naturally evolve within the context of the story.

CHAPTER 15

FREQUENTLY PAIRED TROPES

Because Forced Proximity is such a strong adhesion trope, it is commonly paired with repelling tropes like Forbidden Romance, Short-Term Fling, or the Relational Tropes of Animosity or Sibling's Best Friend. Pairing Forced Proximity with tropes that rely on the history of a couple can be very powerful, forcing them to have long-delayed conversations to clear the air. Second Chance, Secret Baby, or Return to Hometown are good examples.

Any trope that pulls the characters physically together in a shared space can be a strong pairing with Forced Proximity, as long as it is done intentionally. A Work/Community Project can be Forced Proximity, but it is not inherently so. Same for most marriage tropes (Marriage of Convenience, Arranged Marriage, etc.).

The additional subtropes of this category have their own frequently paired tropes as well, and we've outlined them within each entry.

COMMON PLOT DEVICES

Ticking time bomb: Any factor that moves up the timeline for resolving the main conflict is par for the course in these stories. This might be a change in schedule that results in a need to finish the project sooner, an injury or illness that makes escaping isolation a matter of life and death, or the end of temporary shared living arrangements. These elements function to enhance and complicate the intensity of the situation.

Caretaker: One character requires caretaking from the love interest, instantly deepening their connection. This could be from illness, injury, or emotional distress.

Secrets revealed: One or both characters have secrets that are gradually revealed, adding intrigue and tension to the story. The unveiling of these secrets will inevitably impact the romantic relationship, for better or worse.

Each subtrope also has unique Common Plot Devices listed within the entry.

FORCED PROXIMITY TROPES

ROAD TRIP

SHARED LIVING ARRANGEMENTS

STRANDED TOGETHER

ROAD TRIP

The Road Trip variation of this trope can involve any situation where characters are compelled or unwittingly choose to travel together. As they embark on a journey together, the combination of shared experiences, challenges, and victories creates space for a romantic connection to form.

The Road Trip trope may be used on a micro or macro level, but when used as a Storyline Trope, it refers to the main premise of the romance involving two characters who embark on a journey together. Usually these characters travel by car, but they may be on some sort of rat race journey by plane, boat, foot, or any other mode of transportation—in historical romance, this may be done as a long-distance train ride or carriage ride. The main component of these stories is the extent to which the story revolves around this journey, meaning most of the action of the story takes place while the characters are traveling.

The shared journey serves as a backdrop for character growth and increasing intimacy, allowing the characters to bond, face challenges, and discover more about each other. The road trip provides ample opportunities for the characters to engage in meaningful conversations, share personal stories, and open up to each other in ways they may not have done otherwise. Whether it's late-night conversations under the stars, impromptu pit stops at roadside attractions, or heartfelt confessions during long stretches of highway, the journey fosters moments of vulnerability and connection between the characters while they explore hidden gems off the beaten path, trying new foods, activities, and experiences.

You might have guessed that settings are a major part of these stories, and in fact, we will discuss this trope further in our Romance Settings Tropes book. The setting, and the journey itself, serves to isolate these characters from their everyday lives in such a way that forces a shifting of typical roles and often carries many Fish out of Water elements.

WHY READERS LOVE IT

The Road Trip journey is a metaphor for the growth of the character. As the characters go on their adventure, they are not only traveling to new destinations but also confronting their fears, insecurities, and unresolved issues. The road trip serves as a transformative experience, pushing the characters out of their comfort zones and forcing them to confront their inner demons, ultimately leading to personal growth and self-discovery—and of course, romance.

The relationship between the characters evolves as the setting changes along the journey. The constant movement and change of scenery provide a dynamic backdrop for the development of their romance, with each destination offering new opportunities for connection, intimacy, and shared experiences. Whether it's exploring breathtaking landscapes, trying new activities together, or navigating unexpected challenges along the way, the characters' bond is strengthened through their shared adventures and the memories they create together.

Obviously, this trope falls under the main Forced Proximity entry, and that is another huge appeal of the trope. Characters are confined to small spaces (or constant companionship) for extended periods of time in a way that sometimes feels more natural or relatable than Stranded and Stuck in a Snowstorm stories. They have near-constant interaction and opportunities for intimacy, which typically accelerates the pace of the romance. What's *not* fun about being stuck in a space that puts you no more than an arm's length away from the person you're attracted to?

Confined space makes avoidance pretty much impossible. The characters must communicate, and conflict resolution is a natural consequence of having to look each other in the stupid face every moment of every day, no matter how mad or hurt they may be. In fact, one of the funnest things about these stories is the illusion of privacy that traveling in an enclosed space gives these characters. This often opens the door for characters to talk and share parts of themselves that the other character didn't expect, and it creates an opportunity for unconscious desires to make themselves known.

These stories often feel very escapist, with the characters getting away from some negative aspect of their normal life, making space for character growth and changing perspectives. Readers love to adventure in unknown or unfamiliar places through the narrative. And readers can easily put themselves in the car (or train or boat) with the characters, with most of us having experienced such a journey, even if not on the same scale.

READER EXPECTATIONS

Anyone who's been on a road trip knows it is not ever smooth sailing from start to finish. Just as in real life, relational and external conflicts are bound to arise along the journey, presenting the characters with challenges, obstacles, and tension to overcome. Whether it's addressing disagreements, dealing with car trouble, or the tense moments of navigational challenges, these situations test the strength of their bond and their ability to overcome adversity together.

As the characters spend extended periods of time in close proximity, the flames of attraction burn hotter. Whether it's a lingering glance across the car, a playful exchange of banter, or a shared moment of vulnerability, the Road Trip setting amplifies the tension and intimacy between the characters. Lean into the tension for the ultimate reader experience.

Road Trip romances are generally expected to be filled with moments of humor, laughter, and fun. Mishaps, misunderstandings, and awkward moments provide ample opportunities for comedic relief, adding levity to the narrative and endearing the characters to readers. Whether it's getting lost on a detour, encountering quirky roadside attractions, or navigating the complexities of a dysfunctional GPS, the misadventures encountered along the journey inject humor and whimsy into the story, making the road trip experience feel authentic and relatable. Through lighthearted banter, playful teasing, and witty dialogue, the characters share moments of camaraderie and joy that bring levity to their journey and deepen their connection with each other.

Readers who pick up these books are often eager to experience something new about the destination or the places along the route. Readers expect to be along for the journey, from sampling regional cuisine to experiencing local traditions and customs. The destinations provide rich opportunities for immersion, whether it's the vibrant street markets of a bustling city, the quaint charm of a small-town diner, or the breathtaking beauty of a natural landmark. By incorporating vivid descriptions, sensory details, and evocative imagery, authors can transport readers to far-off locales, allowing them to vicariously experience the sights, sounds, and flavors of the road trip adventure.

POTENTIAL PITFALLS

Low stakes: Your characters should have compelling reasons to stay on the journey together rather than walking away, ensuring that the stakes remain high and the tension palpable throughout the story.

Ignored conflict: With the amount of time characters spend together on a road trip, it's unrealistic for them to totally avoid confronting conflicts and misunderstandings entirely. Characters should address and resolve issues as they arise (or without too much delay).

Lack of chemistry: Given the prolonged proximity between characters, there had better be sparks flying between them. Without chemistry, the romance may feel flat and unconvincing, failing to engage readers emotionally.

Slow pacing: To avoid stagnation, it's crucial to vary the pace of the story and incorporate interactions with side characters and subplots. Getting characters out of the car and engaging in different activities will keep the narrative dynamic and engaging.

Flat dialogue: Given the amount of time these characters spend buckled into their seats, there tends to be at least a handful of scenes that are really dialogue heavy. If these scenes come up time and time again with flat or uninteresting dialogue, it tends to highlight the weakness of dialogue (and the romantic connection) in other places in the narrative.

FREQUENTLY PAIRED TROPES

The Road Trip (like other Forced Proximity tropes) is a strong adhesion trope, so it is often paired with repelling tropes like Animosity, Opposites Attract, Second Chance, or other Off-Limits Relational Tropes like Boss/Employee or Sibling's Best Friend. When this storyline puts two characters from disparate groups together, the recognition that they have no other reason to be together outside of their journey adds a sense of urgency and tension to the narrative.

The Eccentric Character Trope is one that often appears in Road Trip romances. The quirky character shines in the confined space and dynamic setting.

Sometimes this trope is paired with the Time Travel trope, where the journey through time becomes the mode of transportation. In this case, the time travel not only has a clear purpose and mission, but there is a concrete destination point and point of return for these characters. In this case, both characters would be traveling through time together rather than one character doing so and falling in love with an individual from the past.

While the usual iteration of this trope is a lighthearted, often comical, journey for the characters, that isn't the only option. A high-stakes version of the Road Trip trope might be a Survival (Stranded) trope that involves travel to achieve rescue or survival. Including the elements and reader expectations mentioned in that trope alongside the ones mentioned here will make for a satisfying reader experience and a unique story from the layered tropes.

COMMON PLOT DEVICES

Unexpected or unplanned detours: Characters may encounter unplanned stops or detours due to road closures, car trouble, or other unforeseen circumstances. These detours often lead to new adventures, challenges, and opportunities for the characters to bond. Characters may even find themselves stranded in a remote location along the road, compelling them to rely on each other to reach their destination or even to survive.

Overnight stays/just one bed: Financial constraints, weather challenges, or last-minute changes may result in characters having to share accommodations such as a single hotel room or a cozy cabin. This is often where a long-hidden confession occurs, or a moment of confiding in each other that leads to increased emotional intimacy.

Romantic scenes in a picturesque setting: Whether it is castle ruins, a beach cliff, or another breathtaking landscape view, a gorgeous setting is used to enhance the romantic atmosphere.

Competing objectives: Characters are sometimes given conflicting goals or motivations for embarking on the journey, creating tension and leading to sabotage and other obstacles along the way.

Eccentric characters: Along the journey, characters often encounter quirky or eccentric individuals who leave a lasting impression, and often by pushing the characters out of their comfort zones, work to push them together.

Deadline/ticking time bomb: Characters must be to the destination or returned by a certain date and/or time. This plot device adds urgency to the narrative and forces characters to prioritize the objective over their desire to linger along the way.

KEY MOMENTS

Inciting incident: In a Road Trip romance, the premise and goal of the road trip is established. The characters typically decide to embark on the trip at this point, and a portion of the first act will center around the preparations for the road trip. In a shorter format like a novella or in a faster-paced story, this may happen quickly enough that the inciting incident includes the actual departure for the trip.

Turning point: Early in the journey, your characters will encounter their first significant obstacle. This may be a disagreement, unexpected obstacle or delay (often paired with the first detour), or a misunderstanding. This usually hits as a no way beat where characters have begun to get comfortable with each other and are suddenly pulled out of that rapport by the reintroduction of very overt conflict.

Dark moment: The dark moment often occurs when characters have reached the end of their journey or is tied to the purpose of the road trip. In either case, the characters are forced to confront their true feelings and hesitancy to make a place for one another in a shared future.

POTENTIAL THEMES

Adventure/exploration
Living in the moment
Working together
Finding joy in the mundane
Acceptance

SHARED LIVING ARRANGEMENTS

In these stories, the key to the Forced Proximity is that the characters are living together in some way. This also applies to characters who "live together" at work, but it should be in very close quarters, like a shared office.

Characters may end up sharing a living space due to circumstances such as needing a roommate because of financial constraints, vacation hotel room mishaps, visiting a friend, unexpected homelessness, or displacement. They may also be brought together due to family events (think a week-long family camping trip that the brother's friend tags along for), special occasions (family Christmas, anyone?), social gatherings, or caretaker situations.

Sharing living space creates unique opportunities for blurred lines between characters that other scenarios do not. In these cases, the characters are free to leave and interact with the world outside, but they have to come back to the shared space frequently, forcing interaction at the most inopportune times and leading to the progression of emotional and physical intimacy.

WHY READERS LOVE IT

In addition to readers' general love of Forced Proximity for reasons mentioned in the main entry, readers love these stories because of the dynamics of sharing living space. It leads to delicious tension between the characters. In clean and Christian stories especially (but even in other heat levels), there is something inherently taboo about living in a space together. It feels intimate, likely due to the opportunity for vulnerable moments. Characters are witness to the other in their most authentic state—perhaps sick, upset, partially dressed, without makeup, or other unguarded moments. These unexpected moments of the "behind the scenes" of another person are incredibly powerful intimacy builders, and readers are totally here for it.

Living together often leads to moments of domesticity and everyday intimacy that resonate with readers and draw the characters together. From cooking meals together to sharing household chores, these mundane yet meaningful interactions humanize the characters and make their relationship feel authentic and relatable. Readers enjoy witnessing the characters navigate the complexities of living together, from negotiating personal space to learning each other's habits and quirks as they navigate the ups and downs of daily life, even in a temporary situation. Characters get a glimpse into what life would be like with this person, complete with moments of comfortable silence and just cohabitating a space.

READER EXPECTATIONS

While there is more physical space for these characters to move around (and apart), they are still forced into interaction with each other by the nature of their living arrangements. This leads to serious discomfort for your characters, bordering on claustrophobic sensations of not being able to get far enough away from the love interest in their most vulnerable moments. The key is that characters can't escape each other (other than temporarily).

Don't forget this is a Forced Proximity story, so it can't be all roses and sunshine. These characters have to face this person on a daily basis, and they'll generally fight against the other invading their personal space. Amidst this backdrop of tension, the small moments of domesticity, thoughtful gestures, chemistry, and fun together gradually pull the characters through the romance arc. Whether the characters start off as strangers, acquaintances, or old friends, they are bound to find themselves embroiled in misunderstandings, disagreements, and heated arguments as they navigate the challenges of living together.

FREQUENTLY PAIRED TROPES

In addition to the tropes mentioned in the main Forced Proximity entry, Shared Living Arrangements is often paired with Relational or Storyline Tropes that can be twisted to require cohabitation, such as Nanny, Sibling's Best Friend, Fake Relationship, Marriage of Convenience, Vacation Fling, or Instant Family.

POTENTIAL PITFALLS

Instant lust: Just because there is a bed nearby doesn't mean your characters automatically fall into it together. Make sure any physical intimacy is warranted based on the situation and character arc.

Domestic bliss is boring: As mentioned in the Reader Expectations section, don't make your characters too comfortable together early on in the story. Going about daily life in a shared space can quickly feel repetitive or predictable. Be sure to shake things up for your characters by introducing conflict through side characters, subplots, or personality clashes. If your characters start the book in a shared comfortable shared living arrangement, introduce the conflict early on (at the inciting incident) that will flip this dynamic upside down.

Setting fatigue: Too many scenes together in one space can feel flat. Challenge yourself to switch up the setting by getting the characters out of the house together or just varying the details for the same space by orchestrating scenes at different times of day or in different rooms.

COMMON PLOT DEVICES

Temporary visitor: These stories often begin with a temporary living arrangement. A roommate who brings in a sibling from out of town, a vacation arrangement, a short-term crash pad, or a building renovation.

Surprise meet cute: Nothing gets two people off on the wrong foot like being surprised by someone suddenly invading your space. It is very common for these stories to start with an unexpected meeting, with (one or both of) the characters only discovering after the fact that they will be sharing the living space.

Accidental eyeful: This is a microtrope that shines within this storyline. We're talking about an accidental view of the other person with no shirt, a towel only, or all the way up to full-on nudity (depending on your steam level). It's an image your character can't get out of their head, and no matter how much they want to push the other person off the balcony, they can't deny the physical attraction.

KEY MOMENTS

Inciting incident: Whatever event or circumstance brings these characters together into the shared living arrangement will serve as the inciting incident. Sometimes this is immediately followed by the characters being introduced in the meet cute and getting settled in their new living arrangements.

Turning point: Near the midpoint of the story, one or both of your characters will reveal or hint at the emergence of their feelings. This declaration of love will come after a series of meaningful interactions, emotional moments, or shared experiences that deepen the love interests' connection and strengthen their feelings for each other. It sets the stage for the romance to move forward and for both protagonists to confront their true feelings.

POTENTIAL THEMES

Vulnerability
Being fully known
Embracing the unexpected
Man was not made to be alone
Acceptance

STRANDED TOGETHER

In the Stranded Together variation of this trope, characters find themselves stranded in a usually remote location due to weather or catastrophe—this may be a shipwreck, plane crash, natural disaster, storm, or even an attack from some external force, such as a kidnapping or act of war. In these stories, the characters must work together to survive, creating a tension to nearly every scene and uniting even the most adversarial characters under a common goal. In Survival stories specifically, characters must navigate life-threatening situations or deal with the immediate aftermath.

The hallmark to Stranded stories is the inability of the characters to *safely* leave their location, and this highlights the varying levels of discomfort your characters will feel. Your couple won't exactly feel stranded if they're temporarily forced to remain in a luxurious mansion in the south of France with every amenity under the sun. Ask yourself what necessities your characters will be cut off from if this temporary situation becomes an extended circumstance—food supplies, heat, water, medical care? And what danger do your characters face if they attempt to leave this place early? Even if the story is lighthearted and is mostly a cozy few days curled up by the fire as the roads are cleared, people are not used to being cut off from the outside, and that reality should make your characters uncomfortable.

It is the discomfort (or outright miserable and dangerous circumstance) that brings the characters together to overcome tangible physical threats in these stories. These story settings add a layer of tension, urgency, and vulnerability to the romance narrative and provide a unique backdrop for characters to discover not only their own strength but also the depth of their connection with each other.

They say you don't really know someone until you've seen them at their worst, and these characters have a front row seat to their love interest facing their worst fears, nearing their physical limits, and probably hungry (which for many of us is the definition of being at our worst!).

WHY READERS LOVE IT

Readers love the anticipation of a romantic connection developing against the backdrop of such challenging circumstances. Life-or-death situations specifically add a layer of urgency to the connection and often allow the characters to let go of insecurities and other obstacles to working together, as they feel they are left with no other choice.

Most of these stories draw readers in with an exciting combination of Forced Proximity and adventure or high stakes. While the story may or may not be suspenseful, there are likely to be non-romantic scenes that get your readers' hearts racing. These high-stakes stories really shine in the Forced Proximity vein, as these characters have everything to lose if they don't learn to cooperate. With the intensity of the conflict, intensity of chemistry naturally follows, so don't fail to deliver on the heart-pounding romantic moments either. After all, this is still a romance novel—not a thriller.

When characters face the potential end of their lives, they often develop courage to bring hidden feelings or secrets into the light. Something about the realization that you might never get a chance to resolve all the loose threads of your life creates an urgency and willingness to throw caution to the wind and make sure you don't leave anything unsaid.

We can't ignore the appeal of a strong, capable hero who steps up in situations like this. Whether he is gathering firewood, fishing for their dinner, wrenching debris off of the heroine's legs, or using an ancient navigation method to help guide them to civilization—there is so much opportunity to emphasize a masculine hero. While readers don't want a helpless or whiny heroine, we do love a man who handles the unexpected with resilience. Readers appreciate protagonists who face challenges head-on, learn from their experiences, and find strength to move forward—especially when they choose to do so together.

READER EXPECTATIONS

Stranded and Survival stories should be well-researched, believable, and fitting to the setting and premise of the narrative. Establish the stakes of survival early on in the first act, gradually building the sense of urgency and tension as you lead up to the climax. The high stakes of these early scenes will not only grab the readers' attention, but it will keep them invested in the characters' journey and outcomes.

If the stakes require it, showcase how characters navigate challenges such as finding food, water, shelter, and other resources. This adds an element of authenticity to the circumstances and helps the reader to connect to the situation. It also provides an opportunity to highlight the characters' resourcefulness, smarts, and resilience in the face of adversity.

The setting and proximity should foster emotional intimacy between characters through moments of vulnerability and shared experiences. In situations where characters are forced into isolation, whether stranded on a deserted island, trapped in a snowstorm, or stuck in an abandoned building, characters must confront isolation and survive together. This setting intensifies emotions and accelerates the development of relationships.

POTENTIAL PITFALLS

It's too heavy: While Survival stories are intense, an overwhelming focus on despair and hopelessness can be emotionally draining for readers. Balancing challenges with moments of resilience and hope is important.

Sensationalized survival story: Overemphasis on the disaster itself, without due consideration for the characters' emotional journey and relationship development, may result in a story that feels more like a disaster film than a romance.

Outrageously unbelievable: Some survival stories stretch the bounds of credibility, either through improbable scenarios or unrealistic character actions. While your characters are sure to be stretched by the circumstances, your scrawny programmer probably can't suddenly lift a tree off of your heroine. Avoid unexplained skills, medically inconsistent injuries, or other over-the-top actions or circumstances.

FREQUENTLY PAIRED TROPES

In addition to the tropes mentioned in the main Forced Proximity entry, the Stranded storyline is often paired with tropes that play on the setting or Character Tropes that lend themselves to wilderness or danger. This includes Cowboy, Lumberjack, and Men in Uniform as well as Mountain settings or Christmas stories with a snowed-in theme. The Tough Guy tropes shine in the high-stakes circumstances as well.

COMMON PLOT DEVICES

Caretaker: One character requires caretaking from their love interest, creating the opportunity to deepen their connection. In Stranded stories, this is typically a result of injury or illness related to their circumstances, and the heightened intimacy is felt immediately.

You can't go out there: One character is more impulsive, or at least set on escaping their situation, and insists on braving the external circumstance that has left them stranded in order to seek help or get home. The other character is practical and attempts to talk them out of it due to the danger or uncertainty that awaits them *out there*.

We're doomed: This plot device (often used during the dark moment) features an escape attempt or rescue that is unsuccessful. The long-term implications of the situation leave the characters in a hopeless or desperate state, leading them to reassess their priorities and feelings.

KEY MOMENTS

Inciting incident: Typically this scene is shaped by whatever events leads the characters to be stranded together (eg. the crash, the shipwreck, the drive through the blizzard and desperate arrival at an abandoned mountain cabin). Lean into the adrenaline of the situation with vivid descriptions and the emotional reactions of your characters.

Turning point: Once the characters have spent some amount of time together and been given the opportunity to learn about each other (the good and the bad), they will be faced with some kind of physically threatening situation that throttles them into the zone of truly caring for one another (or at the very least valuing each other's lives).

Resolution: Survival or success. Whether it's rescue, escape, or survival—the external conflict is wrapped up. This scene should provide that taste of what freedom and happily ever after look like. It typically occurs at the resolution, but sometimes it comes at the end of act two. When the rescue comes before the romance arc is resolved, the characters will continue to wrestle with what the relationship looks like after the intensity of their shared experience.

POTENTIAL THEMES

Resilience
Bravery
What doesn't kill you makes you stronger
Sacrifice
Determination

CHAPTER 16

I LIKE THE WAY YOU WORK IT

TEAMWORK TROPES

These tropes center around the characters working toward a specific goal, and themes of teamwork, mutual respect and support, and transformation are heavily featured. These stories are pretty project-based, which does give them flexibility in the pacing and length of the story, but they tend to focus on long-term projects in order to give the romance some space to grow.

RENOVATION

SAVE THE TOWN/FARM/BUSINESS

SHARED GOAL

RENOVATION

The Renovation trope is a very popular trope in the romance genre, as it provides plenty of opportunities for cooperation between characters, mishaps, and transformation. In these stories, characters work together on a renovation or restoration of a property such as a house, family property, or business.

The story typically centers around the characters working together to transform a run-down or neglected property into something meaningful. While these characters may (or may not) have the goal of renovation in common, their reasons for being involved in the project, their goals for the renovated property, and their methods for achieving success can vary widely and may even oppose each other.

Ultimately, this is an adhesion trope, pulling our characters together over and over again as they work together, make decisions, and tackle obstacles in pursuit of the completed vision.

WHY READERS LOVE IT

Is there anything women love more than romance novels? If there is, it's probably HGTV. Now don't get us wrong, we're not pigeonholing the modern woman into being obsessed with romcoms and Joanna Gaines, but the stats don't lie—both of these forms of entertainment are sky-high in popularity among Western women. So why not bring these things together? That's exactly what the Renovation trope does.

Even if readers are the furthest thing from handy or DIY-capable on their own, we love characters who are—hero or heroine. Men with power tools and rolled-up work shirts? Yes, please. Plus these stories are super relatable—we've all daydreamed about which walls we would knock down or strolled through the hardware store and trailed our fingers along the quartz countertops.

One of the things that makes this trope a ton of fun is the way that writers can use design choices and style as an extension of the character's personality. This not only gives the reader a unique way to connect with them, but it almost makes disagreements between characters with different personalities and different visions for the project completely inevitable. And when these characters are also insanely attracted to each other? All the better.

In the same way that design mirrors personality, the Renovation also echoes the growth arc and emotional journey of your characters. Two characters learning to work together and come to a place of agreement on their vision for the renovation is symbolic of their two hearts coming together in a shared vision of the future.

Renovations are a high-emotion undertaking. Anyone who has tried to work on a DIY project with their significant other can tell you that the tension leads to frequent conflict, as well as moments of intense vulnerability and openness as the intimacy increases during their time together.

READER EXPECTATIONS

This is an example of a trope that naturally follows the typical story arc of a romance novel—especially if we're comparing it to something like a home renovation show (which we unashamedly are). As we jump into the story, we get to connect with the characters and their current circumstances, but we also really need to understand their dreams and goals in order to understand the significance of the renovation project.

Within the first act, our lovers are brought together and the renovation gets underway if it hasn't already started. It's worth noting that in order to realistically span the length of a novel, this project should be a true renovation. While a bathroom remodel could theoretically do the trick, it will be hard for readers to believe that it would be dragged out long enough for the two characters to fall in love.

Anyone who has attempted a home improvement project probably understands that nearly every project will involve some unexpected complication, and our fictional renovations are no different. In fact, they're all the more fun if you can really play up those complications to ramp up the romantic tension. As your characters work together to overcome these obstacles, readers want to see them connecting in meaningful ways and putting aside poor dispositions and first impressions.

We get a glimpse of success and the potential for transformation near the midpoint, where naturally our lovers hit their own romantic high. But before our characters can get too high on their horse, they must overcome one last major hiccup. As the characters near the climax, there is typically a juxtaposition of mounting success in the renovation project while the romance becomes increasingly strained. Since many readers are specifically interested in the transformation aspect, this is a great time to highlight the character and style of the emerging project.

POTENTIAL PITFALLS

Neglecting character arcs: This is an inherently external conflict-driven trope, so it is important that you do not prioritize the Renovation plot over the character arc. We can capitalize on the HGTV phenomenon without short-changing the expectations of our romance readers. You may find that pairing these stories with a strong Character Trope will be helpful in achieving an impactful character arc.

Contrived conflict: Some stories may rely too heavily on introducing any and all conflict as the primary source of obstacles without developing other aspects of the story. This can make the plot feel contrived and formulaic, but in a Renovation romance, it may also make your reader wonder whether this building will be safe to inhabit after the characters are done with it. If every single attempt at the renovation goes awry, we will seriously consider whether you've set the right people to the task of safely renovating a property.

Bob the Builder hero: While it may be incredibly impressive for your hero (or heroine—let's call her Barbara the Builder) to be an expert at electric, plumbing, drywalling, demolition, and construction, it's also not totally realistic that they would handle every one of these aspects on their own. Be sure to bring in other parties, and don't be afraid to use it to enhance tension, conflict, and stakes.

FREQUENTLY PAIRED TROPES

This trope is often paired with a Small Town setting, but it could work just as easily with an Urban or Western setting. The property being renovated is often part of an Unexpected Inheritance, and the character must renovate the property to bring it to its former glory and (usually) be accepted as part of the community as a symbolic claim of their inherited position.

When the renovation requires an extraordinary amount of time together, the trope can be paired with Forced Proximity for lots of fireworks. Animosity tropes, Opposites Attract, and Second Chance tropes are also common pairings.

COMMON PLOT DEVICES

Unexpected delays: Delays may occur due to unanticipated complications with the construction/renovation project, budget constraints, or inspection or permit problems. These delays and complications are great for increasing tension and giving the story a "ticking time bomb" energy.

Competing interests: It adds interest and conflict if the characters have competing goals or motivations. Perhaps one character wants to tear down the ramshackle library, while the other is determined to save and renovate it. Or one wants to sell the old farmhouse after the renovation and the other wants to operate it as a bed-and-breakfast.

Community impact: The renovation project is often seen as a benefit to the immediate community, and it may even already be an important place in the community. This infuses some sentimentality to the place and increases the stakes of the project.

Completion party: A common way to wrap up these stories (and provide an opportunity for grand gestures or other subplot resolution) is for the character to host a housewarming or open house party celebrating the completion of the project and showing it off to the community.

KEY MOMENTS

Inciting incident: This moment usually coincides with the meet cute in a Renovation romance. The characters will probably meet for the first time with the renovation as the backdrop, and it is often a humorous, awkward, or memorable encounter.

Call to action: This is when the characters decide to (perhaps reluctantly) work together, or swear to oppose the other if they have conflicting goals.

Dark moment: The dark moment in these stories usually coincides with the seeming impossibility of completing the renovations. Budget woes, some sort of disaster wiping out progress, permitting issues, or other obstacles stand in the way of the character and they doubt they can complete the goal, but it must coincide with an overwhelming weight or tension that creates a rift in the romantic relationship.

Resolution: The characters come together and complete the goal, solidify the happy ending, and enjoy the fruit of their labor. This scene almost always needs to happen in the freshly renovated space.

POTENTIAL THEMES

Transformation
Embracing imperfections
Second chances
Resilience
Community

SAVE THE TOWN/FARM/BUSINESS

Save the Town occurs when one character (or both) are actively and strategically working to save an entity such as a town, community building, business, or a property such as a farm or ranch. Characters are propelled into action to rescue a beloved entity from some kind of external threat that will lead to its closure, destruction, or downfall.

Whether it's fighting to preserve a small town's heritage, revitalize a struggling business, or protect a cherished property from looming threats, this trope explores the lengths to which individuals will go to safeguard the places and people they hold dear. When both characters find themselves working together, it creates a sense of camaraderie and shared purpose—but this isn't always the case, as we'll see in the Common Plot Devices section.

From encroaching developers to natural disasters and bureaucratic red tape, the obstacles the characters face are as diverse as they are formidable. Yet it is in the face of adversity that the true character of the protagonists shines through as they rally together to devise creative solutions, forge unlikely alliances, and confront their own fears and limitations in pursuit of their goal, all while finding love.

This trope is an adhesion device, throwing your characters together with shared purpose, or at the very least, a shared proximity. Themes of loyalty, sacrifice, and perseverance are interwoven with elements of romance and personal growth. As characters navigate the trials and tribulations of their mission to save their town, they not only strengthen their bonds with each other but also reaffirm the power of community and the resilience of the human spirit in the face of adversity.

WHY READERS LOVE IT

Characters in these stories are passionate about their cause and fight for what they believe in. They put their money where their mouth is—even if they have no money! Whether it is organizing protests, getting their hands dirty to do the work needed, or finding another solution to appease the entity trying to destroy the town, these characters are strong-willed, clever, and unashamed of their convictions. Even if we don't agree or would never tie ourselves to a tree to protest a logging operation, we can admire a character who does.

Readers love to see the collective effort of characters and side characters coming together toward a common goal. There is a universal appeal in witnessing individuals set aside their differences and unite in solidarity, demonstrating the transformative power of community and collective action.

The underdog element adds an additional layer of intrigue as the protagonists defy expectations, saving the community, business, or property that was deemed irrelevant and worth destroying. Through their collaborative efforts, characters not only save their town or business but also inspire readers with the belief that positive change is possible when people come together with a shared purpose.

The close-knit relationships and genuine camaraderie depicted in these tales evoke a sense of warmth and nostalgia. Whether the story takes place in a small town or not, the allure of tight-knit communities cannot be overstated. Through vivid descriptions, colorful side characters, and unique history, these stories shine when the bonds of friendship and community are highlighted. Consider The Shop Around the Corner from *You've Got Mail.* While the shop was in New York City, the community of customers and employees gave it a very Small Town feel. Even though Meg Ryan wasn't able to save her bookstore, everybody was rooting for her.

READER EXPECTATIONS

Your character is not an island, despite our extensive praise of their strong-willed and passionate nature in the previous section. These stories require a strong sense of community and some measure of support. Even if everyone in town feels the fight is not worthwhile, there must be someone(s) in the story who understands the character's motivation for at least making an impossible attempt to save the thing.

The inciting incident of these stories typically comes in the form of an external threat or force that the characters recognize as destructive to the entity that they care deeply about. This may be a corporate takeover, natural disaster, economic downturn, or some other negative force, but whatever it is, stopping it from coming is outside of the characters' control. What they must do instead is prevent it from toppling everything.

To be clear, in the case of something like a corporate takeover or a buyout, your character's *realistic* goal will always be to maintain control, even if they have fooled themselves into believing that they can stave off the vultures. The buyout will eventually be presented, and it will still feel like a very real solution to hardship, but the entire buildup to this point in the story will be to prove that the characters can make it on their own rather than taking the easy way out.

SAVE THE TOWN

Your character must be personally invested. Typically there is a sense of the character's identity rooted in whatever they are trying to save. If it is the old town clock tower, why do they care so much? And being a history buff is probably not a strong enough reason. The reader should get the sense that the character believes if they are unsuccessful in their goal, it will be like losing a significant part of themselves. This personal investment in the outcome will make the stakes of the story dramatically higher and the passionate actions of the hero or heroine in pursuit of the goal that much more believable.

POTENTIAL PITFALLS

Unlikable characters: These characters are often hardheaded (*ahem* strong-willed); they really must be in order for us to believe that they would so tenaciously attempt a goal as lofty as saving a town or business. But they should not be impenetrable, or readers won't be able to connect with them, let alone the love interest. Understanding their motivations is key here. The external threat should be powerful and realistic.

Low stakes: The reason for investment for these characters must be very real and clear to the reader. We have to believe that they would put their life on hold and throw all of their efforts at this goal, so make sure it matters to them and is guaranteed to be destroyed if they don't act.

Underdeveloped setting and side characters: Because the tight-knit community or family-like sentiment is at the heart of these stories, readers really need to get the full sense of this community and the individuals in it in order to buy into the investment with the same fervor the characters do.

Unrealistic solution: If your character is spending the entire length of the novel coming up with or executing on the solution to their problem, then it better be worth the journey for the readers. Avoid having the solution be too easy or convenient, or the resolution to the story will fall flat.

FREQUENTLY PAIRED TROPES

The no-brainer pairing for this trope is the setting of a Small Town. This is the plot of so many Hallmark movies, we couldn't even begin to list them all. But this trope also pairs well with other settings like Western, Urban, or even Regency.

Adding a dash of intrigue to these stories with Hidden Identity or Hidden Motives (where one character unknowingly falls for the opposition) can be an extremely powerful pairing. This trope is also a strong adhesion trope to layer in with any Relational Trope, such as Enemies to Lovers or Friends to More.

COMMON PLOT DEVICES

Competing goals: One character love is actively working against the goal of saving the community or business. When that character is the love interest, it sets up an Enemies to Lovers dynamic, whereby the characters must learn to compromise.

Town fundraisers: The town or business at risk will often use fundraising to raise awareness about their plight and simultaneously collect resources to save themselves. This may be a gala, a festival/carnival, or any other community gathering that the people can rally behind.

Symbolic landmarks or items: There is often some significant item or landmark/location that symbolizes or otherwise represents the significance of the threatened entity for the characters or the community at large. This symbol often comes back around during critical moments such as the midpoint or dark moment.

KEY MOMENTS

Inciting incident: The threat to the town, community building, or property is introduced, setting the stage for the protagonist(s) to take action and rally support. It's important to clearly establish the personal stakes for your characters if their plan is unsuccessful.

Call to action: Faced with the looming threat, the character(s) devise a plan to save their town, galvanizing the community and igniting hope for victory. By this point, your love interests should have at least one major interaction and will likely be spending much of their time on the page together. Either way, their dynamic should give the reader a hint as to what will have these characters butting heads over the course of the narrative—even if they appear to be working in unison.

Dark moment: As the deadline approaches and the danger escalates, your characters will confront the imminent destruction or loss of their beloved entity, testing their resolve and resilience to the breaking point. This in turn puts immense pressure on the romantic relationship.

Resolution: The character(s) successfully avert disaster and save their town, reaffirming the power of unity and collective action, solidifying their romance at the same time. Alternatively, if they fail to Save the Town, the resolution will require the character to move forward without the identity-carrying entity they were trying to save.

POTENTIAL THEMES

Strength of community
Self-discovery
Determination
Found family
Hope

SHARED GOAL/GROUP PROJECT

The Shared Goal trope involves two characters coming together to work on some sort of project. Sometimes it is for the benefit of their community, or it can also be used in the workplace setting where coworkers are assigned to work together on a task, team project, or even company-wide initiative.

This creates opportunities for them to bond, overcome obstacles together, and ultimately deepen their romantic connection as they collaborate and support each other toward a common goal. Their own motivation for wanting to achieve the goal will likely come into play in the conflict of the story, but the key in these stories is that the characters are working together—unlike in Save the Town, where the characters may have opposing goals.

While we refer to them as "Group Projects", the task at hand can really be anything pulling the characters together. Examples of community projects that fit this trope are fundraisers, festivals, events, parties (including weddings!), or performances. The common tie between the characters could be a school, town, church, friend group, or any other social connection.

As for work, the possibilities are also endless. Characters can be thrown together to win workplace competitions, tackle school assignments, plan conferences, execute product launches or software integrations, conduct audits, complete budgets or strategic plans, or any other workplace initiative.

In fact, any time you throw characters together with a shared goal, some of the tenets of this trope will apply. The key is that they are working together, either reluctantly or by choice.

WHY READERS LOVE IT

While this isn't a Forced Proximity trope, many of the things readers love about those tropes also ring true for the Work It tropes. Characters are more or less stuck with each other if they want to achieve their goal. While either of them could theoretically walk away at any moment and there's no *external* force keeping them together, their own goals and motivations propel them forward, even amidst difficult working conditions.

As characters work together, they find common goals and bond over shared experiences, creating opportunities for moments of passion, intimacy, and vulnerability.

These stories really shine when these elements work to highlight the strengths of your characters—and while we expect flawed and nuanced characters, we want to find all the reasons to love them too! Working toward their common goal, your characters are incentivized to recognize each other's positive traits as well and to find the areas where their strengths complement one another and their weaknesses are supported by the other character's skills.

These stories are very relatable, probably because of our shared trauma of group projects in school. The dynamics of working together to achieve a goal with another person (or group of people) can bring out the best and the worst in people. Personalities clash and work styles conflict. Add in some irresistible chemistry, mutual respect (eventually), and shared victories or defeats? It all comes together for a satisfying story with solid conflict, romantic arc, and character growth.

READER EXPECTATIONS

Characters may or may not know each other prior to starting the project, and they may choose each other as partners or be paired together; whatever the case, the key to this trope lies in the tension between the need for collaboration and the inevitable disagreements and tensions that will arise from any long-term cooperative effort.

Throughout the project, readers anticipate the emergence of various conflicts and obstacles that challenge the characters individually and as a team. These challenges can stem from external sources, such as project setbacks or unexpected hurdles, as well as internal sources, such as personal insecurities, unresolved feelings, or group dynamics.

As the characters navigate these challenges, readers look for signs of growth and development, expecting to see the characters overcome their differences and grow toward one another. Typically the amount of time characters are spending together will coincide with the romantic connection—the more intimate things get, the more time they find to spend together. This creates a beautiful cycle in which they can't help but to find excuses to be together, which only pours fuel onto the fire of their passions and ultimately causes them to spend even more time together.

The culmination of the project almost always ends in success, but this doesn't necessarily coincide with the success of the relationship. In fact, it's not uncommon for characters to part ways just as they are reaching their peak against the external conflict, perhaps struggling to separate their desire for the other from their desire to achieve their goal, as the two have become increasingly intertwined. Internal and relational conflicts threaten their relationship, even as they overcome the external conflict together.

POTENTIAL PITFALLS

Neglecting character arcs: This is an inherently external conflict-driven trope, so it is important that you do not prioritize the project plot over the character arc. You may find that pairing these stories with a strong Character Trope will be helpful in achieving an impactful character arc, as will giving your character a strong personal motivation for pursuing the shared goal.

Contrived conflict: Some stories may rely too heavily on introducing any and all conflict as the primary source of obstacles without developing other aspects of the story. This can make the plot feel contrived and formulaic. Conflict should arise naturally from the characters' goals, motivations, and personalities.

Project . . . what project? While the project serves as a backdrop for the romance, it should still be integral to the plot and receive adequate attention. Neglecting the project in favor of focusing solely on the romance can leave readers feeling disconnected from the story.

FREQUENTLY PAIRED TROPES

Probably the most common pairings for this trope are the Animosity tropes (Enemies to Love, Hate to Love, and Rivals), but it can also be an effective pairing with Friends to More or Boss/Employee. The adhesion of the Group Project is at odds with the repelling nature of these Relational Tropes, providing lots of internal and relational conflict to balance such an externally heavy conflict trope.

Community Projects are an obvious fit for Small Town and Christmas settings, with the trope lending itself to lots of volunteer opportunities, unique festivals, and charming traditions. However, don't underestimate the power of a Historical or Fantasy setting, especially when the Group Project is something like overthrowing an evil regime or recovering a magical artifact. Nothing like a little noble quest to bring two people together.

COMMON PLOT DEVICES

Late nights: Whether a workplace or other project, the time spent together will often fall outside of working hours, necessitating shared meals, courtesy escorts to a character's vehicle (for safety, of course), and the intimacy that comes from being anywhere together while it is dark outside.

Competition with other teams: Introducing elements of competition, whether within the workplace or the community, adds an extra layer of conflict and excitement to the story as the characters vie for success or recognition.

Quirky side characters: None of these projects happen in a vacuum. These stories often make use of eccentric side characters in the office or community to drive the plot forward, provide comic relief, cause drama, or act as a sounding board when the main character is struggling.

Workplace politics: Incorporating workplace politics or community dynamics adds realism and complexity to the story, presenting challenges such as office hierarchies, power struggles, or interpersonal conflicts that the characters must navigate.

Project milestones: Structuring the narrative around key project milestones, mini-quests, or deadlines provides a framework for the plot's progression and creates opportunities for tension as well as smaller victories as the characters work toward their goals . . . and fall in love, of course.

KEY MOMENTS

Inciting incident: Characters are typically given the goal and the parameters at this point. This scene sets the stage for their collaboration and establishes the initial context for their interactions. Sometimes it coincides with the meet cute, but the characters may not know who they are working with or be introduced to each other until later.

Midpoint: Since the external plot of these stories is so heavily focused on the project, the midpoint typically revolves around the romantic connection finally being established or made genuine (they kiss), regardless of what point in the project the characters are at.

Turning point: Whether the project is completed or facing a major setback, your characters will face a moment toward the end of the second act where tensions are escalated, emotions are high, and your characters are forced to confront their fears, insecurities, or doubts. This could force them to prioritize competing demands or make difficult decisions that impact their future together.

Grand gesture: The grand gesture in these stories almost always requires characters to compromise on their individual goals or desires for the sake of the relationship or the success of the project. The lead-up to this point typically involves a heavy amount of support or involvement from secondary characters in the community or workplace who offer guidance, encouragement, and perspective.

POTENTIAL THEMES

Collaboration
Better together
Community
Mutual support
Compromise

CHAPTER 17

IT'LL NEVER WORK

INCOMPATIBILITY TROPES

Each of the tropes in this section center around the external circumstances (or internal convictions) that make a long-term match unlikely. These characters must demonstrate that their bond is stronger than the multitude of obstacles that stand between them. The more challenging the journey to love, the greater the emotional payoff when your lovers finally overcome those obstacles, reinforcing the idea that love is worth fighting for.

FALLING FOR THE MATCHMAKER/

MATCHMAKER GONE WRONG

FORBIDDEN ROMANCE

LONG DISTANCE

SHORT-TERM FLING/VACATION ROMANCE

STAR-CROSSED LOVERS

FALLING FOR THE MATCHMAKER/ MATCHMAKER GONE WRONG

While the use of a third-party Matchmaker is more of a microtrope, there are plenty of situations in which the matchmaker *becomes* the love interest. These are the tropes we'll cover in this volume.

The Falling for the Matchmaker trope is typically depicted as the person receiving the matchmaking service developing feelings for the individual trying to find them a perfect match. In this case, the story revolves around the recipient of the matchmaking dodging any real attempts at connection with anyone other than the matchmaker and continuing the process for the sake of spending time with their true love interest.

The Matchmaker Gone Wrong is a version of the trope where the matchmaker falls first and usually intentionally sabotages other potential matches. Sometimes both characters harbor feelings for each other, even if they are still making an honest attempt at the matchmaking process. A third variation of this trope is the Cyrano retelling (only with a decidedly happier ending), which we will not cover in this edition.

The matchmaker may be a friend, colleague, family member, or a professional—but in the Matchmaker Gone Wrong tropes, you will want to steer clear of family members falling for each other . . . for obvious reasons. But the key to these stories is that the matchmaker's involvement in the other character's life often leads to misunderstandings, unexpected twists, and ultimately the realization of the romantic connection between the main characters.

WHY READERS LOVE IT

Very little is as fun for readers as one or both people desperately fighting their attraction for the other. In these stories, the nuance of two characters working toward a goal that readers know is fruitless brings a mix of humor, drama, and anticipation. As the relationship between the matchee and the matchmaker evolves (whether it starts as a polite professional arrangement, friendship, or downright animosity) readers love waiting for both characters to eventually openly (or at least internally) admit that the matchmaking process is nothing but a charade.

If the matchmaker is a professional, then readers love witnessing the dilemma of crossing professional boundaries or fear for the consequences of failure. On the other hand, if the matchmaker is a friend or coworker, then readers enjoy the evolution from denial of attraction or the gradual shifting of perspective as they suddenly view the person as a potential match for themselves instead of for someone else.

As their relationship shifts, then so does the motivation that guides the characters' choices and the opportunity for subtext, blurred lines, and a back-and-forth dance of honoring the original goal or embracing their new feelings. The matchmaker becoming personally drawn into the romantic equation leads to internal conflicts, dilemmas, and challenges as they navigate their own feelings while orchestrating the romantic connection. These tropes introduce humor, especially when the matchmaking efforts go awry (intentionally or otherwise) or when there are comedic elements in the situations created during awkward setups and ridiculous dates.

Readers especially look forward to the buildup of romantic tension between the main characters. However the matchmaking scenario came about, at the beginning of the story, the characters either didn't know or couldn't admit their feelings for one another, so the matchmaker's interventions should heighten the anticipation of the characters realizing their feelings for each other.

READER EXPECTATIONS

The matchmaker or the character seeking a love match should struggle with the duplicity of continuing to be matched by (or continuing to find matches for) their true love interest. The motivation for continuing the charade is an unwillingness to admit their feelings and a desire to continue spending time with the other person. Often they might offer additional time together—for the purpose of finding their match, of course. It might be dating lessons, a makeover or—shopping trip, or "last-minute cancelations" by the supposed date that just happens to leave them with two tickets to tonight's game. For this reason, the Falling for the Matchmaker and Matchmaker Gone Wrong tropes are a mix between repelling and adhesion.

The character arc of the matchmaker shifts from focusing on the happiness of others to discovering their own romantic desires. This is especially true if they are a professional matchmaker or have sworn off love for some reason or another. During the course of the relationship, the matchmaker overcomes their deep-seated wound and discovers that love isn't something they want to miss out on, acknowledging that their friend or client is the only one for them.

These stories have a central thread of unexpected romance between the matchmaker and love interest. Whether the matchmaker learns to view their friend in a new light or caves to unanticipated desire for their client, the key is that they didn't see it coming. Be sure to highlight those moments of unexpected connection and the characters' reactions to them.

The internal conflict and external complications that arise from the potential failure of their matchmaking mission need to be significant. Lean into the reasons that the matchee was willing to be matched in the first place or that the matchmaker was pushing them into it. Other tropes may help in this area, providing somewhere to lean into relational or external conflict.

POTENTIAL PITFALLS

Artificial conflict: In some cases, the Matchmaker trope can introduce artificial conflict or misunderstandings solely for the purpose of creating drama. If not well-executed, these contrived elements may feel forced or unrealistic, leading to a less satisfying reading experience.

Dumping on the intended match: When the intended match is swoon-worthy in their own right, or just an all-around really great person, it is difficult for readers to root against them. Be sure to use methods such as complete lack of chemistry, incompatibility, or simply not being as likable as the matchmaker to keep readers from becoming too invested in the match that's doomed to fail (unless it is an intentional Love Triangle).

Invasion of privacy or manipulation concerns: Some readers may be uncomfortable with the idea of characters meddling in others' lives, viewing it as an invasion of privacy or manipulation. If the matchmaker's actions seem intrusive or ethically questionable, it can be a turn-off for readers.

FREQUENTLY PAIRED TROPES

Because this trope often relies on some sort of professional matchmaking service, it goes hand in hand with *Money, Money* tropes, where someone is willing to pay an exorbitant fee to find love without the typical mess of dating.

The other common iteration of the trope is a Friends to More combination, often paired with an Unrequited Love or Love Triangle (or Imaginary Love Triangle) twist.

Another common pairing with this trope is Hidden Identity when the matchmaking is a virtual or online service, so when their worlds collide in real life, the matchee doesn't realize they are interacting with the matchmaker at all.

If there are major consequences, like a strict professional policy against falling for a client, then the Forbidden Love trope could also apply.

COMMON PLOT DEVICES

Misunderstandings and mistaken identities: Characters may misunderstand the matchmaker's intentions or mistake someone else for their intended romantic partner. These misunderstandings create comedic situations and contribute to the overall tension in the story.

Forced proximity: The matchmaking relationship brings characters together under a common goal—for at least one of them to find love. While this method doesn't necessarily mean that Matchmaker stories follow the Forced Proximity trope, it will share many of the same elements.

Date debrief: After a date is completed between the matchee and a potential match, the matchmaker and the matchee might meet up to discuss how the date went, often resulting in time spent together that is far more enjoyable than the date itself.

Letters: Specifically in historical romance, the matchmaker may use written communication, such as anonymous love letters or messages, to facilitate the romantic connection. This adds a layer of mystery and anticipation as the love interest tries to discover the identity of their secret admirer.

Disguises and subterfuge: Characters, including the matchmaker themselves, may use disguises or adopt different personas to observe and influence the romantic interactions. This device can lead to humorous and unexpected confrontations.

Bet or challenge: The matchmaker may set up a bet or challenge that the matchee must fulfill, or the matchmaker may have agreed to a bet that they could successfully match the other character. This plot device adds a goal-oriented element to the storyline and sets the stage for character growth, conflict, and tension. Note that this does not necessarily make the story a Bet/Wager storyline, but you may choose to lean heavily into those elements to layer tropes.

KEY MOMENTS

Inciting incident: Early on in the story, readers are introduced to the matchmaker and a plan for finding love is established. This sets the stakes for the plot and includes many of the important details of the matchmaking setup.

Turning point: Revelation of feelings. While there may not be an outright declaration of love, the depth of feelings is acknowledged and creates conflicting emotions in the matchmaker or the character looking for a love match. This moment is made all the more powerful based on how adamantly the characters deny or remain oblivious to their feelings up to this point.

Dark moment: The dark moment of these stories is often tied to the matchmaker's own romantic journey and their reluctance to find love themselves, or feelings of shame for having fallen for the person they are supposed to be finding love for. The events of this moment should force your characters to confront their feelings directly and test the strength of the tenuous bond they have formed.

POTENTIAL THEMES

Unexpected love
Love vs. logic
Embracing love
Love is worth the risk
Authenticity

FORBIDDEN ROMANCE

The Forbidden Romance is a classic trope featuring two characters falling in love, but their romantic connection is socially or culturally unacceptable, or downright forbidden by someone in power (government, employers, or parents). These obstacles can include different social classes, rival families, differences in race or ethnicity, or situations where societal norms or rules otherwise forbid the characters from being together. These stories are emotionally charged, as the characters are forced to choose between their love and societal or familial expectations.

The trope allows for exploration of themes such as societal norms, prejudice, and the power of love to overcome adversity. The characters must decide if love is worth breaking the rules, angering those they love, or facing ostracism.

WHY READERS LOVE IT

The obstacles and challenges that come with the Forbidden Romance storyline create a heightened emotional experience for the characters and, by extension, the readers. The stakes are higher, leading to a more intense and emotionally charged story. The characters will lose something if they walk down the path of the romance. Whether that is family connections, social status, employment opportunities, or something else, the high stakes are a huge part of why this trope is powerful.

The forbidden nature of the romance introduces an element of tension and suspense, and readers are eager to see how the characters will navigate and overcome the obstacles in their path. When every moment the characters spend together means a risk of consequence or disapproval, then every moment is that much more powerful. The characters are choosing with each interaction to continue down the path of their love, or they are fighting against the feelings that are overwhelming but they cannot succumb to. The taboo nature of the relationship is exciting, pulling the reader on an off-limits adventure that they might not be willing to take in real life.

Readers often find themselves rooting for the underdog or the rebel. When the powers that be ordain something as forbidden, it is in our human nature to want that exact thing. When faced with societal norms or expectations that go against the central romance, readers are primed to pull for the characters in the face of the opposition. The story tugs on their sense of empathy and desire to see the characters triumph against the odds.

The Forbidden Romance trope introduces an element of unpredictability, as readers may not be sure how the story will unfold. This uncertainty keeps them engaged and invested in the narrative, eager to discover the resolution of the romantic conflict. Readers can immerse themselves in a story where love conquers all, even in the face of societal constraints, family pressure, or one-dimensional corporate policies.

READER EXPECTATIONS

The central romantic relationship will face significant barriers in a Forbidden Romance. This could come in the form of disapproving family members, societal expectations, or other obstacles that create conflict and tension. In addition to external challenges, readers look for internal struggles within the characters. They want to see the protagonists wrestling with their own emotions, values, and beliefs as they navigate the forbidden nature of their romance.

The readers' love of the back-and-forth dance of *we shouldn't, but we want to* cannot be overstated. Make sure there is plenty of internal struggle with the competing desires of adhering to the rules or expectations while constantly being drawn toward someone they cannot have. Readers expect to see the characters weighing the risks of pursuing their love against the potential fallout, and these stories are expected to evoke strong emotions and carry a fair bit of angst. Readers anticipate a roller coaster of feelings as the characters navigate challenges, leading to moments of heartbreak, passion, and ultimately, joy.

There is often an element of secrecy or hidden relationships in forbidden romances. The characters may need to keep their love affair discreet to avoid societal or legal repercussions. Around others, the use of subtext in conversation can greatly increase the anticipation and the feeling for the reader of being "on the inside of the secret." The stakes of the story must be high enough that characters truly fear (and readers deeply understand) the consequence for breaking the rule and pursuing the relationship despite its forbidden nature. But the reader must root for the characters to break the rule and blur the line anyway.

Readers look for significant character development as the protagonists face and overcome the challenges of the forbidden romance. While the journey may be fraught with obstacles, readers generally expect a satisfying resolution to the forbidden romance—whether it involves overcoming societal norms or finding a compromise, readers want to see the characters' love triumph in the end. Characters may even be required to make significant sacrifices, such as giving up personal aspirations or severing ties with family, to be with their Forbidden Love.

POTENTIAL PITFALLS

Predictability: For some readers, the Forbidden Romance trope can feel overused or predictable. If the storyline follows a formulaic pattern without offering unique twists or fresh perspectives, or if the story wraps up with a convenient solution that doesn't adequately address the challenges set up earlier, it will leave readers dissatisfied.

Frustration with characters' choices: In certain cases, readers may find themselves frustrated with the characters' decisions or actions within the forbidden romance. If the characters repeatedly make choices that seem unrealistic or go against their established personalities, it will make it difficult for readers to connect with or understand the motivations of your characters.

Weak reasoning for forbidden romance: If the force opposing the romance is easily resolved with a conversation or is merely based on the characters' perceived consequence instead of an actual strong cultural, familial, or legal reason that the characters should not be together, then the story falls flat, and the conflict and tension do not deliver. Make sure whatever is keeping your characters apart is truly a large obstacle.

Lack of consequences: Tying the story up in a neat bow at the end isn't a bad thing in the romance genre. However if things fall into place too easily, it can make the entire journey end with a letdown. The characters should face consequences (even temporary ones) when their relationship is revealed, and they need to decide, eventually, that those consequences are worth it.

Excessive angst: A constant focus on external conflicts and obstacles without sufficient character development or emotional depth may lead to a lack of connection between readers and the protagonists. While conflict is a crucial element in any romance, an excessive focus on angst and drama without moments of joy or resolution can wear on readers and make the overall reading experience emotionally draining.

FREQUENTLY PAIRED TROPES

It's not uncommon for these characters to start as adversaries but eventually fall in love, especially if their initial conflict is rooted in societal or cultural differences.

As in the classic tale of Romeo and Juliet, this trope is often paired with Star-Crossed Lovers—lovers who are destined to be together but are thwarted by external circumstances beyond their control. Sometimes the story mirrors the original tale so closely that it's considered a Romeo and Juliet Retelling.

Adding a Love Triangle to the Forbidden Romance can intensify the emotional stakes. The protagonist may be torn between two love interests, complicating the narrative and creating additional obstacles. The non-Forbidden Romance character is the easier choice, but the heart doesn't always choose what is easy.

Forbidden Romance is often paired with Relational Tropes involving some sort of power dynamic that makes the relationship socially unacceptable or forbidden by law or a governing body. Think Boss/Employee, Doctor/Patient, Teacher/Student, or Age Gap romance.

Placing characters in situations of Forced Proximity can enhance the forbidden nature of their romance. This could occur in workplace settings, on a journey, or during other scenarios that make their connection challenging.

COMMON PLOT DEVICES

Secret meetings, marriages, or escape plans: Characters may need to meet in secret to maintain their forbidden romance, adding an element of suspense and clandestine excitement to the story. The characters may choose to elope to escape the constraints of their society or situation, leading to a dramatic and often risky escape.

Threats or blackmail: External forces may use blackmail or threats to manipulate the characters and create additional obstacles to their romance. As a consequence of their forbidden love, characters may even be forced into exile or be banished from their community, creating a sense of isolation and despair.

Forbidden love letters or messages: Written communication, such as love letters or messages, can be a way for characters to express their feelings while facing the challenges of a forbidden romance.

Interruptions or close calls: Near discoveries of the forbidden romance or unexpected interruptions during moments of intimacy heighten the anticipation of the truth coming out and the consequences that are sure to follow.

KEY MOMENTS

Inciting incident: This typically comes when characters experience the first sparks of attraction, setting the stage for the forbidden romance. Characters may or may not realize the forbidden nature of the romance, whether it's because they aren't aware of the obstacles that will later face them or they aren't aware of the identity of their romantic interest.

Turning point: The gradual revelation of the forbidden nature of the romance may come at the midpoint or as late as the dark moment. At this point, the focus of the story shifts from the characters avoiding discovery to confronting the consequences of their romance.

Dark moment: Whether the relationship has already become public before this moment, this point in the story should be intense and pose seemingly insurmountable obstacles that threaten to permanently separate the couple.

POTENTIAL THEMES

Loyalty
Trust
Social expectations
Choosing love over duty
Love is worth the risk

LONG DISTANCE

The Long Distance trope refers to a storyline where the central characters are involved in a romantic relationship and are physically (geographically) separated. Typically these characters are living in different states or countries, but it's possible that they may simply live in different cities a significant distance apart. The distance between these characters must be significant enough that it affects not only their daily interactions, but that it seriously limits the amount of available time they are able to share. The characters must overcome these obstacles in order to maintain their connection and build a successful relationship.

In contemporary stories, these relationships rely on technology such as cell phones, emails, or video calls. The relationship may also start online via dating services or other internet connection avenues. Historical stories often limited visits and letters passed—sometimes heavily featuring epistolary storytelling.

The challenge of growing or maintaining a romance without physical proximity is daunting, and these romances tend to have significant conflict as each character leads an almost entirely independent life that only marginally intersects with their love interest.

WHY READERS LOVE IT

This trope infuses the story with a sense of longing and uncertainty that pulls the reader in and makes them want to root for the success of the romance. These readers spend the entire story in anticipation of those moments of reunion and the intense emotion that accompanies them.

Compared with other Storyline Tropes, these stories are often incredibly relatable, even if your reader has no experience with long-distance relationships. Everyone has experienced the sensation of missing a loved one, and these romances tap into that experience. The relational issues these characters face are fairly typical, albeit amplified by distance and made more entertaining in fiction.

Readers love the other relationships characters depend on for encouragement and support, whether it's the quirky best friend, a work colleague, or a family member. Having secondary characters who are rooting for the couple to make it or who are willing to challenge the central characters when they need it adds depth and helps guide the character growth arc.

Readers often enjoy seeing characters find creative solutions to overcome the obstacles presented by distance. Whether it's surprise visits, thoughtful gestures, or unique ways of staying connected, these solutions show the reader the true commitment of the characters and give readers a glimpse of the happily ever after to come.

These stories highlight the emotional intimacy of characters at a physical distance as well as the physical longing for their closeness. When characters are in physical proximity, all that pent-up physical desire typically results in some intense physical contact.

READER EXPECTATIONS

The number one expectation for these stories is that the path to happily ever after will not be an easy one—but honestly, is it ever in a well-executed romance? *Hint:* The answer is a resounding *no*.

Distance can affect every aspect of a relationship, but it has a tendency to highlight the weaknesses of one or both partners, incompatibilities, and other strains on the relationship. In the worst of situations, it can be a convenient method of avoiding any of those topics—but note, even though characters are avoiding them, these issues only become more intense as time goes on.

In a contemporary romance, modern technology will prove to be a major advantage over communication and travel limitations. In historical fiction, these limitations will be significantly amplified in varying degrees, primarily based on the available technology.

Even in modern romances, there are ways to make these things more difficult than they theoretically should be. Characters may face issues like time zone differences, poor internet connections, limited access to resources, or schedule demands that make it difficult to find more than a few minutes to talk.

While the physical distance may create communication challenges, readers generally anticipate that the characters will find ways to communicate effectively. These characters don't typically have a lot of time on the page together, at least physically speaking, so when they are together, *make it count*! You'll also want to get *really* good at dialogue and subtext, as this is how the majority of their relationship will take place.

The character shouldn't exist solely online, in letters, or over the phone line, so seeing them in the real world with other characters adds dimension and insight to your main characters. When dealing with the characters separately, be sure to explore the emotional toll distance has created. Show the reader how characters grapple with loneliness, yearning, and fear of growing apart. These things are likely to affect their daily lives in small ways, but as they build up, characters may also see the effect in their emotional and mental health. Create shared goals or dreams that the characters are working toward, offering a sense of purpose and direction to their relationship and providing the framework to maintain their bond.

While the journey may be challenging, readers expect a happy and fulfilling ending that includes a resolution to the distance. Whether it involves one character relocating, a change in circumstances, or a commitment to bridging the gap, the story should end with the characters having made it through the obstacle of long distance and moving forward . . . in the same place.

POTENTIAL PITFALLS

Miscommunication: In addition to their shared history (if applicable), communication is about the only thing holding these characters together. While we can believe that characters may avoid communicating altogether in moments of weakness or doubt, or that there may be moments when communication breaks down due to the limitations on their time together, readers don't want to see these same issues crop up with every conflict.

No reason to stay apart: Be sure to give your characters a realistic reason for separation and a compelling reason for staying that way.

Avoid making your characters a retail store manager, a banker, or some other job they could work pretty much anywhere. Readers must be able to empathize with their lives being pulled in different directions.

FREQUENTLY PAIRED TROPES

Pairing with the Ticking Time Bomb microtrope can create a sense of urgency with countdowns or timelines that mark important milestones in the relationship and add tension as the characters work toward a specific goal.

Military romance lends itself well to pairing with this trope with the likelihood of separation due to duty stations or deployment. While less common, some stories involve characters separated by time with a Time Travel or Time Slip trope, creating a unique spin on the Long Distance story.

Long Distance is a strong repelling trope, working to keep your characters apart, and there aren't many Relational or Storyline Tropes that can compensate for that without negating the distance aspect. Therefore, Long Distance is often paired with other repelling tropes like Secret Relationship, Forbidden Romance, or Love Triangle to add even more opposition to the relationship.

COMMON PLOT DEVICES

Unexpected meetings or reunions: Introduce unexpected meetings, surprise visits, or reunions that catch the characters off guard. This can heighten the emotional impact and create memorable moments. Often this is coupled with a misunderstanding, when one character witnesses something and makes an assumption about the other character, leading to a third act breakup.

Parallel storylines: The physical distance between these characters may give both the readers and characters the impression that they are living separate lives. To amplify this, some authors may highlight each character's own experiences and challenges in their respective locations. This can showcase individual growth and struggles, adding complexity to the overall romance narrative.

Nonlinear timelines: When characters are separated by distance and experience significant limitations on their ability to communicate, authors may use a nonlinear timeline to bring in important moments of the characters' past as well, especially as it relates to the romance.

External threats to the relationship: External factors or threats that put additional pressure on the relationship might include interference from friends, family, romantic rivals, or external circumstances that make the long-distance commitment even more challenging.

KEY MOMENTS

Inciting incident: These stories may begin with the initiation of the long-distance relationship or a shift in an existing relationship to a long-distance arrangement. Occasionally they simply begin with the relationship already present as a long-distance relationship. In those cases, there should be something that shifts the status quo, making it impossible for the relationship to remain static through the story.

Turning point: A critical decision point is reached where the characters must choose between pursuing their individual goals or prioritizing their relationship, creating an increased pressure to close the distance. This may be spurred by external factors such as meddling friends, family pressure, or the introduction of a potential rival, creating obstacles that strain the relationship and cause characters to grapple with doubts and insecurities about the viability of their relationship.

Grand gesture: Reunification. In order for your readers to believe that these characters have a lasting future together, we must see the evidence that they will, in fact, be reunited at some point. This moment is full of emotion, but it also takes decisive action and deliberate maneuvering in order to pave the way for a future together. Whether one character gives up their job and moves to be with the love interest or both characters start fresh somewhere new, this moment should involve a bold declaration of commitment and force one or both characters to sacrifice something for the sake of a future together.

POTENTIAL THEMES

Communication
Sacrifice for love
Trust
Ambition and independence
Perseverance in overcoming challenges

SHORT-TERM FLING/VACATION ROMANCE

The Short-Term Fling or Vacation Romance trope is sometimes called the Summer Romance trope, but it doesn't necessarily need to occur during the summer or even on vacation. Regardless of the time or season, the settings of these stories are often picturesque—in areas like beach towns, ski resorts, or some other vacation destination where characters are free of their usual responsibilities and routines. It can also take place in familiar settings if two people are thrown together temporarily and unintentionally fall for each other.

The key element to these stories is that both parties recognize the temporal nature of the connection, knowing they will have to return to their normal lives at some point. This shouldn't be confused with the Relational Trope we call No Strings Attached, where two people quickly decide to get involved with the intention of withholding an emotional connection. In a Short-Term Fling (unless paired with No Strings Attached), there is an openness to a true connection despite knowing it will be short-lived.

WHY READERS LOVE IT

Subtext is everything to readers of this trope. A key component is the tension of characters saying and believing that they can form a temporary connection while (between the lines) they are actually falling into an absolutely forever love. The reader knows they are going to end up together (this is a romance, after all), so we're just waiting with bated breath for the characters to figure it out too.

The lack of long-term commitment for these characters often allows for a spontaneity that isn't always present in relationships. Readers get swept up by this spontaneity and the adventures characters find themselves on as they explore their connection. Despite (or possibly because of) the seemingly temporary nature of these connections, characters tend to develop feelings for each other quickly. Whether they believe the relationship has a week, a month, or longer, the romance arc is constrained by time, even though it won't be resolved until after the end of the designated time.

READER EXPECTATIONS

There should be palpable chemistry between the main characters, sparking attraction and igniting the passion that drives the fling. Readers want to feel the tension between the romantic connection and the reality of having to return to their lives. Every interaction should be colored by the recognition that this won't last. Whether that makes your character desperate to grab at significant moments that much more fully or has them holding back for fear of getting hurt—it will impact them.

Sometimes it isn't physical distance that will keep the lovers apart at the end of their fling but societal expectations or some other external obstacle that will make their romance impossible and their lives incompatible. Whether due to geographical distance, impending obligations, or other obstacles, the characters should be aware that their time together is limited. As with the Star-Crossed Lovers trope, this brevity heightens the impact of the time the characters have together. These aren't typically heavy, angsty stories though. Especially a Vacation Romance should be about the character (and therefore, the reader) escaping the mundane, embracing new adventures, and taking a walk on the wild side . . . even if "wild" for them means ignoring their responsibilities to lay on the beach and get a tan.

These stories can be a bit of an emotional roller coaster for readers and characters, with the highs in moments of passion and adventure and the lows in places of uncertainty and longing. It's the bond of shared experiences that carries the characters through their doubts and urges them to let the romance take its course.

POTENTIAL PITFALLS

Convenient resolution to separation: When the solution to the characters' separate lives comes too easily, it feels unearned and forced. Make sure the characters struggle with how to make it work and that there is real sacrifice to earn the eventual happy ending.

Rushed romance: While the connection and even interest between these characters tends to happen quickly, readers may find the story inauthentic and unbelievable if authors don't take time to build tension, develop chemistry, and allow the romance to naturally evolve through the storyline.

Someone back home: If your character has someone they are involved with back home, tread carefully to avoid having the character cheat (physically or emotionally) with their vacation fling. If readers can't trust the protagonist to be faithful, it can undermine their investment in the romance.

FREQUENTLY PAIRED TROPES

This trope is often combined with a No Strings Attached Relational Trope, especially in steamier subgenres where a nonemotional physical connection wouldn't be out of place. In a Love Triangle pairing, one character may have someone back home who they are expected to join their future with. The love interest disrupts these plans and ultimately forces the character to make a choice.

This trope is often combined with Setting Tropes of Beach, Mountain, or Christmas, but can also be combined with Small Town in a temporary twist on the Coming Home trope or a Work/Community Project, like if an external consultant were brought in for the project and falls for the Hometown representative.

Sometimes these tropes can be powerfully combined with an inciting incident trope that launched one of the characters into their vacation or short-term situation, such as Jilted, Runaway Bride, or Time Slip.

Depending on the location and cultural context of the vacation, these stories may include a Fish out of Water character. This is often used in young adult romance where a character is sent to stay with a family member for a time and they form a connection with someone who helps them feel accepted or established in this new place.

COMMON PLOT DEVICES

Matching itineraries: These characters find themselves being forced together because of having similar or identical trip plans.

Excursions, parties, town events, or wedding guest festivities—embrace the time together to increase their connection.

Double-booked room: One of the most common setups for the meet cute in these stories is a snafu with the rooming situation on vacation. This is often double-booked rooms (Shared Living Arrangement), but it can also be wrong room numbers leading to an unexpected confrontation, or a lost reservation altogether and a kind gesture from someone who offers to share.

KEY MOMENTS

Inciting incident: Meet cute. These stories may open just before the character embarks on their trip, but they should quickly move into the moment when characters meet during the trip or at least en route to the destination.

Turning point: Characters recognize their true connection. One or both characters often declare their feelings at this point, laying bare their emotions and vulnerabilities. This pulls what has often become a comfortable rapport into chaos, as characters must decide whether to continue investing in their relationship or decide to pull back before the inevitability of heartbreak becomes reality.

Dark moment: Inevitable farewell. At the climax of these stories, the lovers must face the reality of their situation, and one or both must choose to walk away either because time has run out or to break things off before it's too late to avoid a broken heart. (*Spoiler:* By the time the characters have reached this point, it's *always* too late to avoid a broken heart.)

SHORT-TERM FLING

Grand gesture: Whether your characters commit to a long-distance relationship or one character flips their life upside down in order to be together, this moment should demonstrate the characters' willingness and commitment to working toward a permanent future together.

POTENTIAL THEMES

Everlasting love
Sacrifice
Adventure
Choosing happiness
Finding joy in the unexpected

STAR-CROSSED LOVERS

The name of this trope comes directly from the original Star-Crossed Lovers romance—Romeo and Juliet.

"From forth the fatal loins of these two foes, A pair of star-cross'd lovers take their life. Whose misadventured piteous overthrows doth with their death bury their parents' strife."

Although these stories (almost always) eschew the death scene—see more in Common Plot Devices—they still carry a sense of tragedy all the way through to the very end. The quote above packs so much about the story into only four lines of the opening sonnet of the second act: enemies to lovers, caught in the midst of a family feud, having endured a series of misadventures (read *disasters*), finally reaching their tragic end.

In the stories we'll discuss, this is represented by the dark moment (see more in Key Moments) as a *seemingly* tragic ending, which the characters almost miraculously overcome in order to find their happily ever after.

For these stories, it is important to know that the happily ever after may not look like a typical happy ending. If you choose to write a Star-Crossed Lovers story, you may choose to have them miraculously overcome the impossible odds and find their happy ending. But it is equally likely for the resolution of the story to eschew the genre expectation of riding into the sunset together. Instead, readers are left with an ending that shows the enduring nature of the characters' love and that these characters are better off for having loved one another despite the difficult and painful circumstances of their journey.

WHY READERS LOVE IT

There is a special breed of readers that love this type of story. They are also the type to love shows like *This Is Us* and having their heart ripped from their chest over and over again in the most excruciating fashion (figuratively, of course). Let's call them emotional masochists. These stories are so emotionally poignant, there is nearly no way around it.

The emotionally charged nature of the Star-Crossed Lovers trope is one of the things that immediately grabs readers. They become hooked by the tragic circumstances the characters find themselves in from the start of the novel. In addition, the romantic connection is passionate and intense. Because they know the odds are stacked against them, these lovers take full advantage of the brief moments they do get to spend together. Their willingness to fight against all odds for the sake of love makes the happily ever after of these stories feel especially well-earned.

These stories deliver on the promise that true romantic love is precious and something to be deeply nurtured and cherished. Readers who feel this way connect quickly with the characters because in order to enter into the relationship, these characters must be of the mind that it is better to have loved and lost than to never have loved at all.

READER EXPECTATIONS

Throughout their story, the lovers have been drawn together by their love for one another, and yet they've simultaneously been pulled apart by external forces and pressures. Characters usually enter these romances recognizing the risk and likely brevity of their relationship, knowing that the chances of making their love work are nearly nonexistent.

Readers should get the sense that if it weren't for their love story, these characters never would have met. They come from different worlds or are on opposite life paths. In fact, they are usually on a path they don't want to be on. But there is a sense that the love interest completes them and guides them toward the person or path they long to be (on).

While love is an immensely important part of shaping who they are, it should not be shied away that choosing love at all costs is a painful journey. These stories have not just one, but many moments of intense heartbreak, only to be matched by the moments of intense passion and connection that sustain both the readers and the lovers through the tumultuous plot.

POTENTIAL PITFALLS

Too much drama: There is no way around the fact that some readers simply don't enjoy this storyline. If you don't enjoy these stories, you will likely have a difficult time writing one as well.

Contrived conflict: Some stories may rely too heavily on introducing any and all conflict as the primary source of drama without developing other aspects of the story. This can make the plot feel contrived and formulaic.

FREQUENTLY PAIRED TROPES

This trope is so commonly paired with the Terminally Ill Lover microtrope, the two have become nearly synonymous. Examples include *The Fault in Our Stars*, *Five Feet Apart,* and *A Walk to Remember* (please please please see note on "The Death Scene" in Common Plot Devices).

Forbidden Love is often used as a fundamental obstacle to the relationship, especially in stories that replicate the Romeo and Juliet model.

Speculative trope elements such as Time Travel, Immortality, or supernatural mismatches (like falling in love with a ghost) are also potential combinations that emphasize the impossibility of the romantic pairing.

COMMON PLOT DEVICES

Sacrifice: One or both characters are often forced to make significant sacrifices for the sake of being together. This raises the stakes of the story.

Physical tearing apart: These characters are so drawn to each other by their love that they cannot help but steal moments together, but even if their union is not outright forbidden, there is something so incompatible about it that the people around them are willing to forcibly remove them from the situation. This often occurs in the second half of act two when a parent or someone else discovers the romance and deems it inappropriate or harmful for the lover in their charge.

Symbol of love: There is often a physical item that symbolizes the lasting union of lovers in these stories. This item serves as proof the love existed, even if society deems it illegitimate or does not recognize its existence. One example is the blue diamond necklace Rose wears in *The Titanic* and throws back into the ocean at the end of the movie, symbolizing that she has found peace and let go of Jack's death. While society or life circumstances may be successfully keeping these characters apart, it can't erase the fact that they love (or loved) each other.

Actual death: We've saved this plot device for last because, as you might imagine, it is probably the most controversial plot device in all of romance fiction—readers are, after all, looking for a happily ever after. While you will never see either of us (Tara or Jessica) recommending that writers end a romance with death, it hasn't stopped the writers of Star-Crossed Lovers stories from attempting it time and time again. The problem is, few succeed at it the way that Shakespeare did. When these stories end with one character dying, the emotional impact of the story must be such that the impact is intense and *lasting*. Sometimes this is the best choice for a story, as the brevity of the relationship may be what gives the relationship its intensity and impact. But the love story must give the reader a sense of satisfaction through its legacy or enduring impact on the rest of the story world.

KEY MOMENTS

Inciting incident: Because these stories are all about the intersection of two nearly incompatible life paths, the inciting incident of these stories almost always occurs with the meet cute. From their very first scene together, these characters should have an immediate and strong connection, though these stories are not necessarily Instant Love.

Call to action: The characters have already been presented with and recognized the odds against them, but they choose to prioritize their love.

Dark moment: Whatever the root cause of the odds stacked against the couple, it will come back in the worst way possible in this moment. The possibility of living out their love will feel absolutely impossible, and if characters make it to their happily ever after, it is usually due to a shocking twist of fate (and careful plotting).

Resolution: However you choose to end the story, the key to the resolution of this trope is providing proof of their everlasting love and the fact that these characters are better off for having loved one another, despite the difficult and painful circumstances of their love journey.

POTENTIAL THEMES

Destiny/fate
Better to have loved and lost
Everlasting love
Sacrifice
Impossible choices

CHAPTER 18

I DON'T BELONG HERE

OUT OF PLACE TROPES

These Storyline Tropes center around a complete upheaval of the characters' lives and comfort. The vulnerability of characters in these circumstances lends itself to a powerful and resonant growth arc and compels the protagonist to grow and adapt to these challenges rather than succumb to them. These stories tap into themes like identity, embracing the unexpected, and the transformative power of love, making them staples of the romance genre.

AMNESIA

FISH OUT OF WATER

RAGS TO RICHES

UNEXPECTED INHERITANCE/LOST HEIR(ESS)

AMNESIA

In an Amnesia story, one partner suffers from permanent or temporary amnesia (memory loss), forgetting all or part of their life. This memory loss can stem from various causes, including traumatic events, accidents, medical conditions, or even magical influence.

The amnesiac character often finds themselves thrust into a world where familiar faces and places hold no recognition, leaving them grappling with a profound sense of disorientation and confusion. The memory loss may be complete or encompass only a more recent period of weeks, months, or years.

As the protagonist struggles to piece together the fragments of their past, they may encounter challenges in reconnecting with loved ones, rediscovering their identity, and reestablishing the bonds that once defined their existence. The impact of amnesia on the dynamics of the romantic relationship is profound, as both partners navigate through the complexities of love, loss, and the quest for restoration.

WHY READERS LOVE IT

The Amnesia trope is a journey of falling in love all over again, where the heart rekindles what the mind has lost. The commitment to love, even when faced with the challenge of being a stranger to the one you once knew, provides hope for real-life romance where long-term relationships start to feel more foreign than familiar. Readers are drawn to the characters' willingness to fight for a lost connection, to delve into the depths of their emotions despite the uncertainty and fear of rejection.

Within the realm of Amnesia romance, painful, awkward, and/or humorous situations can occur. Picture the protagonist being presented with their former favorite peanut butter and banana sandwich, only to realize that they now think it is disgusting.

Alternatively, imagine the awkwardness of confessing love to a partner who has no memory of the relationship and the uneven footing of one character being at the final stages of emotional intimacy while the amnesia sufferer is only at the beginning. Or the constant back and forth of hope and crushing disappointment as the memories fail to return.

The juxtaposition of rediscovery and revelation amidst the fog of forgotten memories adds a layer of mystery to the narrative, enticing readers to unravel the truth alongside the characters. This emotional depth fuels the journey of self-discovery and the exploration of past connections, leading to moments of both joy and heartache.

The central theme of love prevailing over even the most daunting of physical obstacles resonates deeply with readers. As the characters navigate through the complexities of their forgotten past, readers witness the triumph of love meant to be, the affirmation of one true love enduring against all odds. In essence, the Amnesia trope carries a memorable blend *(pun intended!)* of emotional depth, mystery, and the unwavering power of love. It's a journey of rediscovery. And it's this journey, filled with twists and turns, laughter and tears, that keeps readers turning the pages, eager to witness the ultimate triumph of love reclaimed.

READER EXPECTATIONS

Generally speaking, these stories are not simple comedies. There is a real emotional toll on the character struggling with memory loss, and readers expect some raw emotion as they reconnect with their life. While the story can certainly have lighthearted moments, it will also have some poignant interactions and internal angst, even for the most positive and upbeat character.

The loss of memories will have a significant impact on characters' relationships and daily life. There may be job consequences, people who are offended the character doesn't remember them, promises inadvertently broken, or habits and skills the character has forgotten. Conversations will be confusing without the proper context of assumed knowledge, and locations may be unfamiliar or seem to have changed suddenly. The focus of the story should be on rebuilding connections and the character discovering who they were—and who they are now.

The resolution of the Amnesia storyline can happen in various ways. Gradual recovery of memory (and their revelation to readers) is a common way, with small glimpses of memories returning across a period of time. Alternately, the character may have one big flash of remembrance, but despite what the characters may think, remembering the past isn't a magic bullet that fixes everything.

The character may also end up with no memory recovery at all, learning to accept the loss and move forward with their life focusing on the future. However you choose to resolve the Amnesia storyline, it should be believable. The character is probably not going to get a second bump on the head that suddenly brings back the memories.

POTENTIAL PITFALLS

Unrealistic cause, treatment or resolution of amnesia: Amnesia remains a huge medical mystery that gives authors a fair bit of leeway in storytelling, but if the memory loss is due to medical trauma, be sure to familiarize yourself with traumatic brain injuries. In any case, make sure the cause, treatment, and resolution of the amnesia is realistic for the setting of your story.

Insensitivity by romantic partner: While having your partner lose their memory is certainly difficult, it reflects poorly on the love interest if they are too concerned with their own pity party to be sensitive to the struggle of the amnesiac character. This is their opportunity to show their patience and commitment, not be a self-centered jerk.

No change to daily life: Your character will simply not be able to continue their normal life. Even if they return to work or home quickly, the side effects of amnesia will make themselves known, and the character's (likely) external goal of recovering their memories will impact their decisions.

Return of memory: It can be tempting for your character to regain their memories at times that are simply too "convenient" to be believable. If your character remembers something, it isn't likely to be when they are trying to remember it or desperately need that piece of information to escape dire circumstances.

Limited agency: These characters are in a physically vulnerable state, in addition to their mental state, which will probably leave them relatively dependent on others for a time. Make sure that they maintain some measure of authenticity by finding ways that they can maintain their own identity, even if they don't know how or why they came to be that way.

FREQUENTLY PAIRED TROPES

Tropes like Second Chance and Love on the Rocks provide the perfect backdrop for the redemption and fresh opportunity an Amnesia storyline provides.

Mistaken Identity or Disguise mesh easily when paired with a character who does not know who they are or who has otherwise lost some portion of their memory. While the mistaken identity may be an unintentional result of trying to identify the amnesiac, the Disguise trope is typically used by a character who takes advantage of the fact that the character with memory loss has little reason to believe that they aren't who they say they are.

The introduction of a new love when there is a worried old flame floating out there in the world somewhere looking for their partner makes the Love Triangle trope a good choice to pair with Amnesia. The confrontation of the pre-amnesia lover may result in the rediscovery of identity or memories, or it may cause additional trauma to the patient.

COMMON PLOT DEVICES

Messages from the past: Journals, letters and messages (voice or text) are commonly used in Amnesia stories to help the character regain old memories or find a sense of identity.

Parallel timelines/flashbacks: This device is sometimes used to juxtapose a character's life before and after the event that caused memory loss. Details of the past are usually slowly revealed in order to illuminate and give significance to the circumstances the amnesiac finds themselves in post-memory loss.

Unclear memories: Because the return of the memory does not happen all at once, the bits and pieces of lost memories that return to the character are easily misunderstood or distorted. It is also possible for trauma, individuals, or the events of the present to influence these memories so that the patient sometimes fills in the gaps of their memory themselves with false memories, further confusing their reality.

KEY MOMENTS

Inciting incident: These stories may start with the events that cause brain trauma and amnesia, but that should quickly be followed by the Amnesia character waking up in confusion and realizing they have lost some or all of their memories. This is a very emotionally charged scene, and the reader should feel the visceral reaction of the character as they recognize that they have lost an entire portion of their lives.

Turning point: As your character begins uncovering elements of their past or regaining past memories, they will be forced to confront issues that were left unresolved or that they cannot reconcile to their current memories.

POTENTIAL THEMES

Identity
Healing
Soulmates/meant to be together
Forgiveness
Trust

FISH OUT OF WATER

The Fish out of Water trope puts the character in an unfamiliar and/or uncomfortable situation or environment. For obvious reasons, this setting is typically different from their usual surroundings, social circle, or lifestyle. Think a city girl stuck in the country, or a gangster suddenly hiding out at a church camp.

In the context of romance novels, this trope is often used to create conflict, humor, or tension in the story. It allows for the exploration of how the character adapts to their new environment and interacts with others who may have different backgrounds, values, or ways of life. The romance that develops in such a scenario typically involves the character finding love or connection with someone unexpected, leading to personal growth and a deeper understanding of themselves and others.

WHY READERS LOVE IT

This trope is almost universally relatable, with the Fish out of Water character's struggle to navigate unfamiliar territory or adapt to a new environment, creating an instant connection between the reader and the character. The very nature of so blatantly plucking a character from their comfort zone and into a new routine, environment, or culture helps the author to develop a strong hook and capture the reader's attention from the first chapter. Who wouldn't want to see how the presumed librarian navigates being thrust into the dragon-riding academy?

One of the things readers love about these stories is the opportunity for unfamiliar situations and cultural clashes to arise from the character being out of their element. Will the character rise to the challenge or crumble under the scrutiny? Readers not only appreciate the comedic effect of these moments, but they revel in the awkwardness, the unexpected, and the utterly ridiculous reactions of the characters when they encounter them.

The stark differences between the Fish out of Water character and their romantic interest, as well as the other individuals in their new environment, create opportunities for delicious tension and chemistry. The contrast between backgrounds, values, and lifestyles creates an engaging dynamic and easily lends itself to conflict and opportunities for the character to grow, which tends to pull readers quickly and deeply into the story. The unexpectedness of the romance itself is fascinating, whether it's tantalizing or a total trainwreck, and readers love to see the journey of two seemingly incompatible people learning to complement one another amidst an unlikely connection.

READER EXPECTATIONS

Because this trope relies so heavily on the change of the character's surroundings, it often involves world-building in order to introduce readers to new settings, cultures, or social circles. The reader is brought into this new world right along with the character, expanding the scope of the story and providing the backdrop for the romance to unfold. This is especially important when the Fish out of Water character's new environment involves a different culture or set of societal expectations.

Readers will expect the character to face challenges as they navigate the unfamiliarity. They made need different social skills (like the brash New Yorker who must learn to bite his tongue in front of the queen), physical skills (like the supermodel who suddenly needs to chop wood to prepare for winter in the Alaskan bush), and the hardest challenge of all—overcoming their own insecurities to push toward their goal.

The unfamiliarity of this new world should ultimately serve as a catalyst for character growth and transformation through the action of adapting and coming to understand the people and circumstances of their setting. Through this growth, readers expect characters to reach some kind of internal resolution to their initial discomfort in the environment. This may involve reconciling differences, overcoming obstacles, and finding a sense of belonging. The very crux of this trope is the character discovering that they aren't a Fish out of Water at all, but that they belong in the environment in which they initially felt so out of place.

POTENTIAL PITFALLS

Lack of originality: As one of the oldest and most classic tropes, this trope can easily fall into the overused or cliché category when not executed well. Readers may get a sense of déjà vu and lose interest if the story is not infused with fresh or inventive elements. Another way to avoid this pitfall is to add depth to the story with well fleshed-out characters and conflict.

Unrealistic premise: In some cases, the premise of a character being completely out of their element may seem unrealistic or contrived to certain readers. If the scenario feels forced or lacks authenticity, it can hinder the reader's suspension of belief. Combat this by creating a strong character the reader cares about, and take some care when crafting the reason for the character's sudden presence in a new place.

Lack of chemistry: If the romantic relationship lacks chemistry or if the connection between the characters feels forced, readers may struggle to invest in the love story. Authentic and believable romantic dynamics are crucial for reader engagement.

Stereotypes: It can be easy to lean on stereotypes of a specific place or people: uncaring, too-busy-for-you nature of interactions in the city, or old-fashioned, backwoods, or simple thinking in an isolated small town. But these stereotypes are not universal truths, and side characters and settings should be considered individually for how they serve your story and your characters.

FREQUENTLY PAIRED TROPES

The difference in backgrounds, culture, and lifestyle easily lends itself to the Opposites Attract trope. While this may initially lead to tension or outright conflict, the differences in the characters should eventually lead to an appreciation of how they complement each other.

Societal or cultural expectations can make romantic relationships not only difficult with an outsider, but it may lead to an outright Forbidden Romance. When this pairing occurs, the overcoming of these obstacles becomes the central focus of the story.

Academy is an excellent Setting Trope to use with Fish out of Water. It adds extra relatability to the reader, because most of us can readily identify with the first day of school jitters and the difficulty of finding your place within a large system like an institution. And if the academy also happens to introduce the character to creatures or magic they never knew existed? Well, they are all the more overwhelmed with the change.

When paired with something like a Fresh Start microtrope, wherever a character runs from all they know in order to start over, they might also take up a Secret Identity. It is also often paired with something like a Billionaire romance, Rags to Riches, or Lost Heiress trope, where an ordinary character suddenly finds themselves entering a world of wealth and privilege.

In speculative romance, it is incredibly common to see the Fish out of Water paired with something like a Time Slip or Time Travel—even a Time Loop will be so unfamiliar and out of sync for the character that you will see elements of the Fish out of Water trope in the character's attempt to adjust to the unexpected situation.

COMMON PLOT DEVICES

Unchartered territory: The Fish out of Water may struggle with societal expectations and norms in the unfamiliar setting. This can include navigating high society, dealing with aristocratic traditions, or adapting to a new social class. Family dynamics and expectations can also play a significant role. The protagonist may need to contend with the expectations or disapproval of their own family or the family of the love interest.

Crisis of identity: Your character will often grapple with an identity crisis as they try to reconcile their true self with the expectations of the new environment. This internal conflict will drive character development and growth as they wrestle with who they are at a base level when everything familiar is stripped away and assumptions about themselves or the world are challenged.

Side characters: The character may form unexpected alliances or friendships with characters who help them navigate the challenges of the new environment. These alliances can influence the romantic plot and contribute to the protagonist's personal growth. On the flip side, there may be busybodies or outright antagonists who ruffle at the introduction of an outsider, making things difficult or otherwise creating trouble and discord in relation to the love interest.

Part of the club: As your character adapts to their new community or environment, they may go through rites of passage or challenges specific to the new environment, contributing to their personal growth and transformation. They may even be given responsibilities to test them or to demonstrate that they have been welcomed into the community.

KEY MOMENTS

Inciting incident: This typically occurs when the character enters (or plans to enter) their new environment. While the character may enter this environment off the page, if you don't give readers a picture into the world they've come from, they may find it difficult to fully understand the contrast and significance of the Fish out of Water character's struggle.

Turning point: While the first half of act two is bound to bring struggles, misunderstandings, and social fumbles for the Fish out of

Water, the closer you get to the midpoint, the more your character should start to find triumph and acceptance more within reach.

Climax: At the transition of the second act to the third, the protagonist likely faces a critical decision point where they must choose between their old life and the new one, and this choice often has implications for their personal happiness and the romantic relationship.

Dark moment: When the challenges, pressures, or self-reflection imposed by their new environment seems impossible, the character will wrestle with the implications of their new life, what they've accomplished and failed to accomplish in their new environment. Their insecurities or lie will feel so insurmountable that they will likely express some semblance of regret that they ever found themselves in the new environment.

POTENTIAL THEMES

Identity
Self-discovery
Community
Home is where you make it
Adaptation

RAGS TO RICHES

The Rags to Riches trope involves one or both characters going from meager living or financial conditions to suddenly finding themselves in posh circumstances, or at least with the money to live lavishly. This is a very archetypal storyline going back centuries, and while the intersection with romance does enhance a few elements of the classic storyline, it remains very much intact.

The key component of these stories is that it happens *quickly*, by the end of the first act or sometimes just before the story begins. Traditionally, the characters gain wealth or status, lose it, then regain it by the end (along with their happily ever after).

The character arcs in these stories may involve Billionaires, Royalty, or Lost Heirs, which you can read more about in the Encyclopedia portion of *Romance Character Tropes*.

WHY READERS LOVE IT

These stories can have a bit of a Cinderella feel to them—a meek hero or heroine who has almost always become content with their poor financial state suddenly comes into money (but manages to maintain their goodness). Readers love to see someone receive a windfall like this, and even if the character happens to falter, readers will happily accept a great redemption arc.

The very notion of the Rags to Riches story is embedded in Western culture with ideals such as the American Dream that suggest anyone can find success if they work hard enough. These stories are often not a result of hard work (though they might be a combination of hard work and luck), but they *are* about good people finding a way up the social ladder and finding true happiness in love.

Whether readers actually play the lottery or not, most of us have considered the daydream of what would happen if we suddenly had a handful of extra zeros at the end of our bank account. How quickly circumstances can change, the impact of money on relationships and motives, and the sheer fun of seeing a character navigate the windfall are a few reasons readers love these stories. The dynamic of how a life of poverty and a life of wealth brush up against one another is one readers enjoy.

Ultimately, though, these stories serve as a reminder that money cannot solve all problems and that it cannot buy true love. Characters in these stories find a love that stands for richer and for poorer and extends beyond social classes.

READER EXPECTATIONS

In order to be a true Rags to Riches story, readers must be able to connect with and understand the character in their initial living conditions. Readers want to understand not only the physical squalor of the character's living conditions, but they must understand how this has affected them mentally and emotionally. Even if the story starts after their sudden rise to the top, readers must understand how it has defined or influenced who they are and how they live. If not in the present, this can be shown through internal narrative coupled with the character's actions or dialogue, or through the use of flashbacks, or other characters from the past and their reactions to the changes in circumstance.

These aren't typically stories of hard work and dedication paying off. They are windfall stories of characters coming into money and trying to navigate their newfound financial freedom—which often comes to feel like just as much of a burden as living with nothing. Because of this, when the dark moment arrives and everything is stripped from your character, it's because they haven't yet earned their fortune. So authors should use this moment as the final catalyst for the character to overcome their internal obstacles—the great lie or the deep-seated wound—and complete their transformation arc.

While a Rags to Riches story *can* be have an Unexpected Inheritance storyline, these two tropes should not be confused as one and the same. The character experiencing a windfall of changed financial fortunes will likely have quite a different growth journey depending on the avenue by which they got rich. This in turn will directly influence the trajectory of the romance arc. While there is a certain measure of responsibility inherent in the Unexpected Inheritance and Lost Heir(ess) storylines, Rags to Riches devices like lottery, celebrity, and sheer luck tend to have a very different focus on the impact of fortune in an individual's life and its ability (or lack thereof) to provide any true happiness or fulfillment.

POTENTIAL PITFALLS

Rushed romance: Sometimes the focus of the narrative rests so heavily on the external circumstances that the culmination of the romance feels fabricated and falls flat. Forcing the romantic relationship to develop too quickly or without sufficient emotional groundwork can make the story feel rushed and unsatisfying. In addition, readers may be turned off if the romantic elements feel forced or unrealistic given the severity of the circumstances. The relationship should naturally evolve within the context of the story.

Money solves everything: Don't prioritize the character's external transformation over the growth that needs to happen internally for them to truly overcome the obstacles before them. Money is a tool the character now has at their disposal, but it will not fix their insecurities or heal their deep-seated wounds.

Lack of realism: This is an inherently fantastical trope. While there are plenty of examples of Rags to Riches stories in the real world, this transition typically takes decades of hard work and success. Find other ways to ground your reader in reality by emphasizing the absurdity of the situation, using known vehicles of windfall fortunes such as the lottery, inheritance, or viral success from the internet.

Weak romance arc: As a storyline that has been told for centuries across all genres of story, it is easy for writers to unintentionally or subconsciously follow the key moments of the Rags to Riches plot without giving enough priority to the romantic storyline. Make sure that you give some thought as to how your characters' unique romantic journey will fit into this classic storyline.

FREQUENTLY PAIRED TROPES

Placing your character in unfamiliar or high society settings highlights their outsider status, making this a natural choice for pairing with the Fish out of Water trope. This combination creates opportunities for humor, conflict, and personal growth as they navigate their new environment.

When the Rags to Riches character falls for a previously wealthy or powerful character, obstacles such as social class and familial expectations sometimes come into play. This can be played up in a pairing with the Forbidden Romance trope. Alternately, the suddenly wealthy character may be an unexpecting mark for a Hidden Motive story.

As mentioned, this Storyline Trope is often paired with Character Tropes such as Billionaire, Lost Heir(ess), or Royalty.

COMMON PLOT DEVICES

Transformation scene: This isn't always a physical transformation where the character gets a glow up; sometimes this is a scene of total transformation in their way of life, such as the peasant who moves from their hovel to an elegant estate.

Mentor: The protagonist may receive guidance, mentorship, or financial support from a benefactor or mentor figure who helps them navigate the path to wealth and success. This person may or may not turn out to have ulterior motives, but they will serve to help the character acclimate to their new living situation.

Climbing the social ladder: Their new financial situation may require the protagonist to strategically navigate social circles and events to network with influential individuals and gain access to opportunities for advancement, often encountering challenges and setbacks along the way.

KEY MOMENTS

Inciting incident: These stories typically open right up as the character comes into money, power, or status. While you still have time to introduce the characters and establish the story world, the inheritance of money or the circumstance that triggers your character's Rags to Riches transformation will be the first major turning point of your narrative.

Midpoint crisis: As an archetypal storyline adapted for the romance genre, these stories often use a midpoint crisis rather than a midpoint victory. This means that the initial goal of the character will prove to be futile, and they must pivot their strategy or the goal itself in order to find fulfillment.

Dark moment: The Rags to Riches character is not only threatened with the loss of their wealth, but this also usually coincides with a loss of love.

Resolution: The character regains at least some measure of their wealth, and the romantic relationship is restored.

POTENTIAL THEMES

Hope
Ambition
Identity
Money can't buy happiness
Integrity

UNEXPECTED INHERITANCE/ LOST HEIR(ESS)

In these stories, the main character unexpectedly inherits a large sum of money, a property, or a title, which leads to significant changes in their life. As the character navigates their newfound wealth or status, they find love along the way. The character may or may not be familiar with the kingdom, fortune, or property they are inheriting. They may already have a life in the same kingdom, work for the company, or live nearby the property they inherit. More often, though, the Lost Heir(ess) is completely uninformed about the inheritance and its implications.

These romances often involve a vacant throne or a throne occupied by an antagonistic figure who needs to be ousted. It's important to note that the inheritance does not necessarily grant the character immediate access to the throne (or other object of inheritance); it only provides them with the ability to claim it. The protagonist must not only embrace their new identity as heir, but overcome great challenges to claim their title. During this quest, they are proven a worthy leader, both to themself and to others.

The complications to their inheritance may be a competitor swooping in to purchase the family business while it is in turmoil, a family member contesting the will, or the protagonist themself clinging to their former life. In these stories, the romance may be facilitated or complicated by the inheritance, with the main characters' worlds intersecting when they otherwise would not have, or the heirs' new circumstances threatening to rip them apart.

In the end, though, the Lost Heir(ess) will find their happily ever after and (typically) embrace their inheritance.

WHY READERS LOVE IT

This storyline has its roots in the fantastical "ripped from your ordinary life" kind of reader wish fulfillment. The idea that anything is possible and your life could change at any moment is one of the most powerful draws to the art of story in general. Readers love the escapist fantasy that someday the mundane could be replaced with an adventure and an identity you didn't even know was possible.

These stories are typically high-stakes. Inheritances can come with strings attached, family drama, or unexpected challenges, which create tension and conflict in the story. Power, money, and love all come into play in these stories, and the stakes have the reader rooting for characters to overcome all the obstacles to claiming their happy ending.

Since the inheritance serves as a catalyst for the protagonist's transformation or redemption, characters get to go along for the journey as a flawed, usually very relatable and down-to-earth hero(ine) is thrust into a complicated situation. The conflict stretches and almost breaks them before they overcome it to restore peace to the kingdom, save their fortune, and/or reclaim family ties. Plus, don't forget they find or claim their true love as well.

READER EXPECTATIONS

Lost Heir(ess) stories typically begin with the revelation of the inheritance, and there should be a moment of disbelief or shock for the protagonist when they learn of it. If they do not discover this information until later in the story, there is typically some method used by other characters to pull them into the ongoing events revolving around the fortune or title. Either way, when the revelation is made, it should be shocking to the character.

This revelation serves as a catalyst for the narrative, propelling the protagonist into a world of intrigue, conflict, and self-discovery. Whether it's inheriting a vast fortune, a prestigious title, or a powerful estate, the protagonist will experience a whirlwind of emotions as they come to terms with their newfound wealth or status.

There should be significant conflict surrounding the inheritance itself, presenting obstacles for the protagonist to overcome. Whether it's a usurper on the throne, family members contesting the will, hidden conditions attached to the inheritance, or the protagonist struggling to adjust to their new circumstances, the road to claiming their inheritance is fraught with challenges. These conflicts force the protagonist to confront their fears, insecurities, and limitations, pushing them to rise to the occasion and prove themselves worthy of their inheritance.

When the inheritance is a title or a throne, the journey for the character often becomes about growing into leadership, learning to rule effectively and empathetically, and earning the position through integrity, courage, and compassion.

Along the way, romance should be either facilitated or complicated by the inheritance, bringing the two characters together with a common goal, pitting them against one another in opposition, or ripping them apart as one character is pulled into a new world of status. You'll want to pay close attention to the dynamics between the main protagonists to strike your desired balance of romantic arc, character arc, and external conflict in the story.

POTENTIAL PITFALLS

Weak arcs: No matter what the inheritance is, money and status can't fix everything for your characters. Their character arcs and the romance arc must feel complete and well-earned for the story to be satisfying to the readers.

That was too easy: Make sure whatever obstacles your character must overcome are realistic and challenging. Whether it is the snooty socialites who snub their noses or the usurper king on the throne, the character must fight the battles and resolve them, and solving the problem shouldn't be too easy. Make your character work for it and grow through it.

The plot hole: This is one Storyline Trope where we need to be extra aware of plot holes. If the heir was hidden away, why? If someone knew about their existence, why didn't they blow the whistle? If this magical artifact allowed someone to claim the throne, why hadn't it been used by anyone else before now? Ask a beta reader to try to poke holes in your story and make sure your Lost Heir(ess) story can hold water.

FREQUENTLY PAIRED TROPES

While Unexpected Inheritance is not inherently a Rags to Riches story, it is a common pairing, as is the Fish out of Water trope, with the character suddenly thrust into an entire new world, social class, or family as they navigate their inheritance.

Obviously, Royalty/Regency is an incredibly appropriate pairing for this trope. These settings tend to have an extremely high emphasis on bloodline and inheritance customs, which create ample opportunities for the Lost Heir(ess) trope to shine.

This storyline is also commonly found in Fantasy settings, where the fate of entire kingdoms rests on the unknown heir fighting for their inheritance. The main character could also inherit other things, like superpowers, magical artifacts (Frodo anyone?), or a blood feud they were unaware of!

COMMON PLOT DEVICES

Orphaned hero or heroine: Unknown parentage due to being orphaned is a common plot device in these stories, or at least losing a parent at a young age. The heir may also have difficulty drawing a straight line back to the arbiter of the inheritance because of physical or relational separation that has limited their time with extended family.

Reading of the will: These stories often utilize a dramatic scene where the will is read, revealing them as the heir. This might also be an ordinance in Royalty situations that determines the line of succession to the throne. These moments have especially shocking impact if the Inheriting character is distanced by many degrees of separation from the benefactor.

Revelation of family secrets: This storyline often relies on things being hidden (after all, the heir was lost for a reason!), so long-buried family secrets are commonly used to drive the plot forward, add intrigue, and challenge the protagonist.

Challenges to the inheritance: Money, power, and other inheritances are not usually gladly handed over to the rightful heir. These stories often use other family members, competitors to the inherited domain, or legal complications to create external conflict for the character pursuing their inheritance.

KEY MOMENTS

Inciting incident: These stories often start with the Inheriting character being identified as the heir(ess); sometimes they don't find out until later though. If they do not know of their inheritance at the inciting incident, your characters are otherwise dragged into the situation—sometimes this is the moment the character meets their benefactor without the knowledge of how radically this relationship will change their life.

Turning point: The heir(ess) takes their place or begins the process of inheritance (maybe decides—in the face of opposition—that the inheritance is something worth fighting for).

Dark moment resolution: Many times, the dark moment involves the character wrestling with impossible odds in the fight for their inheritance and/or the loss of their love. Often the conflicts to the inheritance must be dealt with to open the door to romance, and the character must overcome their deep-seated wound or great lie to claim both love and their rightful position.

POTENTIAL THEMES

Identity
Family ties
Chosen family
Self-confidence
Trust

CHAPTER 19

THROUGH TIME AND SPACE

BENDING TIME TROPES

All of the tropes in this category deal with the bending of the space-time continuum, though some instances are intentional (such as the Time Travel trope), while characters stumble into others (Time Slip and Time Loop). In any case, these tropes involve characters experiencing different time periods. The key difference between these three iterations of the *Bending Time* tropes lies in the manner of temporal displacement and the level of control characters have over their journeys through time.

Time Travel: Characters actively and intentionally travel through time, often using some form of technology, magic, or supernatural means.

Time Slip: Characters or objects experience a spontaneous and involuntary shift through time, often without any control over the process, at least until they understand the details of the slip.

> *While some authors, publishers, and readers will refer to Dual Time or Split Time novels (which feature two separate timelines) as Time Slip stories in marketing material and blurbs, that usage in incongruent with the common and well-established use of the phrase across other genres of fiction and nonfiction.

Time Loop: Characters get stuck living an amount of time (usually a day, but sometimes it's an entire lifetime) and must figure out how to break the loop to resume time and move forward.

We will first evaluate *Bending Time* tropes as a whole, and then dive in to each specific iteration.

WHY READERS LOVE IT

In Time Travel and Time Slip stories, readers of historical fiction appreciate the world-building and immersion of a modern character into a historical setting. The same can be achieved when characters travel into the future in order to appeal to readers of speculative fiction or science fiction. In contrast to non-time travel historical or futuristic settings, these stories typically allow the reader to really imagine themselves in the place of the character.

For readers who gravitate towards speculative fiction, the fantastical elements inherent in Time Travel stories offer a thrilling escape into worlds where the boundaries of time and space are fluid, allowing for extraordinary adventures and unexpected encounters.

However, even readers who may not typically explore speculative genres find themselves captivated by the prospect of exploring timeless love and the inherent drama and intrigue that accompanies such journeys. By blending elements of romance with the mystery of nonlinear time, these stories offer a fresh and imaginative take on the themes of love, destiny, and second chances, appealing to a wide range of readers seeking an escape into the unknown.

These stories have an inherent added complexity with the paradox of time travel (or time loops) and unexpected twists, which makes these stories incredibly gripping. The stakes are high and the possibilities for what happens next are endless.

READER EXPECTATIONS

The biggest thing readers need from these stories is a set of logical time travel rules. While they are suspending disbelief to some extent to embrace the stories (since as far as we know, time is still linear and no one gets a redo!), but as the author, it is your job to make the impossible seem possible, at least within the confines of the story.

Magic is a perfectly reasonable explanation, such as a magical being forcing your character to relive the same day over and over until they "get it right" and learn the lesson. Time travel machines, rips in the time-space continuum, hidden portals to the past, time travel artifacts, or a single building existing in two timelines—whatever the mechanism is for the non-linearity needs to be consistent and logical, even when that logic makes things inconvenient in the story. As Bluey and Coco say in the episode "Shadowlands":

"You can't change the rules. The rules make it fun."

CHAPTER 19

POTENTIAL PITFALLS

Underdeveloped settings: Inaccurate or superficial portrayals of historical settings can undermine the immersive experience readers expect from time travel romances. Authors should strive for authenticity in their depiction of different time periods, conducting thorough research to ensure accuracy in details such as language, customs, and historical events.

Not enough focus on romance: The romantic relationship at the heart of the story must feel genuine and compelling for readers to become emotionally invested. Rushed or contrived romances lacking in chemistry or depth will leave readers feeling unsatisfied and disengaged from the narrative.

Low stakes: The stakes of the time journey and its impact on the characters' lives must feel significant and compelling to hold readers' interest. If the consequences of time travel are trivial or inconsequential, the story may lack tension and fail to engage readers on an emotional level.

BENDING TIME TROPES

TIME TRAVEL

TIME SLIP

TIME LOOP

TIME TRAVEL

The Time Travel trope involves one or both main characters traveling through time and encountering a love interest from a different era. This trope allows for a blend of historical and contemporary romance elements as well as exploring themes of fate, destiny, and the power of love transcending time and space. When this phenomenon occurs by accident or unexpectedly, it is considered a Time Slip storyline (see details in the next entry).

Characters may have a specific purpose or goal in mind when traveling through time, such as altering the past, preventing a future disaster, or simply exploring different historical periods.

Time Travel is a common trope in many genres, but to satisfy the Time Travel trope in romance, the key is that the characters who fall in love are from different eras and must overcome that particularly huge obstacle to find their happily ever after.

WHY READERS LOVE IT

One of the reasons this trope is so popular lies in its ability to bridge the gap between historical and contemporary romance. While these stories are typically set in the past, they are often written in a very contemporary voice. While these stories are inherently more appealing to contemporary readers, the world-building aspect of the past (or future) destination is still critically imported. Readers want to be *transported* to a different time along with the characters themselves. Vivid settings, high stakes, and clear motivations help the story feel tangible to the reader.

Readers who enjoy adventure themes are likely to enjoy Time Travel stories, as they often have a very mission/quest-focused external plot. These characters have intentionally utilized some method of time travel for an express purpose, and readers love to go on the journey of victories and setbacks as they try to reach that goal (or another, as the story moves along and the goal shifts, often to one of survival or returning to their own time.)

READER EXPECTATIONS

In contrast to the Time Slip trope, the characters of these stories are often prepared (at least to some degree) for the situation that awaits them on the other side of their journey through time. In many cases, they've studied the time period and customs or even researched the people they will interact with in the time period.

The method of time travel should make sense within the context of the story world.

When the Time Traveler falls in love with a character from the past, readers will expect certain obstacles to be addressed such as societal expectations, cultural differences, and most importantly, the fact that the character has an entire life waiting for them in the future.

Depending on the rules of time travel that you implement (and we could probably write an entire book on all the different ways this is done), it is likely that you will need to address what consequences will come into play if your character changes anything about the past. It's worth noting that if you are writing a story where the time-traveling character falls in love with someone from the past, your character cannot be operating within a time-traveling world where they are a simple observer unable to have any effect on the events of the past.

POTENTIAL PITFALLS

Inconsistent rules: Failing to establish clear rules or boundaries for the time travel or time slip mechanism can lead to confusion and inconsistency within the narrative. Readers may become frustrated if the rules governing time travel change arbitrarily or if there are glaring inconsistencies in how time travel is depicted.

Underdeveloped settings: Inaccurate or superficial portrayals of historical settings can undermine the immersive experience readers expect from time travel romances. Authors should strive for authenticity in their depiction of different time periods, conducting thorough research to ensure accuracy in details such as language, customs, and historical events.

COMMON PLOT DEVICES

Butterfly effect: Sometimes the Time Traveler must grapple with the consequences of their actions in the past, knowing that even small changes could have significant ripple effects on history. This usually works as a catalyst for the growth arc.

Quest or mission: In some variations of the trope, the time travel element is part of a broader quest or mission that the characters must undertake together, adding layers of adventure and danger to their romance.

Parallel timelines: Occasionally, time travel romances explore the concept of parallel timelines or alternate realities, where the actions of the characters in the past have the potential to create entirely new futures.

FREQUENTLY PAIRED TROPES

These stories sometimes have a very Star-Crossed Lovers feel, with everything stacked against an eventual happy ending. These stories can also be paired with the Group Project trope, pairing two characters who share the same goal despite being from different times.

The story can become a Road Trip through time as two characters complete their journey through one or many different time periods. The characters may use a Fake Relationship to achieve the objective of the time travel mission.

KEY MOMENTS

Inciting incident: The inciting incident usually occurs when characters stumble upon, create, or otherwise discover some mechanism of intentional time travel. This usually involves a scene which highlights the implications and risk of choosing to embark on this journey, and it may be immediately followed by your character starting their time travel journey.

Turning point: Due to some complication or perceived benefit, your characters can't (or won't) go back to their time. This may be used at nearly any pinch point in the novel, including the call to action at the end of act one, the no way beat, the midpoint, or during the falling action in the second half of act two.

Dark moment: In a moment of true despair, your lovers will be separated (or face inevitable separation) by time and space. Whether your character has already returned to their own time, having completed their initial quest, or whether there is nothing left to keep them in the past (other than their great love, of course), these characters are faced with the choice to completely upend their lives and fight against all odds if they choose to be together, or walk away forever.

Resolution: Because this is the romance genre, your characters must find a way to be together at the end of the story.

POTENTIAL THEMES

Destiny/fate
Timeless love
Consequences
Embracing the unexpected
Living in the moment

TIME SLIP

Unlike Time Travel, where characters actively choose when and where to go, Time Slips typically happen unexpectedly, leading to confusion and disorientation for the characters involved. Time Slips usually occur when characters encounter a specific location, object, or event that triggers their displacement in time.

These stories involve a character becoming temporarily immersed in the past (or occasionally the future), experiencing life in a different time period before returning to their own time. Time Slips can also occur when objects travel through time without a character (think Pen Pals through time with a Time Slip mailbox) or certain places that exist in multiple timelines, unintentionally allowing interaction between characters from different points on the timeline, but the characters return to their own time when leaving the Time Slip location.

WHY READERS LOVE IT

One of the reasons this trope is so popular lies in its ability to bridge the gap between historical and contemporary romance. These stories are typically set in the past, but they are often written in a very contemporary voice. While these stories are inherently more appealing to contemporary readers, the world-building aspect of the past (or future) destination is still critically important. Readers want to be *transported* to a different time along with the characters themselves, if that is what is happening in the story.

TIME SLIP

These stories explore the potentially thin barrier between our time and another, drawing characters into the mystery and romance of interacting with another time. The character is thrust into the past (or suddenly begins interacting with it), which gives readers an adventure in which they can escape the mundane reality of "the now."

READER EXPECTATIONS

Since we've already established that these characters are inadvertently sent back to the past, readers expect to see quite a bit of shock and confusion upon arrival in a different time. These characters not only don't know how they got there, but they often must figure out *where* they are and in what time period. They must adjust to different customs, social expectations, and possibly languages, giving these stories a very Fish out of Water feel. If the character remains in their own time but interacts with the past or future in another way, it will typically involve a fair bit of time for them to discover what is happening, and the realization will be accompanied by disbelief, doubt, and hesitancy to continue the interactions.

The goal for the Slipped character(s) is almost always to return to their own time, if the Time Slip takes them somewhere (somewhen?) else. In the other iterations of Time Slip, the characters' motivations may initially be curiosity, but as they grow closer to their romantic interest in the other time period, their goal may change to understanding and harnessing the small-scale Time Slip so they can use it to time travel intentionally. Other iterations of Time Slip may involve multiple slips, with the character(s) pulled from time to time without warning.

POTENTIAL PITFALLS

Too easily resolved: When the character(s) are too easily returned back to their own time, or when the solution to separation from the one they love feels too convenient or easily earned, it will leave your readers feeling short-changed. To avoid this, authors must not only make sure that the resolution (such as the character being able to travel back to their own time) is plausible, but it must make sense within the story's context.

Inconsistent rules: Failing to establish clear rules or boundaries for the time travel or time slip mechanism can lead to confusion and inconsistency within the narrative. Readers may become frustrated if the rules governing time travel change arbitrarily or if there are glaring inconsistencies in how time travel is depicted.

Underdeveloped settings: Inaccurate or superficial portrayals of historical settings can undermine the immersive experience readers expect from time travel romances. Authors should strive for authenticity in their depiction of different time periods, conducting thorough research to ensure accuracy in details such as language, customs, and historical events.

COMMON PLOT DEVICES

Butterfly effect: Sometimes the Time Traveler must grapple with the consequences of their actions in the past, knowing that even small changes could have significant ripple effects on history. This usually works as a catalyst for the growth arc.

Parallel timelines: Occasionally Time Slip romances explore the concept of parallel timelines or alternate realities, where the actions of the characters in the past have the potential to create entirely new futures.

Letters/communication through time: Often the method of interaction between time periods is done through written communication. This is used when characters remain in their own times or can be used as a plot device to help a character stranded in the past communicate with the present to find a way back.

FREQUENTLY PAIRED TROPES

These stories sometimes have a very Star-Crossed Lovers feel, and the characters must fight against all odds, including the barriers of space and time, in order to find their happily ever after. Fish out of Water is an obvious pairing for a character accidentally thrust into a different time.

This trope could also be paired with Amnesia, Mistaken Identity, or Stranded as you play with the circumstances of the character's welcome into the Slipped timeline.

Giving the characters in the historical timeline their own complex goals with an intriguing Storyline Trope can be a very effective way to enhance the story also. Using one character with a Secret Identity (perhaps another Time Traveler who is there on purpose) or a Lost Heir(ess) pursuing their throne creates opportunity for the Slipped character to get wrapped up in the other character's story as they try to find a way home.

KEY MOMENTS

Inciting incident: Your characters may not actually experience their time slip or travel through time, but the inciting event should involve a significant enough moment that the readers recognize (possibly only in retrospect) that the barrier in time has been ruptured. Basically, someone or something crosses through the fabric of time.

Turning point: Due to a complication or some perceived benefit to staying, your character can't (or won't) go back to their own time. This creates tension and provides plenty of opportunity for conflict, but it also gives your readers extra time to fall in love.

Dark moment: In the most desperate moment of these stories, your characters will find themselves separated by time and space, believing that the obstacles to their future are too impossible to breach.

***Grand gesture*:** In order to be together, characters must either discover or manipulate some aspect of the time slip continuum to cross back into their love interest's time. This may involve the historical character finding their way to the future or the original time traveler finding their way back to the past. In either case, it requires a major sacrifice and usually a miraculous breakthrough.

POTENTIAL THEMES

Courage
Embracing the unexpected
Lack of control
Love conquers all
Temporal nature of life

TIME LOOP

The Time Loop trope plunges one or both main characters into a repetitive cycle of events, trapping them in a perpetual loop where the same moments are relived over and over again. This time-distorting phenomenon often centers around a single day or period with significant impact on the characters' lives, but it may also be a longer period, such as two characters being reincarnated in life after life until they overcome some obstacle that is keeping them from a happy ending that lasts forever.

Whatever the details of the loop, as the cycle resets, the character(s) find themselves navigating familiar scenarios with newfound awareness, prompting shifts in their choices, motivations, and relationships. Characters grapple with the surreal experience of reliving the same moments while striving to break free from the cycle. This unique story structure offers endless opportunities for creative exploration, allowing authors to craft compelling narratives filled with unpredictability and imaginative twists.

At the heart of the Time Loop trope lies the element of unpredictability, despite the repetition of the circumstances. Each iteration brings fresh challenges, revelations, and opportunities for growth, driving the narrative forward with a sense of urgency and intrigue. As characters try to break the loop, they are forced to confront their deepest desires, fears, and vulnerabilities, leading to profound moments of self-discovery and introspection.

As a backdrop for romance, the characters must navigate the complexities of love and relationships within the confines of the repeating cycle. The cyclical nature of the narrative heightens the emotional stakes, intensifying the bonds between characters and inviting readers on a journey of love, redemption, and second chances. As characters strive to break free from the endless loop and seize their chance at lasting happiness, the Time Loop trope offers a mesmerizing exploration of the enduring power of love.

WHY READERS LOVE IT

The Time Loop trope provides unparalleled exploration of character growth and development. Within the confines of the repetitive cycle, each iteration allows the character(s) to confront their flaws, regrets, and vulnerabilities with increasing clarity and insight. With each repetition, readers witness characters making different choices, evolving progressively from selfish and self-serving behaviors to more altruistic and compassionate actions.

These stories often have a dose of humor, as characters find themselves navigating the absurdity and surrealism of reliving the same moments *ad infinitum*. From quirky mishaps and comedic misunderstandings to witty banter and playful interactions, the repetitive nature of the time loop lends itself to a plethora of humorous situations that add levity and charm to the story. These moments of levity serve as a refreshing counterbalance to the deeper themes of love and personal growth, ensuring that readers are thoroughly entertained from start to finish.

The stakes of the romance are inherently high. Continuing to live in the same loop forever isn't an option, so the question is how characters will break free from the time loop and find lasting love. As readers root for the protagonists to overcome the seemingly insurmountable obstacles and seize their chance at happiness, the Time Loop serves as a continuous reel of second chances—chances to make a different choice, take missed opportunities, get a do-over. That's something we have all wished for a time or two. A chance to have that conversation go a different way or to make that first move instead of letting the moment pass you by.

READER EXPECTATIONS

In Time Loop stories, characters generally accumulate knowledge and experiences from each repetition. This unique narrative device allows protagonists the chance to rectify mistakes, improve themselves, and navigate the challenges of building relationships with a heightened awareness of the consequences of their actions. Each iteration of the loop presents new challenges, unexpected events, and plot twists. Readers relish the thrill of uncertainty as they follow the protagonists' journey through a shifting landscape of possibilities, where every difference in choice alters the sequence of events and reshapes the trajectory of the narrative.

Characters trapped in a Time Loop must undergo meaningful growth and development over the course of the story. It is the only way they can find their way out of the loop. Everything within the loop remains the same, with the character(s) being the only variable in each iteration. Without significant change in themselves, the loop will continue forever.

As characters traverse through the Time Loop, they may experience a sense of déjà vu, subtly recognizing the recurring patterns and events without concrete awareness that time is repeating itself. Typically the character becomes aware of the Time Loop and (depending on the length of the loop) uses that to their advantage in figuring out how to escape it.

TIME LOOP

Storytelling in this trope can be choppier and feel slightly disconnected, with only small portions of certain iterations of the loop being shown as the character tries multiple attempts to “get it right.”

While the Time Loop character will develop deep connections with key individuals, such as their love interest, other characters typically only garner shallow interactions. This imbalance of significance and emotion adds layers of complexity to the narrative, as the time loop character becomes more observant, picking up on subtle nuances and cues that others may overlook.

There typically needs to be some sort of explanation for the Time Loop. While “it was all a dream” can be overdone, it can work in these stories along with a coma or some sort of third-party supernatural being orchestrating the Time Loop. In an early script of the classic Time Loop movie, Groundhog Day, Bill Murray’s character was cursed by his ex-girlfriend to relive the same day until he became a better person, but that explanation never made it into the movie, something that still irks some viewers.

POTENTIAL PITFALLS

Time loop doesn’t change enough from one to the next: Readers may become disengaged if the iterations of the loop lack significant variation or fail to introduce new elements that propel the story forward, resulting in a sense of stagnation and monotony. This can also be avoided by skipping the repetitive portions in the storytelling.

Inconsistent responses: If the character does things exactly the same in two iterations of the loop, the result should be the same. If the consequences of characters' actions within the time loop are inconsistent, it can lead to confusion and detract from the believability of the narrative, undermining the tension and stakes of the story.

Rules/origin not explained: Failing to provide a clear explanation for the rules or origin of the time loop can leave readers feeling frustrated and disconnected from the story as they struggle to understand the mechanics driving the temporal anomaly.

Lack of growth arc: We mentioned this in the Reader Expectations section, but it bears repeating here. Characters trapped in a Time Loop must undergo meaningful growth and development over the course of the story. It is the only way they can find their way out of the loop. Everything within the loop remains the same, with the character(s) being the only variable in each iteration. Without significant change in themselves, the loop will continue forever.

COMMON PLOT DEVICES

Trying to break the loop attempts: Characters may make various attempts to break free from the time loop, including experimenting with different actions, seeking help from others, or uncovering the root cause of the temporal anomaly.

Messing around in the time loop: Characters may engage in lighthearted or adventurous activities within the time loop, such as exploring the limits of their abilities, testing the boundaries of the temporal anomaly, using their foreknowledge to win big, or simply enjoying the freedom of endless repetition.

"I've done this before": Characters may experience moments of déjà vu or recognition as they navigate through the time loop, providing opportunities for self-reflection, insight, and growth as they strive to make sense of their recurring experiences.

Parallel storylines**:** Although we've already discussed how each iteration of the time loop can and should be different, it's worth noting that these differences (however minute) are caused directly by the actions of your character. With each decision they make to do something different than they did in the previous loop, it creates a ripple effect for the rest of the events before the loop starts over.

External threat: An external threat or conflict may emerge within the time loop, whether it be directly related to the origin of the temporal anomaly (such as the evil being they must defeat to exit the loop) or as a consequence of characters' actions.

FREQUENTLY PAIRED TROPES

One of the love interests may forget what happened in previous iterations of the loop, giving it a bit of Amnesia flavor, though the love interest will never regain their memories of the previous iterations.

Sometimes Time Loops are paired with Second Chance romances, with the main character thrust back in time and given the opportunity for a do-over with the past. Due to the often-similar themes of redemption and becoming a better person, Christmas is a very common pairing with the Time Loop trope, with characters forced to relive Christmas over and over again until they make the right (usually sacrificial) choices.

KEY MOMENTS

Inciting incident: The inciting incident is usually tied to a significant moment which occurs within the loop that your character will be forced to relive over and over again. This moment is directly related to the necessary goal or change your character must make in order to eventually break free of the loop.

Turning point: While your character may not immediately recognize that they are living the same time period over and over, they should come to this realization before the end of the first act. At this point, they begin making intentional choices that alter the course of events, for better or worse.

Midpoint: By the midpoint, your character has gone through the loop enough to find some measure of success in getting what they want in the time loop, but they can't find a way out of the loop. This creates a tension between the freedom of controlling their circumstances (within the loop) and yet being completely powerless to break out of it. This moment also typically coincides with the realization of their feelings for the love interest or an outright declaration of love.

Dark moment: The time loop is nearly always broken when everything seems to be going wrong for the character, often when the character has finally resigned themself to being stuck and given up trying to influence events for the better. This leads to the final catalyst for growth, as the character must realize that they still *can* make their past mistakes right, even without the opportunity to relive those moments and make a different choice—but first they must own up to their mistake.

POTENTIAL THEMES

Selfishness
Introspection and self-growth
Priorities
Second chances
Redemption

Part Four

CASE STUDIES

CASE STUDY 1

50 FIRST DATES (2018)

AMNESIA

TIME LOOP

ABOUT THE MOVIE

50 FIRST DATES

Starring:

Adam Sandler as Henry Roth
Drew Barrymore as Lucy Whitmore
Rob Schneider as Ula, Henry's best friend
Sean Astin as Doug Whitmore, Lucy's brother
Blake Clark as Marlin Whitmore, Lucy's father

Release date: February 13, 2004 (USA)
Director: Peter Segal
Screenplay: George Wing

FEATURED TROPES

Character Tropes: Creative, Playboy
Relational Tropes: Opposites Attract
Storyline Tropes: Amnesia, Time Loop
Setting Tropes: Beach

SYNOPSIS

Henry Roth is a commitment-phobic veterinarian living in Hawaii. A serial womanizer, Henry ends each hookup by employing lies such as being married, joining the priesthood, or being a CIA agent.

Henry sees Lucy at a local diner and becomes intrigued. The next day, he returns, only to see her follow the same exact pattern of activities that she did the first time. He works up the nerve to introduce himself, and after hitting it off, the two make plans to meet again for breakfast the next morning. But the next morning, Lucy acts uncomfortable, saying that she doesn't know him. Henry is pulled outside by the café owner who informs him that Lucy has a devastating form of amnesia that keeps her from retaining any memories past the date of her injury.

Undeterred by this obstacle, Henry is determined to connect with Lucy, even if it means reintroducing himself and recreating their initial connection every single day. Initially, Henry's efforts to woo Lucy are unsuccessful, but as he spends more time with her, his interest grows. When he's warned to stay away from Lucy and the café by her father and brother, Henry resorts to roadside hijinx to intercept Lucy as she leaves the café. It's during this time that their relationship deepens (albeit one-sided), and Henry begins to fall for Lucy.

Once again, her family catches on and brings him back to reveal that she has been singing as she paints—but only on the days that she sees Henry. Recognizing that Henry truly cares for Lucy and that he makes her happy, they allow Henry to continue pursuing her. After Lucy has an episode, recognizing that her perception does not match reality, Henry takes her home where they reveal the events of her car accident and everything that's happened in the last year. Henry gets the idea to create a video recap of Lucy's life, hoping that it will help her adjust to the reality of her amnesia without being frozen in time.

His plan is fairly successful, with Lucy seeking him out daily to advance their relationship. Even as Henry and Lucy fall deeper in love, she becomes hesitant to continue the relationship, fearing that she will hold him back from his own goals and dreams. After breaking up with him, she moves into a local memory institute, feeling that she must also remove the burden to her family that her presence causes.

At the end of the movie, Marlin and Doug, Lucy's father and brother, visit Henry's boat to wish him farewell on his research trip and Marlin reveals that Lucy has begun singing as she paints at the institute. Realizing this means Lucy must remember him, Henry turns his boat around and goes to see her. Although she has no idea who he is, she tells him that she recognizes him from her dreams and takes him to her studio where she has painted hundreds of images of Henry. The two reunite, and the ending scene reveals Henry and Lucy, married and traveling on a research trip together with their daughter and Marlin.

KEY MOMENTS, THEMES AND ANALYSIS

The combination of the Time Loop and Amnesia tropes make this movie a fun and unforgettable romp. When Henry and Lucy first meet, he doesn't suspect anything is off with her—but he quickly realizes that he's missing some information when he returns to the café the next day to meet her for breakfast (as they planned). Lucy's anterograde amnesia prevents her from being able to form any new memories, but Henry is determined to win her over day after day—this sets the premise for the Time Loop narrative. While this is a fun twist on the Time Loop trope, it does in fact represent the repeated cycle of events that is inherent to the trope.

In dealing with the Amnesia storyline, the movie even goes so far as to bring in visits to the memory clinic where Lucy is able to receive the explanation from her own doctor and see the images of her brain scans.

Because Lucy remembers everything up until about a year ago, and because she follows the same routine every day, most of the faces and places in her post-amnesiac life are highly familiar to her. This is why it causes such a noticeable disruption (enough that Doug and Marlin recognize something has changed) when Henry enters her life.

Once Lucy has been informed of the events of the last year, she has a gathering with her old friends, where she learns of how much their lives have changed—a stark contrast to the fact that she has been reliving the same day of her life for the past year. Realizing this, Lucy feels that she will inevitably keep Henry from moving forward with his life if they stay together, and she decides to end the relationship.

This movie hits the Amnesia sweet spot of the falling in love all over again theme, as Henry quickly becomes determined to make Lucy fall for him every day (see Key Quotes). Ultimately, this overpowering love connection is what brings Lucy around to considering a future with Henry, as even once he is no longer in her life, he becomes the subject of her dreams and all of her art.

Time Loop and Amnesia fit together perfectly due to the similar themes of self-discovery and learning to move forward, and because it allows Henry's character arc to be formed by the Time Loop and Lucy's to be formed by the Amnesia storyline. The movie employs classic plot devices such as Lucy's journal, parallel events (in which Henry tries the same tactic repeatedly with different, often hilarious results), and Henry's evolution from a selfish playboy to a devoted partner really highlight the ingenious mix of these tropes.

50 FIRST DATES

In a twist of the typical Amnesia inciting incident, it's not Lucy who discovers her loss of memory, but it's Henry who is informed of her condition. This works brilliantly with the Time Loop inciting incident, as it is also the moment that Henry realizes in order to have any sort of relationship with Lucy, he will need to win her affections every day—only made more complicated by the fact that Lucy remembers nothing.

The movie sidesteps a classic Amnesia pitfall of the amnesiac character experiencing no change in their daily life by making the lives of those closest to her revolve around repeating the day of her accident one day after another. By highlighting the absurdity of the notion that Lucy could repeat the same sequence of events daily, and with Henry openly challenging the sustainability of such a plan, they are able to use it to advance the plot.

AMNESIA KEY QUOTES

Henry: So she can't remember anything?
Sue: No, no, no. She has all of her long-term memory. That's a different part of the brain. Her whole life up to the night of the accident she remembers. She just can't retain any new information. It's like her slate gets wiped clean every night while she sleeps.

***

Lucy [after learning about the accident]: I have to talk to this doctor. I need to hear it from him.
Marlin: You have heard it, sweetie, many times.
Lucy: I have?

***

Henry: It's gonna be all right, Luce.
Lucy: Don't call me Luce. I barely know you.
Marlin: Sweetie, you're . . . sorta dating him.
[Lucy visibly shocked]
Henry: Sorry I'm not better looking.

TIME LOOP KEY QUOTES

Sue: She says that every day because each morning she wakes up thinking it's October 13th of last year. She comes here for breakfast because that's what she did on Sundays, and October 13 was a Sunday. She has no idea it's more than a year later.
Henry: She reads the newspaper though.
Sue: It's a special paper her dad puts on their porch every night. It's from the day of the accident. He got hundreds of them printed out. Lucy does the *same thing* every day.

***

Ula: So basically what you're saying is, she's the perfect girl for you. You could hang out with her with no attachment because—
Henry: Her plane leaves every night? There's only one problem with that.
Ula: What is it?
Henry: It's evil.
[The next day he goes to the diner to see Lucy]

***

Marlin: Look, if you know her condition, then you know she can't have a normal relationship with a man because the next

morning, she won't know who he is. And any guy who's okay with that ain't okay with me.
Henry: I'm not looking for a one-night stand.
Doug (Lucy's brother): Anything with Lucy is a one-night stand, numbnuts.

***

[Just after Henry admits he's in love with Lucy, they kiss on the beach]
Lucy: Nothing beats a first kiss.
[the next day they kiss again near a lighthouse]
Lucy: There's nothing like a first kiss.
[and the day after that, they kiss at a pineapple farm]
Lucy: Nothing beats a first kiss.
Henry: That's what I've heard.

CASE STUDY 2

NEVER BEEN KISSED (1999)

HIDDEN IDENTITY

FORBIDDEN RELATIONSHIP

ABOUT THE MOVIE

NEVER BEEN KISSED

Starring:

Drew Barrymore as Josie Gellar
Michael Varton as Sam Coulson
David Arquette as Rob Gellar (Josie's brother)
John C. Reilly as Gus (Josie's managing editor)
Leelee Sobieski as Aldys

Release date: April 9, 1999 (USA)
Director: Raja Gosnell
Screenplay: Abby Kohn and Marc Silverstein

FEATURED TROPES

Character Tropes: Nerd
Relational Tropes: Love Triangle
Storyline Tropes: Hidden Identity, Forbidden Relationship
Setting Tropes: High School

SYNOPSIS

Josie Gellar is a young editor at the *Chicago Sun Times* who still carries the scars of the ridicule and humiliation she lived through in high school. When her boss assigns her to an undercover story at a local school, she becomes excited about the opportunity for a do-over. But on her first day at South Glen South High School, she learns that you can take the nerd out of the classroom, but you can't take the nerd out of the nerd.

Josie is immediately subject to humiliation, made worse by her poor wardrobe choices and weird behavior, but this time she is befriended by a fellow nerd, Aldys, and welcomed into her group, the Denominators. As she begins to find her footing, Josie develops a crush on her English teacher, Mr. Coulson (Sam). However her managing editor, Gus, is not pleased with the progress she's made on her story, and he orders her to infiltrate the popular crowd while wearing a hidden camera—which delightfully becomes the entertainment of choice for the entire office back at the paper.

While attempting to connect with the popular kids, Josie goes to a bar where she sees Sam with his girlfriend, then sits down with some stoners and inadvertently eats a cake laced with marijuana which leads to some arguably ridiculous behavior. The next morning, she shows up to school with LOSER stamped across her face after falling asleep on the admittance stamp from the bar. However when Josie goes to run from school out of humiliation, she (literally) runs into her brother Rob, who has decided to re-enroll in high school as well. Rob instantly becomes cool and helps her get in with the popular crowd.

As Josie gets closer with her teacher and "transitions" into the popular group, she is given a two-week deadline by the editor-in-chief of the paper to get her story in—or she and Gus are fired. Gus insists that Josie focus her story on Mr. Coulson, with a headline of "Student-Teacher Relations: How Close Is Too Close?" While Josie is reluctant, she doesn't offer any alternative story ideas. At prom, Josie is stunned to be crowned prom queen. While dancing with Sam, Josie is about to tell him the truth when she notices that her "friends" are about to pour dog food all over Aldys. She stops them and reveals the truth of her identity, angering Sam who stalks out of the building before confronting her lies.

Heartbroken and left with no scoop for her story, Josie writes a completely different story for the paper about the high school experience and her life as a loser who has never been kissed and fell in love with her pretend teacher. She expresses her regret for hurting Sam and asks that if he loves her back, he will show up at the high school championship baseball game and kiss her on the mound before the first pitch. The newspaper doesn't seem to care about her totally changing her assignment because it tugs at the heartstrings and becomes wildly popular, with media outlets from all over the city coming to see the outcome. At the last second, just as Josie has given up hope, Sam shows up, and they reconcile with a kiss.

KEY MOMENTS, THEMES AND ANALYSIS

We'll admit that the romance between Josie and her teacher (who believes her to be his 17-year-old student) is pretty problematic—but it does fit the Forbidden Romance trope. Josie for her part, plays the Hidden Identity to a tee, and like any good Hidden Identity story, she doesn't really discover her true self until she pretends to be someone else. Josie's own high school experience significantly influences her approach to the undercover story to the point that she vacillates between three identities: Josie Grossie (as she was called in high school), Josie the *Chicago Sun Times* editor and junior reporter, and Josie . . . the 17-year-old sheep farmer from Bali. This is highlighted by the flashbacks to Josie's high school years, triggered by her experiences at South Glen South.

There's no denying that Josie totally loses herself as she strives to, for once in her life, be the popular girl everyone loves, putting the theme of identity front and center in this movie. As she tries to shed the "Josie Grossie" persona, she becomes an entirely different person, losing her connection to the truth—which she ends up writing about in her final article. Meanwhile, like any Forbidden Romance, Sam must push past the idea of who he believes her to be as he begins to fall in love with the Josie—luckily, she is actually a 25-year-old college graduate whose weird charm and intelligence Sam is undeniably drawn toward.

When Josie reveals the truth at prom, Sam confronts her lies. Although this moment does a strong job of portraying the betrayal Sam feels upon finding out her Hidden Identity, it is a bit lackluster at addressing the Forbidden Romance storyline. Since we don't get any scenes with Sam alone, we never see him struggle with his feelings or the inappropriate nature of the teacher-student relationship. Furthermore, when Josie tells Sam at prom that she has to tell him something important (presumably the truth), he tells her that he too has something to share—the viewer can easily interpret this as Sam being ready to cross the line into a romantic relationship . . . with his 17-year-old student. In the end, Sam is too hurt by the truth to feel any relief that he is not, in fact, a total creep for being in love with a student.

Recognizing the damage she's done, Josie attempts to fix everything with the story that chronicles her journey to self-discovery at South Glen South High—revealing her motives, her backstory, and her feelings for Sam. This moment of complete vulnerability and willingness to risk everything for the chance to apologize to him is what makes that final kiss scene hit so hard.

FORBIDDEN ROMANCE KEY QUOTES

[On Josie's first day in class]
Sam: I, uh, I don't think we've met. I'm Sam . . . Coulson. Uh, the school has this thing about letting you guys call me Sam.
Josie: I'm Josie, but I'm pretty sure the school would be okay with you calling me that.

***

Sam: Well, I can tell you that when you're my age, guys will be lined up around the block for you.
Josie: You have to say that because you're my teacher.
Sam: Actually, I shouldn't say that because I'm your teacher.

***

[After Sam overhears George ask about the story on Coulson]
Josie: So . . . surprise!
Sam: Surprise, you were doing a story on me?
Josie: No, I couldn't. I mean . . . Surprise, I was hoping—
Sam: What? You were hoping what? That I'd be happy? Why, because it turns out all of a sudden that I'm allowed to be attracted to you?

HIDDEN IDENTITY KEY QUOTES

Aldys: [talking about hopes and dreams] . . . and I want to go to Northwestern!
Josie: I went there!
Aldys: For what?

Josie: Um. Just once to use the bathroom. They have, uh, a really nice facility.

***

Josie: Gus wants me to be friends with these people, the popular kids. It's impossible.
Rob: Why is it impossible?
Josie: You know what it was like for me in high school. All I wanted was to be accepted. And they just tortured me. I can't go back to South Glen South.
. . .
Rob: You're an adult now, Josie. You're successful. You graduated top of your class. You wash your hair now. You're not Josie Grossie anymore.

***

Josie: All of you people, there is a big world out there, bigger than prom. Bigger than high school. And it won't matter if you were the prom queen or the quarterback of the football team or . . . the biggest nerd in school. Find out who you are, and try not to be afraid of it.

***

Sam: Damn it, Josie . . . Just drop the act. Okay? I mean, every word out of your mouth has been a complete lie. I don't know you at all.
Josie: Look, if-if we could just spend some time together, you could get to know me again.
[Sam turns to leave]
Josie: Wait, please don't walk away.
Sam: I just can't look at you the same way.

CASE STUDY 3

LEAP YEAR (2010)

ROAD TRIP

ABOUT THE MOVIE

LEAP YEAR

Starring:

Amy Adams as Anna Brady
Matthew Goode as Declan O'Callaghan
Adam Scott as Jeremy Sloane

Release date: January 8, 2010 (USA)
Director: Anand Tucker
Screenplay: Harry Elfont and Deborah Kaplan

FEATURED TROPES

Character Tropes: The Grump
Relational Tropes: Love Triangle, Animosity
Storyline Tropes: Road Trip
Setting Tropes: Road Trip, Ireland

SYNOPSIS

Anna Brady, a Boston real estate stager who is frustrated with her boyfriend's lack of a proposal after four years heads to Dublin to take matters into her own hands. However her journey takes a detour when she lands in Wales due to a storm. She charters a boat to Cork, but gets detoured again, this time to Dingle.

Determined to reach Dublin, she strikes a deal with local pub owner Declan O'Callaghan to drive her for a fee. Along the way, they clash over Anna's plan to propose to her boyfriend on Leap Day, a traditional Irish custom.

Their journey becomes a series of misadventures as they encounter obstacles like cows blocking the road, storms, and being robbed. Forced to spend more time together, Anna and Declan develop an unexpected connection during their travels. As they navigate through challenges and share intimate conversations, they begin to question their own relationships and feelings.

When they finally reach Dublin, Declan refuses to take Anna's money. Then her boyfriend finds them in the hotel lobby, and as Declan steps away, Jeremy proposes to her. Anna hesitates in her response and looks for Declan, but he is gone. Anna says yes to Jeremy—after all, isn't this exactly what she wants? Meanwhile Declan confronts his past by retrieving his mother's claddagh ring from his ex-fiancée. Back in Dingle, we see the community rally around Declan and save the pub. In New York, we see Anna and Jeremy at their engagement party. Anna finds out that he only proposed because the fancy apartment building they wanted to live in wouldn't give them the apartment without being engaged.

Disillusioned, she realizes her true feelings for Declan and breaks off her engagement. She goes back to Ireland and confesses her feelings to Declan at his (thriving) pub. Initially he seems to reject her, but he's only left to get his mother's claddagh ring and then he proposes to her.

KEY MOMENTS, THEMES, AND ANALYSIS

For the Road Trip trope, motive must be strong for both people, especially two such characters as Anna and Declan, who get off on the wrong foot almost immediately. Anna is determined to get to

Dublin to propose to her boyfriend of four years. This is a rather spur of the moment decision, after her father reminds her of the Leap Year tradition, and a special evening with her boyfriend (that she was convinced would be a proposal) turned out to be just another date—one which her cardiologist boyfriend had to leave early.

On her journey (as meets the Road Trip trope expectations), Anna finds herself navigating quite a few unforeseen obstacles–one of which connects her with Declan. The turbulence on her flight from New York City to Ireland is diverted to Cardiff, Wales. All flights are canceled, and so are the ferries. She charters her own boat to Cork, but the boat is forced to stop in Dingle instead, where she meets Declan.

Declan begrudgingly rents her a room and feeds her, but he won't go to Dublin due to his own grudge with the city. The next morning, he has a change of heart. We find out that he owes someone 1000 euros, and he agrees to drive Anna to Dublin in exchange for 500 euros. There, we have his motivation established. Which is good, because he needs a serious reason to stick around for this crazy trip.

Let's review all the crazy difficulties along the trip for Anna (and later, Declan):

1. Turbulence on the flight to Ireland. Diverted to Cardiff, Wales.
2. All flights from Wales canceled. All ferries canceled.
3. Chartered boat can't get her to Cork. Stops in Dingle instead.
4. At Declan's pub/hotel, she can't reach the outlet and destroys the bedroom, then causes a power outage trying to charge her phone.

5. There are cows blocking the road. She gets them to move . . . and steps in a cow pie.
6. Trying to get the manure off her shoe, she leans on the car and it rolls down the hill and into the water.
7. They miss the train after a sightseeing excursion and have to stay with the train attendant. To be able to rent the room, they must pretend to be married.
8. The next day, they can't take the train because it doesn't run on Sundays.
9. They are stuck outside in a hailstorm and end up crashing a wedding.
10. Anna accidentally hits the bride with a shoe and then dumps a glass of wine on her.
11. She gets drunk and throws up all over Declan's shoes.

It isn't all awful though. There are some pretty magical moments mixed in along the way. As they wait for the train to Dublin, Declan points out Ballycarbery Castle is right across from the train station. He convinces her to go see it . . . despite her not wanting to miss the train. The view is gorgeous, and Declan (in his delicious Irish accent) tells her the story of the people who lived there. She misses the train, obviously, despite running through the rain and slipping in the mud to catch it. But sightseeing is a moment of intimate conversation, and they get to know each other . . . kind of.

They end up going home with the attendant from the train station, but the wife won't rent them the room unless they are married, so we get some Fake Relationship microtrope goodness in there too. Plus the Just One Bed microtrope. At the bed-and-breakfast, Anna and Declan cook dinner together. We see his hand over hers on the skillet handle, sharing the bottle of wine, and feeding each other tastes of their creation. And of course, Declan and Anna have to kiss at dinner to maintain the ruse of being married.

During these moments of intimacy (the castle, cooking together, dancing at the wedding, etc.), Anna and Declan overcome their animosity and get a deeper understanding of one another. Anna learns about the woman who cheated on Declan and ran off with his friend to Dublin. Embracing the Road Trip trope themes of Adventure, Anna learns to find joy in the journey and not always be so focused on the destination. The two of them embark on their honeymoon by throwing the map out the window.

ROAD TRIP KEY QUOTES

Anna's dad: In Ireland, there's a tradition that in a leap year, a woman can propose to a man on February 29th. One day every four years.
Anna: That's ridiculous.
[Cuts to a scene of her packing.]

***

Worker: Ferry's canceled.
Anna: What's wrong with this country?
Worker: Usually I blame the government, but this one's the weather. Storm, ya see? [Gestures to the torrential rain outside]
Anna: We'll just see about that. I'll find my own boat.
[Cuts to her in a boat in ridiculous waves]
Boat Captain: We're going to have to go into Dingle.
Anna: But I paid for Cork.
[More waves crashing onto the boat]
Anna: Okay, Dingle will do.

***

Anna: I noticed a menu on the bar?
Declan: It's closed.
Anna: Closed. But . . . given the famous Irish tradition of hospitality and generosity?
Declan: I'll do ya a hang sandwich.
Anna: What's a hang?
[Declan walks away]
Anna: Hang is a verb! It's not a sandwich!

***

Anna: What are you, the Lucky Charms leprechaun? You know what? We are done. We're not talking anymore. I'm not paying you to talk, I'm not paying you for your opinion. I'm paying you to drive, so just get in the car and drive.

***

Declan: My Renault 4! Look what you've done!
Anna: What I've done?
Declan: You couldn't just wait for the cows!
Anna: You couldn't just help me?
Declan: It's gonna cost at least 200 to tow her out. That's not gonna come out of my pocket. It's coming out of yours.
Anna: Oh, like h***. You will have to kill me before I pay you a dime!
Declan: There's an idea.

CASE STUDY 4

NO RESERVATIONS (2007)

INSTANT FAMILY

FORCED PROXIMITY

ABOUT THE MOVIE

NO RESERVATIONS

Starring:
Catherine Zeta-Jones as Kate Armstrong
Aaron Eckhart as Nick Palmer
Abigail Breslin as Zoe
Release date: July 27, 2007
Director: Scott Hicks
Screenplay: Carol Fuchs
Based on: *Mostly Martha* by Sandra Nettelbeck

FEATURED TROPES

Character Tropes: Cinnamon Roll, Genius
Relational Tropes: Animosity (one-sided), Opposites Attract (Grumpy/Sunshine)
Storyline Tropes: Instant Family, Forced Proximity
Setting Tropes: Workplace Romance, Urban

SYNOPSIS

Kate Armstrong is the intense, perfectionist head chef at the trendy 22 Bleecker Street restaurant in Manhattan's West Village. When Kate's sister Christine is killed in a car accident, her nine-year-old niece, Zoe, must move in with her. Kate is devastated by her sister's death and her sous chef is due to have a baby any day. Her boss decides to hire a new sous chef to join the staff. Nick Palmer is a rising star in his own right and could be the head chef of any restaurant he pleased. Nick, however, wants to work under Kate.

Kate feels increasingly threatened by Nick as time goes on due to his style of running her kitchen. He loves to listen to opera while he cooks and makes the staff laugh. Kate also finds herself strangely attracted to Nick, whose uplifting personality has not only affected her staff but Zoe as well, who ends up coming to work with her and bonds with him.

After Kate takes a few days off, it's clear that something has shifted. Paula is deferring to Nick more. He is invited out to talk to guests, and Paula chooses wines Nick recommended. Each time he tries to insist that Paula talk to Kate instead and avoids telling Kate the truth. When the truth comes out, Kate confronts him—and she doesn't take the news well. She accuses him of not having the guts to go after what he wants, and he calls her on her distrust of people and tells her that, whatever she might think, the restaurant is just one little piece of her life. Zoe runs away after hearing they broke up, and Kate turns to Nick for help looking. They find her, and Nick informs her that he took a job in San Francisco.

Kate ends up quitting her job. She goes to Nick, and they reunite, eventually opening their own restaurant together.

KEY MOMENTS, THEMES, AND ANALYSIS

The two Storyline Tropes in this movie have almost equal depth and screen time. The Instant Family trope comes first, with an impactful series of short scenes near the beginning of the movie as Kate prepares for a visit from her sister and niece while thriving in the chaos of her kitchen.

When her sister dies on the way to the visit, Kate gets the call in the middle of the dinner rush. She doesn't even want to take the call, but her employee insists. There is no dialogue, but the chatter in the kitchen fades, and you see the shock and concern on Kate's face before it cuts to her running through the hospital and finding her niece there.

When Zoe wakes up and asks if her mom is dead, Kate is clearly not sure how to comfort her . . . she doesn't touch her at all. A letter from Kate's sister is read as an overlay, indicating that Kate is the only person she would want to have custody of Zoe. "I know you'll love my baby the same way I do."

Kate's struggle to adapt to guardianship is right in line with expectations for the trope, with a fun twist from her being a chef and therefore trying to feed Zoe everything from fish that still has a head to duck in her school lunch. Even when Kate begrudgingly tries to serve her niece fish sticks, Zoe won't eat anything. In fact, it is Nick who finally gets the young girl to eat with his disarming charm and non-confrontational manner. Zoe has to wake her aunt up for the first day of school. Another time, Zoe is late for school and once, Kate even forgets to pick her up.

The Forced Proximity of the romance starts off with a bang when Kate unexpectedly stops by the restaurant and finds that her boss (Paula) has taken it upon herself to hire a new sous chef. Her first impression isn't a good one. He's getting the entire kitchen staff to sing opera in the kitchen and generally making all the employees giggle with his theatrics—basically the exact opposite of how she runs her kitchen.

As the movie goes on, there are several short montages of scenes showing the Forced Proximity aspect, slowly transitioning from downright animosity from Kate and hopefulness from Nick, then to the added layer of Zoe being there too and seeing both of them interact with her. Then, Zoe is no longer allowed to come to the kitchen in the evenings, but now Nick and Kate enjoy the time with each other. Throughout the movie, she continually does things she claims she never does, like eat in the afternoons or drink at work. Nick is pushing her out of those self-imposed boundaries.

At one point in the story, Zoe uses a wish (granted by Kate as an apology) to orchestrate Nick coming over for dinner at Kate's house so Nick and Zoe can cook dinner for them all. They put together a tent for a "safari" in the living room. They eat without plates or shoes and play games—all three of them. Zoe falls asleep, and Nick carries her to bed (and Kate gets a glimpse down the hallway). This kind of family togetherness is hitting all the Instant Family goodness.

But it can't all be sunshine and roses. When Kate confronts Nick at the restaurant and he challenges her on defining herself by her position at the restaurant, it creates the pressure that eventually causes her emotional walls to crumble. By the end of the movie, this is the catalyst for growth in Kate's character. She thought the restaurant was her entire identity, but the love she has for her niece and the way in which Nick has disrupted her life make her realize that her identity is so much more complex than she believed it to be.

INSTANT FAMILY KEY QUOTES

Doctor: Zoe's doing great. She's going to be fine.
Kate: Has anyone told her yet?
Doctor: We thought it would be best for her to hear it from someone in the family. Do you know how we can reach Zoe's father?
Kate: He's never been . . . I don't even know his name.

***

[Kate serves Zoe a fish with a head and eyes still on it.]
Kate: What's the matter? Aren't you hungry?
[Zoe shakes her head]
Zoe: Can I go back to my room?

***

Kate [in therapy]: There has to be someone better suited to this. I have no idea what to do with a kid, especially one who's lost her mother. How do their minds work? I can't get Zoe to eat anything I make. What am I supposed to do, force her?

***

[Nick tries to kiss Kate at the breakfast table after their night together]
Kate: Not in front of Zoe.
Nick: Zoe, I am now going to kiss your aunt.
Zoe: This is so embarrassing.
Kate: So how are we going to work together now?
Nick: We'll do what we always did. You'll tell me what to do, and I'll go behind your back and do whatever I want.

FORCED PROXIMITY KEY QUOTES

Kate: Who do you think you are?
Nick: Nicholas Palmer. And may I just say, the world would be a dark and depressing place without your quail and truffle sauce.
Kate [to her boss]: We need to talk.

***

Kate: I need more space.
Nick: Why are you so mad at me?
Kate: I'm not mad at you?
Nick: You're very mad.
Kate: Look, this is my kitchen. I've worked very hard to get here, and I'm not gonna let you take it away from me, okay?
Nick: And what makes you think I want to take it away from you?
Kate: What else could you possibly want?

***

Kate: I never drink at work.
[Cuts to a scene of the two of them splitting a bottle of wine and a plate of cheese and grapes after hours at the restaurant]

CASE STUDY 5

KATE AND LEOPOLD (2001)

TIME SLIP

FISH OUT OF WATER

STAR-CROSSED LOVERS

ABOUT THE MOVIE

KATE AND LEOPOLD

Starring:

Meg Ryan as Kate McKay
Hugh Jackman as Leopold Mountbatten, Duke of Albany
Liev Schreiber as Stuart Besser
Breckin Meyer as Charlie McKay

Release date: December 25, 2001
Director: James Mangold
Written by: Steven Rogers

FEATURED TROPES

Character Tropes: Regency
Relational Tropes:
Storyline Tropes: Time Slip, Fish out of Water, Star-Crossed Lovers
Setting Tropes: Urban

SYNOPSIS

We meet Leopold in 1876 New York City. He is the financially strapped Duke of Albany. Living under the guardianship of his uncle and tended to by the faithful butler, Otis, Leopold is nudged toward a pragmatic marriage to secure his future. Yet, amidst societal expectations, Leopold's true passion lies in his inventive pursuits, exemplified by his design of a revolutionary elevator prototype.

Fate takes a fantastical turn when Leopold encounters Stuart Besser, a visitor from the distant future, during the erection of the Brooklyn Bridge. Stuart, an aspiring physicist, has stumbled upon a gravitational time portal and inadvertently draws Leopold into the vortex, hurtling them both forward to the year 2001.

As Leopold grapples with the disorienting realities of the 21st century, he finds himself intertwined with the life of Kate McKay, Stuart's ambitious ex-girlfriend. Kate, a driven career woman immersed in the bustling world of market research, initially clashes with the chivalrous and antiquated Leopold. However their initial friction gradually gives way to a burgeoning connection, fueled by Leopold's eloquence and genuine charm.

Against the backdrop of a modern metropolis, Leopold and Kate's romance blossoms, punctuated by enchanting moments such as a rooftop dinner and a tender waltz. Yet, their idyllic union is surely impossible, as Leopold must return to the past and continue his life and accomplishments there. Kate and Leopold end their relationship, and Leopold returns to the past.

Stuart and Kate's devoted brother, Charlie, realize that Kate is actually destined to go back to the past with Leopold after seeing her in Stuart's photos of the past. As the clock ticks toward the closure of the portal, Kate gives up the promotion she'd been striving for, and takes the leap into the past, where she bravely interrupts Leopold's engagement announcement. Upon seeing her, Leopold announces her as his betrothed.

KEY MOMENTS, THEMES, AND ANALYSIS

In any Time Slip story, the moment where someone accidentally falls into another time period is pretty important. In this case, Leopold was chasing Stuart, who was traveling in the past. When he tries to escape through the portal, Stuart inadvertently brings Leopold into the future with him. The rip in the fabric of time that Stuart found is explained to open weekly, and it must be jumped into from a great height (specifically from the girder of the Brooklyn Bridge).

The consequences of the unintentional time travel are threaded through the entire movie, with elevators inexplicably not working during the whole movie, since Leopold was not in the past to invent them. It also provided a nice excuse for Stuart to be absent for most of the week, allowing Kate and Leopold to get to know one another and constantly break Stuart's rules about Leopold being allowed out of the apartment.

We certainly see the Fish out of Water trope from Leopold's perspective. During the movie, we get to see him navigate modern technology like television, phones, and toasters—with varying degrees of success. Most notable is his first scene on the streets of New York, bombarded with sirens, loud music, cars speeding by, honking, Rollerbladers, and even helicopters. People around him generally seem to think he is an actor of sorts, and he is even cast in a nation-wide commercial spot, thanks to Kate's job in marketing.

But Leopold's particular flavor of Fish out of Water is exactly what makes him so swoony! He is polite, well-spoken, thoughtful, and romantic. He rides through Central Park on horseback to save her purse from a pickpocket and speaks eloquently about the meaning of each flower as he selects a bouquet. He fashioned a quill (come on, seriously?) and handwrote an apology letter after he messed up Kate's business dinner. Of course, since the movie is set in 2001, Kate's assistant handwrote her acceptance and faxed it back to him.

Like any good Star-Crossed Lovers trope, it seems impossible for these two people to end up together. They are too different. Leopold must return to the past and live out his life. Kate finally has all the things she's been working for within her reach. There is almost an Animosity to their relationship for most of the movie. Stuart is Kate's ex-boyfriend, which immediately makes her suspicious of Leopold. He disagrees with her choice to work in marketing, peddling lies to the people without integrity. She thinks he's actually crazy for a good portion of the movie, until she realizes he's telling the truth about his past. Not only is Kate faced with the decision to give up her friends, family, career, and life to join Leopold in the past, she has to trust her ex-boyfriend enough to jump off the Brooklyn Bridge. It's this idea that their love makes absolutely no sense when analyzed through the lens of logic that makes this the perfect representation of star-crossed lovers.

TIME SLIP KEY QUOTES

Stuart: I found it.
Kate: What did you find?
Stuart: The portal. A crack in the fabric of time. It was over the East River, just where I said it would be.
Kate: You found the portal.
Stuart: A portal into April 28th, 1876. I jumped off the Brooklyn Bridge and took a walk in 1876 today. I followed the Duke of Albany around old New York. Are you listening?
Kate: Avidly.

Stuart: Because here's the twist, Kate. Here's the kicker.
Kate: What's the kicker?
Stuart: He followed me home.

***

Stuart: Geez, Kate. He's from 1876, Kate! He doesn't know our customs! If something were to happen to him, if he doesn't go back to April 28th, 1876, he doesn't get married, he doesn't have children. And you wanna know what? What happened with the elevators today is going to seem like a walk in the park.

***

Kate: Darcy? What is this?
Darcy: It's a reply to Leopold's invitation. You're going, right?
Kate: I haven't decided yet.
Darcy: Oh, you haven't decided if you want to have dinner on your rooftop with a duke?
Kate: Who thinks he's from 1876! No! And I would appreciate it if—
Darcy: Kate, come on, okay? I don't know what this guy did to p*ss you off, but that is the best apology letter in the history of mankind!

FISH OUT OF WATER KEY QUOTES

[Leopold walking away after dog poops]
Police officer: Are you going to remove that?
Leopold: I beg your pardon?
Police office: Pick it up and put it in the trash.
Leopold: Absolutely not.

Police Officer: Maybe you don't understand. It's against the law to leave it there.
Leopold: Are you suggesting, madam, that there exists a law compelling gentlemen to lay hold of canine bowel movements?
Police Officer: I'm suggesting you pick the poop up and throw it away now.

***

Leopold: [Chases down a purse-snatcher on horseback] I warn you, scoundrel. I was trained to ride at the King's Academy and schooled in weaponry by the palace guard. You stand no chance. Where you run, I shall ride, and when you stop, the steel of this strap will be lodged in your brain.

***

Leopold: What has happened to the world? You have every convenience, every comfort. Yet no time for integrity.

***

Leopold [looking at the Brooklyn Bridge]: Good Lord, it still stands. The world has changed all around it, but Roebling's erection still stands! That, my friend, is a miracle!
Sanitation worker: What?
Leopold [points to the bridge]: It's a miracle, man!
Sanitation worker: It's a bridge.

STAR-CROSSED LOVERS KEY QUOTES

Kate: Are you for real?
Leopold: Pardon?

KATE AND LEOPOLD

Kate: Are you for real?
Leopold: I believe so.
Kate: You're a duke?
Leopold: I was born a duke. I've never felt like one.

***

Kate: We're kidding ourselves, Leopold. In point of fact, I still don't know who you really are.
Leopold: You still don't believe I am who I say I am.
Kate: We had a great weekend. That's that. Now it's Sunday. It's over.

***

Kate: Leopold, this was lovely. But I don't know if I can leap, even if I am inspired. People might think I'm brave, but I'm not.
Leopold: The brave are simply those with the clearest vision of what is before them—glory and danger alike—and notwithstanding, go out to meet it.

***

Stuart: Maybe I was supposed to help you find your guy. Leopold. You gotta go back, Kate. You gotta go back there.
Kate: Go back? How?
Charlie: You have to jump off the Brooklyn Bridge within the next 23 minutes.

CASE STUDY 6

SHE'S ALL THAT (1999)

HIDDEN MOTIVES (BET)

ABOUT THE MOVIE

SHE'S ALL THAT
Starring:
Freddie Prinze Jr. as Zach Siler
Rachael Leigh Cook as Laney Boggs
Kevin Pollack as Wayne Boggs
Gabrielle Union as Katie
Paul Walker as Dean
Release date: January 29, 1999 (USA)
Director: Robert Iscove
Screenplay: R. Lee Fleming Jr.
Loosely based on *Pygmalian* by George Bernard Shaw

FEATURED TROPES

Character Tropes: Creative Genius
Relational Tropes: Love Triangle, Opposites Attract
Storyline Tropes: Hidden Motives (Bet)
Setting Tropes: High School

SYNOPSIS

Zack Siler is student body president, jock, and all-around cool guy. When he discovers that his girlfriend, Taylor, has cheated on him, he's left without a date for prom—only 6 weeks away. Laney Boggs is dedicated to her artwork and her family, but she's anxious to move on from the torment of high school.

His friends challenge his hubris by betting him to transform a girl of their choosing into prom queen. Laney doesn't give Zack the time of day when he first approaches her. With advice from his younger sister, Zack decides to invest some time in learning about Laney and her interests.

After Zack joins her at her performance art show, Laney begins to warm up to him. She reluctantly accepts his invitation to the beach, then Zack arranges for his sister to give Laney a makeover before taking her to a party. She's taken in by Katie, one of Taylor's best friends, and Zach's friend, Preston.

When Laney is humiliated at the party by Zack's ex-girlfriend, she is ashamed at having run out of the house in tears. Zack takes her home and clearly becomes conflicted about the terms of the bet. He continues to seek her out as she slowly opens up to him and encourages her to let others in. And she challenges him to make his own decisions, including choosing his own university.

In an effort to sabotage Zack's success in the bet and his relationship with Laney, Dean begins pursuing Laney, eventually revealing the terms of the bet. On prom night, Laney's father convinces her to leave her art for the night and join her classmates at prom.

Dean accompanies her, but his goal all along is to humiliate her. When Jesse, Laney's best friend, overhears Dean bragging about taking Laney to a hotel after prom, he and Zack's sister, Mackenzie, tell him to intervene. They interrupt his speech after he's voted prom king, alongside Taylor, and he rushes out, realizing that they have already left. Zack waits for Laney to return to her home and they reunite.

KEY MOMENTS, THEMES, AND ANALYSIS

At the beginning of the movie, Zack is arrogant and accepts the terms of the bet with no hesitation. He is flabbergasted when he approaches Laney twice and she blows him off, clearly unfamiliar with the notion of being turned down. This banter and pulling/pushing action automatically draws the viewer into the story and lays the foundation for some serious chemistry between Zack and Laney.

Although Zack starts off his relationship with no other goal than to get her attention and fulfill the terms of his bet, we see a subtle shift in the way he sees her almost immediately. That change continues up until the point that Laney is invited to Dean's party, and she ends up running out because of Taylor's cruelty. When Laney opens up for the first time after this, it becomes clear that Zack will start developing genuine feelings for her. In a shift from his "it's just a bet" comment to Dean during the party, he begins defending Laney and downplaying the terms of the bet.

Just before Zack kisses her for the first time, Laney cracks a joke about him trying to win her vote for prom king. Recognizing the influence of his reputation on his actions, Zack leaves before kissing her.

One of the things that makes this couple so enticing is the way that they bring out the best version of each other. While Laney challenges Zack to stop being so wrapped up in what others expect of him, Zack pulls her out of her constant grief and obligation. And while the stakes of the bet weren't particularly earth-shattering (as revealed in the final scene), the ultimate barrier for Zack is his pride and self-perceived legacy—in the end, it's his relationship with Laney that shows Zack just how shallow his priorities are.

HIDDEN MOTIVES (BET) KEY QUOTES

Dean: The guy thinks he can do anything. Let him prove it. What do you say, Zack?
Zack: A bet?
Dean: Yeah, unless of course you're too heartbroken.
Zack: Just name the terms.
Dean: All right, simple. I'll pick the girl, then you got six weeks to turn her into the prom queen.
…
Zack: You got it.

***

Dean: So, what's going on? You mixing a little business with pleasure, or what?
Zack: I hate to break it to you, man. But uh, it's just a bet.
Dean: Yeah, right.

***

Dean: All right, Zack, enough's enough. This isn't cool anymore. I like this girl, and you gotta stop this whole bet thing.
Laney: Bet?
Dean: Yeah, it was so stupid Laney. Look, Zack said he could make any girl prom queen, and you were the one picked, so he thinks that if he takes you to the prom, it'll help him win. People have feelings, man.

SHE'S ALL THAT

Laney: Is it true? Am I a bet? Am I a bet? Am I a ***king bet?
Zack: Yes.
…
[Laney runs out, followed by Dean]

***

Zack: You know I made that bet before I knew you, Laney. Before I really knew me.
Laney: What was it for anyway? I mean, what did you end up losing?
Zack: My best friend. She taught me a lot. Before her, I thought we had to have all the answers right now.
Laney: And now?
Zack: I'm kind of liking the fact that I don't. So . . . can I have the last dance?
Laney: No. You can have the first.

THE ROMANCE WRITER'S ENCYCLOPEDIA SERIES

There's more to "Writing to Market" than calling your hero a Billionaire and putting him in a suit on the cover.

But what if you don't have time to read a dozen Small Town romances or a dozen Cowboy books or a dozen Nanny/Single Dad romances, hoping you can glean the patterns and expectations of these markets?

That's where we come in.

The Romance Writer's Encyclopedia is doing the legwork for you. Using our unique Framework Trope method, which separates tropes into categories based on how they impact your story, we examine each trope, explain why readers love it, and clue you in on the unspoken expectations of the trope, as well as some pitfalls you might encounter while writing.

This is far more than a book with an unexplained list of tropes or broad advice for writing romance. This is an encyclopedia, and each entry is detailed, but easy to understand. It will leave you excited and prepared to write a romance that delivers deep reader satisfaction based on the premise you've designed.

Whether you use the books to brainstorm, plot, edit, or help with marketing your books—this collection is sure to become one with a permanent place on your craft book shelf.

Learn more and see all the available titles in the series at www.thetropebooks.com

Volume 1: Romance Character Tropes

Volume 2: Romance Storyline Tropes

Volume 3: Romance Relational Tropes

Volume 4: Romance Setting Tropes

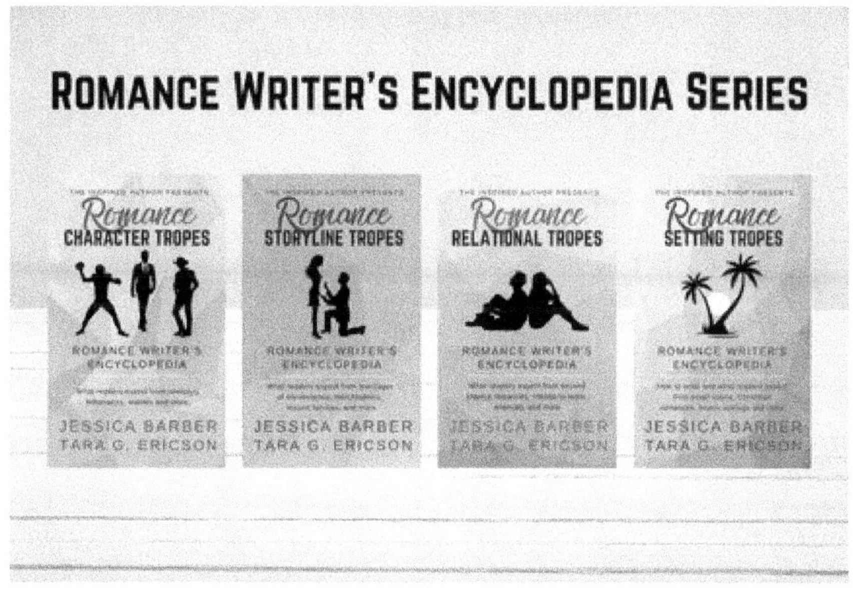

ABOUT THE AUTHORS

Best-selling author and marketing coach Tara Grace Ericson has published nearly twenty novels in Christian romance and romantic suspense. She was a Carol Award finalist for Best Christian Fiction by the American Christian Fiction Writers in 2022. Follow her at @taraericsonauthor on Facebook and Instagram. Her website is www.taragraceericson.com

Jessica Barber is the chief editor at New Life Editing Solutions where she offers editing and story coaching services for both traditionally and independently published authors. She is the author of *Beyond the Beats: How to Write a Romance Readers Can't Resist*. You can view her editing services at www.newlifeediting.com

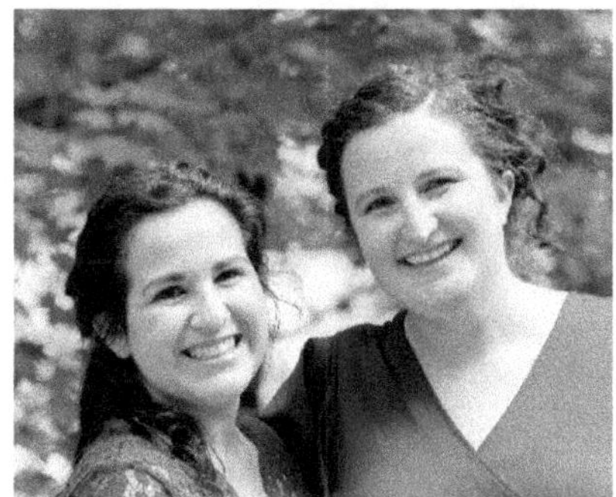

Jessica and Tara co-founded The Inspired Author in 2022 with a vision of creating books, courses, and other resources to encourage and equip authors. Learn more at www.theinspiredauthor.net

MORE FROM THE INSPIRED AUTHOR

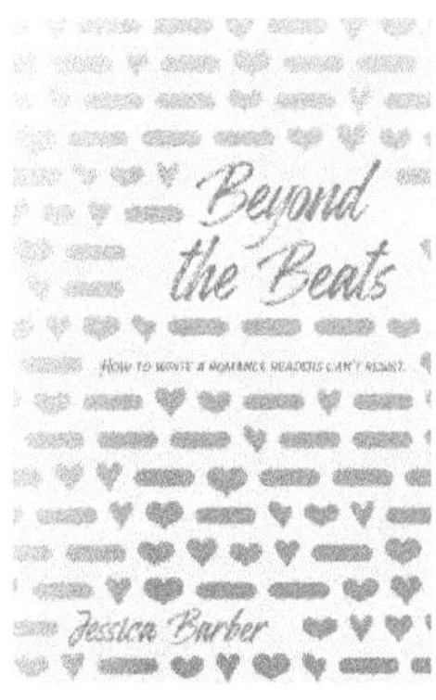

**Beyond the Beats:
How to Write a Romance Readers Can't Resist**

By Jessica Barber

Learn to grab readers' attention when you go beyond the story beats of the romance genre by harnessing the impact of the relationship arc, character arc, conflict, key moments, and other writing techniques.

Based on her experience working with dozens romance novelists over the last decade and insight from reading and studying thousands of romance novels, editor and story coach Jessica Barber has compiled the most lucrative advice for writing a well-developed, engaging novel that will have your readers begging for more.

This book will teach you:

- The guiding principles of the romance genre
- The basic structure and storytelling elements of romance
- Content expectations
- Ways to enhance and improve your storytelling

After reading this book, you can be confident that you will have the tools to take your novel from a good book to a book that readers can't put down.

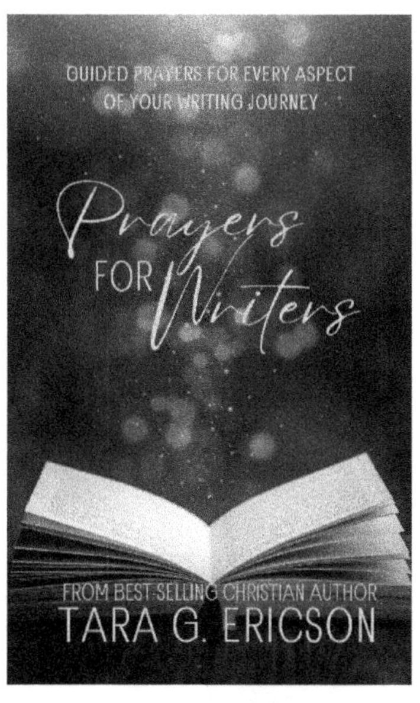

Prayers for Writers:
Guided Prayers for Every Aspect of Your Writing Journey

By Tara G. Ericson

This guided prayer journal is designed for Christian writers of all kinds. Any genre, any age, and any stage of publishing. Whether your writing is a hobby, a business, a forgotten passion, or something you've always wanted to try, this book is for you.

Inside you'll find prayers in four categories:

- Prayers for a Writer's Heart (Priorities, Faith, Humility, etc)
- Prayers for My Circle (Friends, Partner, Teachers, etc)
- Prayers for a Writing Career (Success, Platform, etc)
- Prayers for Specific Times (Evening, Anxiety, Failure, etc)

Along with tons of scripture, reflection questions and journaling space for you to invite the Lord into your writing.

With prayers about your craft, the people in your life, a writing career, and for specific times in your writing endeavors, you'll find countless ways to grow as a writer and as a follower of Jesus. Beautifully designed with journaling space and prayer prompts, this book was developed with the heart of a Christian writer in mind.

www.ingramcontent.com/pod-product-compliance
Lightning Source LLC
Chambersburg PA
CBHW070049030426
42335CB00016B/1840

* 9 7 8 1 9 4 9 8 9 6 6 5 7 *